THE
INFLUENTIAL
—AUTHOR—

How and Why to Write, Publish, and Sell Nonfiction Books that Matter

By Gregory V. Diehl

Foreword by Tom Morkes

D1453836

For permission requests, write to the publisher at contact@identitypublications.com.

Ordering Information:

Quantity sales. Special discounts are available on quantity purchases by corporations, associations, and others. For details, contact the publisher at the address above.

Orders by U.S. trade bookstores and wholesalers. Please contact Identity Publications: Tel: (805) 259-3724 or visit www.IdentityPublications.com.

ISBN-13: 978-1-945884-65-8 (paperback)   **JUN 1 7 2020**
ISBN-13: 978-1-945884-66-5 (hardcover)

Library of Congress Control Number: 2018913387

Cover design and section illustrations by Resa Embutin (www.ResaEmbutin.com). Author photo by Lenin Laviña.

First Edition
Publishing by Identity Publications
www.IdentityPublications.com

Dedicated to every exceptional mind that has ever feared it would not be able to express its full ability to perceive the world beyond the limitations of its time.

"The whole Earth is the Sepulchre of famous men; and their story is not graven only on Stone over their native earth, but lives on far away, without visible symbol, woven into the stuff of other men's lives."
—**Pericles (495 BC – 429 BC)**

"If I have seen further it is by standing on the sholders *[sic]* of Giants."
—**Isaac Newton (1676)**

"The survival or preservation of certain favoured words in the struggle for existence is natural selection."
—**Charles Darwin (1871)**

"A man may die, nations may rise and fall, but an idea lives on. Ideas have endurance without death."
—**John F. Kennedy (1963)**

"The word is now a virus."
— **William S. Burroughs (1998)**

"An idea: a theory or an equation, might sit around unnoticed for decades, centuries, even, before it's rediscovered and put to some use. That's how it works: it makes connections with other ideas, other knowledge, gathering momentum all the time, growing exponentially if it's strong enough."
—**K. Valisumbra (2015)**

Table of Contents

Foreword

By Tom Morkes

───────────

There is no better medium for spreading an idea than a book.

I would typically explain my reasoning behind such a claim, but thanks to Gregory Diehl's *The Influential Author* I can save you time (and the pain of redundancy) by simply pointing you to his book.

Instead, I want to focus on a simple question:

If a book can be such a powerful tool for change in the world, why don't more people write and publish?

Having worked with hundreds of authors (and aspiring authors) in various capacities over the years, it seems to me "failure to launch" comes down to three myths:

Myth #1: You Don't Believe You Have Anything Worth Sharing

Or you don't believe you have the skills to share it properly... or you don't believe it's worth the time, money, and effort... or you don't believe, even if you do publish, that anyone will care.

When you don't believe in the work you do, you will necessarily lack the faith to bring your ideas into being. Everything in life will present itself as a great idea... for someone else.

So if you're waiting for a pat on the back or an "attaboy" from the crowd before you dive headfirst into your creative pursuit, I have unfortunate news for you: no one will believe in you if you don't—nobody bets on the fighter who talks about his forthcoming defeat.

The only way to inspire others is to be the source of inspiration.

If you're not there yet, don't lose hope. Picking up and reading a book like this is a practical demonstration that there is a spark within you. Your next step is to kindle that into a flame that you (and others) can believe in and follow. That takes time and practice. Don't quit.

Myth #2: You Don't Know Where to Start

So you search "how to write a book" on DuckDuckGo and, instead of having the precise path illuminated and prepared for you, you're sucked into the infinite abyss that is the internet: a thousand contradictory ideas that all claim the same perfect outcome, each with a compelling narrative of its viability.

So, instead of moving with a purpose—picking a path and taking the next step—you get sucked into the world of the amateur critic, whose predominant concern is squabbling with others to determine the "right" path. Can you guess what happens next?

Nothing.

Hop onto any Facebook group for self-publishers and you'll see what I mean: thousands of aspiring writers talking about writing, thinking about writing, and criticizing every resource, book, course, coach, or program that's out there to help them start writing... but never actually writing. Here's the thing. There is no "right" path. That's a myth. There are best practices (you'll find them in this book), but besides that the "right" path is nothing more than doing the hard work that's right in front of you.

This takes focus. It's not easy. It is worth it.

Myth #3: You Don't Have Time

You've found a way to believe in yourself—enough to get started, at least—and you've demonstrated the desire and discipline to make progress on your book. You found your focus. Things are going great. So great, in fact, that you decide to give yourself a break. Just this week for the holidays. Then for the month because of an urgent matter at work. Then for the next quarter because your family needs you.

Then for years, because life is full of plug-and-play excuses.

Here's the deal: nothing worthwhile is easy. Worth is manifested through work. And writing a book that's worth reading is some of the hardest intellectual work anyone can undertake. So don't be surprised if you want to take a break or extend your break (indefinitely). You're human.

Here's the solution:

First, remember: you've come this far. You owe it to yourself to finish and ship what you started. You owe it to others, too.

Second, if you're considering taking a break, don't. In fact, do the opposite. Write twice as many words today; finish an extra chapter this week; rewrite the entire thing one more time this month. Whatever your tired, uninspired self wants to do, do the opposite (unless it's writing, then do that).

Third, if you took a decade-long hiatus but still have a whisper of a desire left inside you, sit down for an afternoon and read what you've written and do nothing more. Do this every afternoon—don't stop. The human brain is a goal-oriented, organizational machine that seeks to reduce pain and increase pleasure. If you're fighting your own nature, unless you have the will of a saint you will lose. So stop trying to fight yourself by saying "I need to write" or "I need to finish this." You'll lose. Instead, put yourself in a position where the primary (or better yet, only) thing you're consuming is the book you're writing. Eventually, you'll grow so tired of reading your half-baked ideas you'll find it easier to write than not.

Now it's your turn.

Your mission right now is to read this book. Take it in, take notes, and enjoy. No need to rush.

But when you do finish, you have an even more important mission: sit down and write the book you've been inspired to write. Nobody will tell you twice. So get after it.

Tom Morkes
Author of *The Art of Instigating*
www.TomMorkes.com

Questions to Help You Get the Most from This Book

Many books on self-publishing proclaim that everyone has a book in them. They promote the false notion that anyone can become a successful author with hardly any effort. Such all-inclusive declarations are nonsense.

To write a book, one must invest hundreds of hours into strategizing, writing, and rewriting. To write a good book, one must become an exemplary communicator, using words as tools for a purpose. To become a respected author, one must have a purpose worth fulfilling and not be shy about promoting it.

To write a book is not the path for everyone… but it may be the path for you. The process is a challenge, but if you are determined to put in the necessary work, it is possible to find success as an independently published nonfiction author.

A nonfiction book with a valuable message can feed a specific type of hunger held by thousands of readers for generations to come. It can be a medium of information that adds longevity to the most valuable products of its author's life, even long after they are gone.

If you think you desire to write and publish, you must ask yourself what your book will do that no other book already does. You must inquire about your reasons behind your desire and whether they are strong enough to bring order out of the chaos of your still-unprocessed thoughts.

Is the content of your book unique?

Few people come up with wholly original ideas of any worth. Most just rework and popularize earlier ideas, connecting them in ways few before them have done. Much of what you intend to say, others have already said in some form. What novelty will you add to humanity's encyclopedia of wisdom? If you know the standards set by the other books on your subject, you can improve on them or combine them into an emergent structure.

Are your tone and presentation more effective than other authors'?

Delivery can count for more than complexity or profundity. Many authors can convey the same information in many distinct ways. Each approach will influence minds differently, as no two readers have the same background or goals. Some minds prefer numbers and diagrams, while others may learn best through humor, drama, or long-winded diatribes. Superior arrangement and style improve upon the works of giants before you. Through better framing, you will make the past more accessible to a wider range of readers.

Why are you inspired to bring your message to the world?

You will need the wherewithal to see the writing and publishing processes to completion. If your heart isn't in it, you will grow to resent your book for the enormous demands it places on your time, mind, and finances. You may lose the strength to finish. An inspired message will be worth the effort it requires.

Who needs to read your message and why?

A great book is one that answers questions aching for resolution. The inability to find these answers can lead to everyday practical problems or lifelong existential struggles. Your book can offer a permanent end to someone's malaise. The goal should not be to have everyone on Earth read your book. It should be to reach those readers who will receive the full intended value of your message because they need its insight.

Will you still want to write your book if it makes no money?

Effective marketplace positioning can turn a decent book into sustainable passive income for its creator, but a book written with revenue as its only goal will sacrifice a portion of its integrity. Decide where your priority lies and what your purpose in writing is so you will not sacrifice one for the other. Commercial success will then be only a supplement to the existential reward of communicating your knowledge and ideals.

How will your book change people?

The worth of all creative endeavors can be measured by their influence on living people. Some authors set out to overhaul the way a reader perceives a topic. Some books plant seeds of thought that take time to germinate in new minds. Your book might outline a method by which to change the reader's physical actions, offering a series of gentle suggestions for improvement. It may also continue to affect readers' lives long after they've put it back on their shelf.

How will your book entertain readers?

Even if you think your message is strictly informative, its transmission depends on engagement. No one can absorb information perfectly; you must make it easy for your readers to consume hundreds of pages without losing interest. Each word represents a moment that a reader could have spent in another activity, so work to earn every ounce of your readers' attention by stoking curiosity, evoking empathy, and infusing wit and passion.

Are you prepared to earnestly promote your book?

To find success in self-publishing, you will need to be more than a writer. It doesn't require experience in sales or marketing (though it helps). What you need is an honest willingness to tell people why your book is worth buying and reading. You need to believe this proposition at your core. Do not be content to put the message out there and hope for the best. Own its presentation and promotion. Know there are people who need to read it, as it cures a specific ailment they carry.

I hope the directness of my approach has not scared you off the prospect of becoming a nonfiction author. If you continue, you may have what it takes to rise above the vanity seekers who give self-publishing a poor reputation and enjoy yourself along the way. The conviction to complete your book and bring it to market may change your personal and professional life in ways you cannot imagine. Most importantly, it may grant you a lasting sense of purpose that stays with you all the rest of your life.

If you are ready, destiny awaits you.

Introduction to This Book's Structure and Purpose

We live in a world with access to more information than any generation before. Most of these ideas, once expressed, soon evaporate. Beyond the minor impressions retained by individuals, information tends to wither out of human consciousness, fading from memory as soon as it is transmitted. Both the content of ideas and their mediums are not well-suited for long-term retention. Rarely will an idea come along that is so potent and so well expressed that it rearranges the ideological framework of its time. Only the right conversation, structured in just the right way for the right listener, can achieve any form of permanence in society.

All thinkers, beginning with our earliest intelligent ancestors, have contributed unique pieces to the human story with their ideas. The contributions that accumulate across cultures enable people to live differently than people before them. You need not consider yourself a Shakespeare or a Galileo to influence others with your original ideas. You need only have the patience to arrange your knowledge in a structure some portion of humanity can appreciate.

By connecting to the internet or visiting a library, people today can study human customs and discoveries from the farthest corners of the Earth. They can adopt the wisdom and experiences of bygone eras. The smartest philosophers, scientists, and kings of any previous era would never have believed the volume of stored communication now accessible to common people.

Collective knowledge can also inhibit the spread of new ideas. It can stifle any thoughts that reach too far beyond the norms of their environments. Appropriately, the most influential people in history have been those who were not afraid to speak their minds and focus on their passions, not surrender to established wisdom. We have many brave, untethered individuals, such as the philosophers and inventors of centuries past, to thank for today's developed world.

When you've processed enough of the information from before your time, you may develop the desire to contribute your own ideas to the human story. The same writing technology that brought about the modern world makes it easy to spread new ideas into the unknown future. That is what you can contribute if you are ready to master the communication conventions of your time. You will curate the best of your ideas and share what you know.

Today, due to blogging, vlogging, podcasting, and (most pertinent to our purposes) self-publishing, it is easier than ever to communicate your ideas to the people most desperate to hear them. However, you may never have pondered what your message is, the forms it could take, or its influence upon those who will receive it. You might not yet appreciate the power of your influence over the thoughts and emotions of other people.

As a self-published author, you will be the master of your own destiny. You will need to ask yourself many questions about what you are trying to say. Even if you think you know what you are talking about, do you have a detailed idea of the type of people you are trying to say it to? Do you understand how they should change after having read your words and assimilated your ideas? Without a specific purpose to your actions, your communication will fall flat.

Ideas accomplish nothing without viable presentation. You will need to convince strangers, in moments, that the contents of your book constitute a worthwhile claim on their time and money. Your ideas will need to keep the reader's attention throughout the text, so they will feel compelled to keep the pages turning. An influential author must wear many hats: as the creator, presenter, promoter, and consumer of valuable ideas.

Understanding how human knowledge has been passed on throughout the generations and the importance some books have had for how we think and live pushed me into nonfiction writing and self-publishing. When I realized I had stumbled onto a relatively undiscovered and untapped outlet for meaningful human expression, I started my own publishing company to help people who know they have something important to say write and sell their own influential books. Now, I wish to share with the world what I have learned so far writing my own books, running Identity Publications, and experimenting with countless interesting ways to educate about complex ideas.

The Influential Author examines seven aspects of the relationship between an author and their nonfiction book.

Part 1: Philosophy

Your philosophy about your book is your internal understanding of what you want to say, why it matters, and the social and historical context of your message. Although it may seem obvious that developing your philosophy—or your "why"—is foundational to everything that follows in writing, editing, publishing, and promoting your book, it is the most often overlooked part of the creative process.

Part one of *The Influential Author* addresses:
- What it means to communicate meaningful ideas.
- How communication has evolved since prehistoric and preindustrial times.
- Why books are still the best way to communicate with long-form depth, personality, and precision.
- The many ways self-publishing is better and worse than traditional publishing.
- Why uniqueness and influence matter when choosing what to write about.
- Introspecting about what you care enough to write about and become known for.

Part 2: Strategy

Strategy consists of developing a viable plan for the form the meaning of your message will take. To make a plan for your book, you'll need to understand the modern dynamics of self-publishing so that you'll know what is possible. You'll need to study the marketplace to learn how books similar to and different than yours are received by their readers. Good strategy requires you to think like an entrepreneur on a mission, not solely an artist filled with inspiration.

Part two of *The Influential Author* addresses:
- The angle, style, and unique value of your book.
- The ideal readers and target audience for your unique message.
- Structuring your communication for the ideal scope, length, and focus of your message.
- Comparing the framing of your book's purpose and structure to its marketplace competition.
- Opportunities in your market where reader demand has yet to be fulfilled by other authors.
- The search functionality, subcategory breakdown, and bestseller ranking systems of Amazon and other online book retailers.

Part 3: Creation

Creation, more accurately perceived as transmutation, is the process of turning thoughts into words and capturing them as static writing. The symbols of your writing represent the intangible meaning of your thoughts. You will need to become the kind of person who can achieve this transmutation regularly without losing inspiration, sacrificing the clarity of your message, or succumbing to fatigue.

Part three of *The Influential Author* addresses:
- The importance of cultivating the ideal writing environment and internal state to suit your unique creative nature.

- Arriving at a large word count at a pace that makes sense for your lifestyle and material.
- The functions of a nonfiction book's traditional structure.
- How to craft an outline that captures the essential parts of your message and keeps you focused until you've finished your first draft.
- Keeping your voice authentically yours and avoiding redundancies or omissions.
- Ghostwriters, pre-written content, dictation, and other nontraditional drafting tactics to ease the writing burden.

Part 4: Refinement

Refinement is how you will optimize what you've written to fulfill its purpose. It is the act of improving your message through better structure, style, and presentation and creating more powerful influence for your readers. Getting feedback from external sources and reassessing what you've done so far will help you overcome tunnel vision and self-bias.

Part four of *The Influential Author* addresses:
- The functions of developmental editing, line editing, and copyediting for nonfiction books.
- Learning to love the destruction of your creations for the sake of optimizing your message.
- Rearranging the order of the content of your message for optimal cohesion and retention.
- Working with beta readers and using their feedback to rectify your book's shortcomings and enhance its strengths.
- Reconsidering the focus, scope, and purpose of what you have written.
- Why the pedantic parts of language and proofreading matter for every message.

Part 5: Presentation

Presentation is the impression your message makes when its receivers are first exposed to it. The elements of your book's presentation are the doorway to becoming fully invested in the message within. The way you package your message must capture a specific, actionable kind of attention from the right kind of minds. Your book's title, cover, description, and formatting must all contribute to a complementary and accurate impression.

Part five of *The Influential Author* addresses:
- Avoiding the many pitfalls that make your book look poor quality, cheap, or amateurish at first glance.
- Choosing a title, subtitle, and description that contain the most relevant search terms and entice sales from your target audience without misrepresenting your message.
- Designing a cover that is conventional enough to be recognized for the type of book it is but unconventional enough to stand out from the crowd.
- Formatting the text of your book in paperback, hardcover, and e-book formats.
- Narrating your audiobook or hiring a professional to do it for you.

Part 6: Promotion

Promotion is how you spread your complete and attractive message. It will require you to position your book where it will get attention from the people who can most appreciate it. Today, there are countless ways to build exposure for products online, but only some of them will provide an equitable return of revenue and attention. If your book's outreach is successful, readers will even begin to promote it on their own, creating a sustainable cycle of interest.

Part six of *The Influential Author* addresses:
- Crafting your personal brand and bio as the author of your book.

- Preparing your book's launch date and getting the word out by sharing guest content on the platforms your audience frequents.
- How to determine the ideal retail price of each format of your book with real market data.
- Getting verified, positive online book reviews from readers during and after launch.
- Generating ongoing traffic for your book by running profitable ads where qualified buyers will actually see them.
- Preparing your book for foreign markets through translation and working with foreign publishers.

Part 7: Reward

Your reward is the positive change your book's publication will bring to your life. As a published author, you will come to think of yourself differently than you did before. As well, the world will begin to treat you differently, both challenging and respecting your opinions. Leveraging your book will create many new opportunities in business and in life. Sustainable passive income from your book royalties will liberate your time and labor.

Part seven of *The Influential Author* addresses:
- Dealing productively with results that aren't as good as you'd hoped and understanding the many forms success can take.
- Reframing your self-conception and social narrative as an *authority* on your subject.
- Recognizing the new levels of personal meaning that come with being the face and voice behind important ideas.
- How professional life changes with reliable passive income and the other opportunities a book makes possible.
- Repurposing your book's content for videos, courses, and other mediums to expand your influence.
- Planning your next publications without letting your initial success or lack thereof become a creative trap.
- The unknown but optimistic future of self-publishing and spreading important ideas.

This book's purpose is to help you see the value of your ideas from the perspective of your readers. In addition to honing your ability to communicate through the written word, you will learn about the practical economics of self-publishing and promoting yourself as an originator of a message that really matters. Though they may seem foreign and overwhelming to you now, the knowledge and skills required to complete the task of writing and publishing will seem easy once you are ready.

Best of all, you will not have to surrender creative or monetary control of your work to an outside party. Your expression and its rewards will be yours alone to reap and manage.

PART 1:
PHILOSOPHY

CHAPTER 1:

The Historical Influence of Writing

The practice of targeted communication has been as essential to mankind's sanity as it has to our survival for as long as we have been social creatures. By putting our ideas about the nature of existence into words and images, we can create agreement among our tribes about our shared values. We can collaborate on projects that are beyond the scope of a lone actor (whether it be toppling a mammoth, erecting a skyscraper, or instigating a social revolution). Effective communication gives people a shared sense of identity.

It's easy to forget that for most of human history and prehistory, the only way to communicate was through primitive sounds and pictographs. Absent the aid of electronic amplification, speaking was limited to listeners within natural earshot of the speaker. Any information accumulated across more than one human lifetime would be passed on through myths and stories, from older generations to their offspring. Such enormous amounts of talking constituted a large demand on time and energy.

Early societies maintained their cultural identities through the values practiced among their inhabitants. Parents repeated to their children the wisdom of their parents before them. Political and spiritual figureheads commanded attention and dictated the lifestyle choices of their tribes. Such was the power of their words to influence those who would listen.

Throughout our history, writing has proven to be our most influential communication medium. It is because of the written word that we have been able to draft a history and a narrative for humanity. Our story maintains its continuity across moments, generations, and ages. Primitive cave paintings, the development of the printing press, and the rise and fall of mass market bookstores have all played vital parts in shaping society's cohesion.

Influence does not work differently in our world today, despite the many modern trappings that we think differentiate ours from the primitive eras of the past. The difference today is that our technology for transmitting ideas and their associated values is greater than ever before and still growing. Through sounds, words, and moving or still images, we are better able to convey to other people what we know, believe, and care about. With modern power to influence come modern responsibilities.

If you choose to enter the role of influencer through the dissemination of information you care about in the form of a book, it is wise and worthwhile for you to understand the historical context that has allowed you to consider the path before you. Knowing where things came from and where they may next be going gives context to your role as an author. The right context will make the lengthy endeavor ahead of you all the more rewarding.

The Social Power of Reading and Writing

The advent of the written word forever changed the way we communicate and, thus, changed all civilization. Writing made keeping a record of history possible. On a local level, it allowed groups to maintain an impartial account of information beyond the biases of human memory over time. On a global level, writing has allowed anyone who can read to access information produced thousands of years before them or oceans away.

Because of writing, no longer did communication rely upon the double coincidence of both parties offering and desiring the same information, in the same place at the same time. For the first time, speaker and listener could be separated by time and space. Writing allowed information to spread independently of the mind of its originator. Writers could send out as much information as they wanted, but readers could only receive it at a different time from a distant source. Regardless, the written word has been the primary catalyst for the evolution of human society, understanding, and technology.

In the modern age, where it seems everyone in the developed world owns a personal computer and maintains an online persona, it is humbling to remember that for thousands of years literacy was quite rare in the world. Both reading and writing have almost always been available only to the wealthy and educated, not the common people of any given society. Writing was power. Anyone who could write held more social influence than anyone who could not, for their ideas could spread to more minds. Those who could write persuasively held the most power of all.

Social Thought Policing

The written word has been so important to society (even before widespread literacy), that cultures throughout history have imposed approved thought patterns and barred incongruous ones by destroying books, scrolls, and other forms of documentation. The most powerful institutions on Earth have always been terrified by writing that contradicted what they wanted the people under them in their social dominance hierarchies to believe. For centuries, the Roman Catholic Church maintained their domination by approving for publication only books that would not "harm correct faith or good morals" with a special Imprimatur ("let it be printed") license.

Within the modern Chinese government, the General Administration of Press and Publication can imprison anyone who publishes or imports books or other written materials (whether physically or digitally) that contradict their officially sanctioned version of Chinese history or promote unapproved cultural values. Classics ranging from *Alice's Adventures in Wonderland* by Lewis Carroll and *Green Eggs and Ham* by Dr. Seuss have been banned within China for the dangerous effects they might have on impressionable Chinese minds. To this day, public book burnings remain an accepted practice. You'll learn more about how this affects you as a self-published author seeking international distribution when I discuss foreign promotion strategies in part six of this book.

Because the world changes so quickly now, there is more wisdom to pass on with each generation. More is written than will ever be widely read. The more quickly information evolves, the harder a person must work to keep up with the standards of their culture. Without the aid of modern communication technologies, a single mind can only take in or put out so much knowledge. Left only to our organic faculties, we would never be educated enough to live a modern life. A child today consumes knowledge at a rate that would seem impossible to their ancestors.

Consider that before the printing press, books were treasured possessions. Each one had to be written painstakingly by the hands of professional scribes. The only book most people ever saw in their lives for most of history was the Bible. It's no accident that the text most available to people for so long was the one that acted as the primary source of their worldview, identity, and social values. The Bible and other religious texts like it are living demonstrations of the power of written information to shape societies.

Social Power Expansion

When Johannes Gutenberg introduced a superior version of the printing press to the world in the 15th century, he revolutionized book production. Mass printing dropped the consumer price of books and other printed materials. For the first time in history, written information was becoming affordable and accessible to the masses, not just the elite. Economies of scale emerged in the information market. An original work could be reproduced countless times for nominal extra cost.

Though he likely could not recognize the importance his work would carry, Gutenberg's printing press had opened the door for the common person to adopt cultural influences from endless new sources. The exchange of information was now limited only by the transportation technology for physical pages. A global integration had begun. Then Samuel F.B. Morse introduced the telegraph and Morse code to the United States, revolutionizing long-distance communication. By the mid-1800s, the transatlantic telegraph wire would send the first messages to Europe without the months-long journey required by boat.

Through Thomas Edison, we received the phonograph, the first portable sound recording device. By the 1920s, music was being pressed into vinyl records and transmitted through radio waves across America, allowing over two million homes to listen to what they wanted on demand for a marginal cost. It's rather telling that throughout the Great Depression, despite a general decrease in consumer spending, the popularity of radio grew as people craved more entertainment in uncomfortable times.

In the late 20th century, widespread use of the telephone would replace the telegraph. Real-time auditory reproduction of the human voice allowed conversations to occur in two directions across any distance. New technologies captured more of the nuances of communication, closing the intimacy gap in a world that grew more detached from its close-knit tribal beginnings.

Today, ordinary people rely on handheld electronic devices for written, audio, and visual communication, surpassing the options of all prior generations. We take for granted invisible communication networks like cell towers and satellites that grant instant access to nearly the entire portion of civilization that participates in these networks. Communication interfaces like social media platforms have sprung up to facilitate humanity's identity transition from the physical to the digital realm. Film, television, and recorded music can be streamed online to hungry minds around the world. Real-time local phone calls across town have evolved into live global video interactions in high definition.

We have all but erased the gaps that distance and culture once held over humanity. Culture can be dispersed geographically and intermingled in countless unpredictable ways because of our advanced communication technology.

Books as the Gold Standard for Ideas that Matter

In 1686, at the insistence and expense of his friend, astronomer Edmund Halley, physicist Isaac Newton agreed to write and publish his three-book series, *Philosophiæ Naturalis Principia Mathematica* (which, in English, translates to "mathematical principles of natural philosophy"). Newton's work began simply as a discussion with Halley about the laws that govern planetary motion. It would go on to become what many consider to be the most important scientific text ever written.

Principia, written in Latin (a language known largely by academics at the time) and in a dense mathematical style, was never meant to be a bestseller. It was never even popular in Newton's lifetime. It was meant to disclose his theories about what he called "the frame of the system of the world." We know it today as the laws of classical physics: the axioms of mass, force, momentum, and universal gravitation, proving that the written medium ensured that the influence of his ideas would go on to matter after his death.

Less than a century after publishing, Newton's laws became directly responsible for the technological and economic boom of the Industrial Revolution. Every subsequent breakthrough in chemistry and biology is possible because of the publication and eventual spread of Isaac Newton's *Principia*. Had Edmund Halley not convinced him to proceed and himself funded Newton's book, we would live in a much less developed world today, and it would not be technologically possible for you to be reading this right now.

In January 1776, an anonymous pamphlet about the philosophical basis for American independence was published in Philadelphia and disseminated throughout the 13 colonies. Thomas Paine's *Common Sense* challenged the institution of the British monarchy and became the bestselling book per capita in American history. Perhaps most impressively, because it was anonymous, Americans were able to evaluate Paine's ideas on their own merits, not on any perceived authority of the author.

Because its language was clear, purposeful, and persuasive, *Common Sense* accomplished an amazing feat: changing the minds of millions of people toward an unprecedented cause. It made the American Revolution (and all social progress that followed) a desirable outcome instead of an obscure fantasy. Less than six months later, the Declaration of Independence would be signed by Paine and his contemporaries. Their change in the structure of society would inspire similar advancements in nations the world over.

If there were any doubt about *Common Sense's* contribution to independence, fellow founding father John Adams had this to say about the matter: "Without the pen of Paine, the sword of Washington would have been wielded in vain." Paine demonstrated that the right idea presented to a ready audience could change the world.

Affluence of Opportunity

As there are now more communication channels available than ever before, people have too many ways to make their voices heard. We tend not to appreciate such power because it's what modern generations have always known. We forget that when we strip away communication technology, our ability to be heard drops to only whoever is within earshot. Our influence then is the same as that of our primitive ancestors.

Every communication medium that has come in and out of fashion throughout history has done so for specific reasons in the context of the time that they were popular. Each medium offers unique advantages and disadvantages. Modern social media platforms give us the ability to create facsimiles of ourselves online. Blogs serve as written collections of experience or expertise

9

on a subject. Video channels rocket ordinary people to minor celebrity status by displaying their personalities on camera for all the world to see.

Though the methods for producing books have improved, their fundamental function has not. Printed books have remained popular in the digital era because they have symbolic importance beyond any other medium. Books are the gold standard of communication that matters. Sitting down with a book in hand is an intimate experience that we have romanticized and adored across countless subcultures. The sacredness of books in human minds is incomparable to other forms of content. There's a reason the idea of burning a pile of DVDs isn't nearly as traumatic as the idea of burning a pile of books.

Long-Form Communication

Books also persist because they serve long texts of tens or hundreds of thousands of words better than any other medium. They provide the space needed to elaborate on every relevant angle of a subject in a logical progression. By the time the reader reaches the final pages, they should feel that their knowledge of the subject is complete enough to be applied in the world. Such a comprehensive education is not possible with snippets of ideas trimmed down for virality and digestion.

Interconnected Ideas

The structure of books enables writers to cover multiple complex, connected ideas. Different sections, chapters, and subheadings make it easy for readers to categorize the information in front of them, skimming back and forth between concepts as needed for reinforced integration. Readers can take notes, mark pages, and refer to earlier passages whenever they need to. Books, more than any other medium, make it convenient for consumers to navigate information at their own pace and in their own ideal way.

The evolution of communication standards and technology is a double-edged sword. Every new medium suffers from rapid self-obsolescence. The way people watch videos or listen to music changes within several years, as generational trends and portable storage technologies move on. Audio and video content have inherently shorter shelf lives (recordings of major historical events notwithstanding). Vinyl records, 8-track tapes, cassettes, CDs, Betamax and VHS tapes, and DVD and Blu-Ray discs are subject to a decline in accessibility from the moment they are created.

Timeless Appeal

More than any other medium, paper books subvert the effects of entropy and obsolescence. In fact, many timeless books just appreciate with age. Books today are still made roughly the same way as hundreds of years ago. Binding techniques and the composition of paper may change with the generations, but the information in old books is as convenient to consume as it is in modern ones. The consistent standards of books make them more collectible than any other medium, either privately in homes or publicly in libraries, stores, and museums. Despite the advances of the digital era, there is no reason to believe that the timeless appeal of books will wane anytime soon. It remains to be seen how the digital evolution of e-book distribution will change how we treat physical books. My belief is that it will only increase the total demand for books, not consume a larger fraction of a fixed number of possible readers.

On the personal level, readers can return to the books they owned when they were younger throughout their lives. Our favorite books become a part of us, as we have put a little bit of ourselves into them. Modern homes proudly display large collections of cherished books. These personal libraries are shrines to the values that have taken hold in our minds. An old book is a renewable spring of positive influence, maintaining the same personal resonance it did decades prior.

On the social level, books from ages past help us appreciate the eras of their authors. Writing styles change. Values shift with the generations. Cultural touchstones go in and out of relevancy. Reading *Common Sense*, we can imagine what life in the American colonies must have been like for Paine's words to spurn such strong support for independence. Books offer a static recreation of the minds of human history, beyond the mere facts and statistics about their existence.

Cost-Efficient Transmission

Without relatively cheap and efficient book publishing, the revolutionary ideas of the Newtons and Paines of the world may never have taken off. Long-term transmission would have been too difficult. We will never know how many other great minds have had ideas of equal worth but lacked the opportunity to publish a book and harness such influence. Books and the information they carry can literally outlast empires.

For almost four centuries, it has been difficult for ordinary people to become published authors, as even small publishing contracts required enormous faith and investment in the author. Only a few organizations had the production, distribution, and marketing capacity to turn an unknown author into a success. Many of the most successful authors today only got their big breaks after struggling for years, penniless, to find someone willing to take a chance. If a writer did not already have a connection to someone in a position of authority at a publishing house, their chances of even being considered were slim.

If you understand the unique and important advantages afforded to you by the creation and distribution of your own books, you only need to determine the best way to harness them.

The Evolution of Traditional Publishing into Self-Publishing

The mass publishing of printed books in America began in 1638, when a printing press was imported to Cambridge, Massachusetts from England.

Since then, it has grown to over 2,500 publishing houses and billions of dollars in revenue each year. In Philadelphia, founding father Benjamin Franklin maintained a print shop, authoring and publishing countless books. By the 19th century, New York City had become the publishing capital in the United States, seeing the rise of such prolific publishing houses as Harper, Scribner, and Putnam.

The 1970s brought about big chain bookstores, such as Barnes & Noble, who established deals with publishers allowing them to sell books cheaper than independent bookstores. From there, it was only a matter of time before Amazon and other online book retailers would prevail as readers realized they would rather browse and order books from home. E-books likewise rose to prominence when it became clear many readers preferred them to the physicality of paper books.

When self-publishing became commercially viable, it was because technology entered the market to replicate what, previously, only large publishing houses could do. Print-on-demand services now make processing print runs of many thousands of copies of a single title irrelevant. Authors working on a shoestring budget do not have to invest thousands of dollars up front just to stack copies of their work in their garage. Now, authors can order as few or as many copies of their professionally bound books as they want for just a few dollars each (plus the cost of shipping).

To the dismay of many large publishing houses, online marketplaces like Amazon.com have democratized book marketing and distribution. Authors with only a basic knowledge of internet marketing can find creative and inexpensive ways to get their book in front of their ideal readers. Amazon and its affiliated companies take their cut of the purchase and automatically send the order to be printed and shipped, or delivered instantly over the internet in the case of digital formats like e-books or audiobooks. The barrier to entry for aspiring authors is all but gone.

Self-Publishing Challenges

Still, self-publishing is the most recent industry change for books. It has not been perfected or fully embraced by readers. Self-published authors can carry negative stigmas of amateurism that traditionally published authors do not. The common perception is that any book that a "real" publisher wouldn't pick up is not worth reading. Without a barrier to entry, the seal of quality offered by large publishers is absent. Anyone, no matter how terrible or revolutionary their message might be, can sell their book on the same platforms as *War and Peace* or the *Harry Potter* series.

What all this means for aspiring authors is that if they are willing to deal with the stigmas and difficulties associated with self-publishing, they no longer need to search for years or know people in the right places to have their book published. Everyone has an equal opportunity at making their voice heard, so long as they learn to make use of the resources available to them. For better or worse, the doors have been opened permanently. There is no turning back from here. No longer do a few ruling minds determine for everyone else who or what can be presented to the masses. Overcoming these hurdles is what I will show you how to do if you believe your message is deserving.

Traditional publishing appears appealing to authors who strictly want to focus on writing, though even this is misleading because large publishing houses still expect the author to assist with the marketing of their book. Publishing houses do, however, have professional sources in place for professional editing, graphic design, and copywriting. Authors who choose to go it alone will have to either handle all these supplementary tasks themselves or outsource the parts they don't like to professionals. The self-published author necessarily wears many hats.

Traditional publishers may take over most of the heavy lifting, but their involvement carries great costs. Not only will the author's book royalties be of a significantly smaller percentage than they would if they self-published, but the author will not even retain total control of their intellectual

14

property. The publishing company they sell their rights to decides how or when they release and promote the book. Additionally, the author's agent makes their money as a percentage of the advance (if any) and royalties for the book (typically 15%).

Creative Control

When a writer signs a deal with a publishing company, the company owns the print license, while the writer owns the copyright. Giving up the print license means the publisher has control over the title, cover, content, pricing, promotion, and distribution of the book. They may require substantial modifications to the content and tone of the work, diminishing the authenticity of the message.

If an author's point of view is unconventional, they may have a hard time convincing a traditional publisher to leave it as is. Just like big Hollywood movie studios, publishers take a risk every time they purchase the rights to a book and expend their resources producing and promoting it. They aren't in the business of gambling on unknown authors who don't fit the mold of what they know turns a profit. Publishers will likely require significant modifications to an uncommon book (if they are even interested in publishing it), unless the author has somehow proven their work's saleability.

The thought of someone else having the final say on what will go in their book is unbearable for many authors. Their name and face are going to be associated with whatever ends up in print. If their publisher doesn't understand the unique, personal appeal the author intends, they will tarnish the message. The revisions could be minor and valuable, like the fixing of problematic punctuation and superfluous vocabulary. They could also be large and deconstructive, like an overhaul of order, theme, title, style, and cover design. Traditional publishers may be right and they may be wrong about their revisions, but they're going to have final say even if the author disagrees.

Traditional publishers tailor their books to the standards they can predict a large audience will respond to. They don't care what an author thinks their book should look like or the philosophical implications of the message. Many publishers are willing to sacrifice artistic integrity and risk misleading buyers if they believe that doing so will create greater intrigue. The publisher is happy with the higher sales, but disappointed buyers can destroy the author's brand.

Royalty Splitting

A traditional publisher pays its authors 7–15% royalties on book sales (minus the literary agent's 15% of the author's 15%, typically a total of 2.25% of the sale price). Through self-publishing, authors keep most of the royalties from each sale. When an author enters into a private agreement with a retailer like Amazon, the retailer keeps a portion of the book revenues for the privilege of listing the book on their site, allowing users to leave reviews and adding the book to their category rankings. If an author publishes their e-book through Amazon's Kindle Direct Publishing (KDP) and prices it between $2.99 and $9.99, they will receive 70% royalties for their book. For any retail price outside this range, author royalties from Amazon drop to 35%, which is still vastly superior to the maximum 15% that traditional publishers offer.

For physical books, KDP Print (Amazon's department for print-on-demand paperbacks) charges a printing fee of one and one-fifth cent ($0.012) per page for black and white books and seven cents ($0.07) per page for color books. They also add 85 cents for the printing of the cover of every book. Authors publishing paperbacks can expect a 250-page black and white book of any page size to cost less than $4 per copy to print. Amazon then keeps 35% royalties of the retail price of KDP Print paperbacks when sold on their platform, leaving the author with a profit of about 50% of the book price in royalties (which is, again, far better than the 15% or less available through large publishing houses). The exact amount will depend on retail and printing prices of the book.

These are the same rates and policies once implemented by CreateSpace, Amazon's former print-on-demand subsidiary company that was integrated with Kindle Direct Publishing in late 2018. Other print-on-demand companies like IngramSpark and Lulu have their own pricing structures, which sometimes allow the author or publisher to set their own wholesale discount rates.

Publishing Timeline

A traditional publisher may require 12–18 months to publish a book from the time they acquire the rights to it. In fact, a book project could get caught in development hell and be delayed for years, if not abandoned altogether. If a book's subject is topical and timely, its content may be outdated by the time the gears of conventional publishing finish turning. If a book is tied to other aspects of its author's professional life, delayed release could mean the loss of new business and opportunities. Book marketing efforts will be fruitless if an author cannot predict when their book will be available. Through self-publishing, an author can have their book on Amazon within days from the time the final draft is ready. It is seldom desirable to rush a book's release so much like this, but it's always an option. The self-published author will not beckon to anyone's timetable but their own.

The burden of self-published authors is to achieve the same level of professionalism as their traditional counterparts. Self-publishing, therefore, requires authors to be responsible for much more than writing. They must aspire to conquer the many responsibilities of publishing if they are to achieve success. Even the world's most skilled writers cannot handle cover design, formatting, editing, presentation, or sales and marketing with the same effectiveness. They will need to outsource at least some parts of the process. It is the only way to produce a book approaching the standards set by traditional publishers that readers expect when they pay $20 for a paperback or $30 for a hardcover.

Many aspects of the book refinement, presentation, and promotion processes are difficult to predict for self-publishers. Editing can happen in one quick round of feedback from a critical mind, or an author can belabor it for months on end, with dozens of readers pointing out ways to improve individual sentences or alter the structure of a book's message. An author can cut entire chapters. They can move the end to the beginning or the beginning to the end. They can even end up rewriting their book from scratch once the first draft has been thoroughly eviscerated.

Then there are all the skilled creative decisions that go into cover design, title selection, and interior formatting. Assessing all the creative alternatives, finding and paying the right talent, or putting the many required hours of their own labor in could extend their book's release date by weeks or months, even after the content is finalized. To self-publish, an author must get comfortable managing these kinds of decisions, as though they were the architect and foreman behind the construction of a house. The challenges that govern both traditional and independent publishing will change in the years to come. It will gradually become easier for communicators to release their messages as profitable books without sacrificing the integrity of what they intend to communicate. The unrealized societal potential of these shifts is massive. Now it's time for you to realize it with your book and your message.

Summary of Chapter 1

Reading and writing have played immensely important roles in maintaining a progression of culture and knowledge across generations and communities for all of human history, even in the face of recent technological advances in audio and video communication.

— — — —

Books have organically emerged as the standard for transmitting important ideas due to their durability, portability, low-tech design, ability to accommodate long messages, social perception of authority, and inexpensive cost of production.

— — — —

For centuries, the means to print and distribute books profitably was held by relatively few major publishing houses. In recent decades, self-publishing technology has made it easier and cheaper for independent authors to produce, publish, and promote their own work without giving up the royalties or creative control for their work.

CHAPTER 2:

Introspecting What to Write About

Are you sure you want to write a book? Are you certain you have something unique and amazing to communicate and that the effort will all be worth it when you are done? Out of all the things you could possibly write about, how will you rationally decide which is the best one for you to start your journey as an author with?

There is no reason for you to proceed with the long and difficult journey of book writing and publishing if your words add nothing new to the library of human thought. Lazy writers seek to copy what has been proven to work by the most popular authors in their genre, leading to countless clones of groundbreakers like *The 7 Habits of Highly Effective People* by Stephen Covey or *The Secret* by Rhonda Byrne. If what you have to say can be (and has been) better said by another author, find something else to say. To know what is right for you to make the focus of your first book, you'll need to be willing to introspect far deeper than most wannabe authors ever do.

As you'll see, writing about a subject for which you know there exists a demand is only one important factor in a complex equation for success and meaning as an author. To the benefit of all communicators, anyone can express old information in new ways that alter or add to the value it conveys. If you aren't writing about things never written about, you can still write about common things from a new perspective or arranged in an innovative structure. It takes great skill as an educator to add a new spin to something familiar without appearing redundant or derivative.

Whatever your subject, readers will judge your book against the backdrop of similar books. If you do not understand what already exists in your genre or what already caters to your receivers' psychological needs, you will not be able to see your work as strangers see it. You will be likely to repeat overused themes and clichéd approaches to familiar material. The key to your successful communication is to find a hole in the library of humanity and fill it.

When you look at popular nonfiction books on Amazon.com or in a local bookstore, can you tell what is uniquely appealing about them? If you were to ignore all forms of preconception and social proof, how much clarity would there be about a book's real utility? What does one book offer that another book a few places over on the same shelf does not? You must have clear answers to these questions about your book before you ever begin outlining.

If you can analyze the purpose of books independently of their authors' personal narratives or public hype, you will see that many fail to contribute anything new to human discourse. When you publish your book, you should do so with the assumption that you will never win any popularity contests or make it into Oprah's book club. You may never become famous for your views or associations. If your message can stand on the merits of its meaning alone, these contests won't matter to you.

The message of your first book is wholly up to you, but whatever you choose to write about will likely be some combination of the following:

- Interpretations of the meaning of life.
- Philosophical insights from your unconventional experiences.
- Practical advice about an area you have professional experience in.
- How to make progress in a domain of personal or interpersonal development.
- The promotion of a new lifestyle movement or philosophy.
- Documentation or analysis of an important worldly phenomenon.

Whatever your book ends up as, certain principles, processes, and skills will work to your benefit as a goal-oriented communicator. The processes and advice I've included throughout *The Influential Author* are meant to help you integrate the qualities you're going to need in order to find success as an independent and influential source of written knowledge.

Why You're Motivated to Write and Communicate

Would you rather write a good book or have written a good book?

Some authors want to write. They are addicted to putting words down on paper. It is cathartic and entertaining. They love the social identity that comes with the territory of being "a writer." Such people define themselves by their struggle as bleeding artists for a noble cause that few others can understand. Talking about the book they are working on provides the same social reward as actually writing the book, so they follow a very inefficient yet outspoken path to finishing it.

The opposite of this is the author who cares only about making the finished product work the best it can be. An outcome-oriented approach may seem counterintuitive to writers who have learned to love the journey of writing, not the destination they thought they were traveling to. It's natural for us to associate greater value with things that require greater effort of us. While there are many scenarios in life where focusing on the process of creation is the ideal choice, it can become your worst enemy as an author undertaking a large and intensive project with the intention of finding philosophical and financial success.

When a writer focuses on the process of writing, they create roadblocks to production. They just want to "do," never to "be done." The same habit manifests in every area of life where we fall into patterns of chronic problem-solving. We cease to look for permanent solutions that would liberate us from the tyranny of symptom fighting. This is a fundamental flaw in the human psyche that keeps most people locked into narrowly defined cycles without significant progress in any of life's domains.

Some writers refuse to let their babies grow up, obsessed with perfecting their work to the point where they are making mindless nitpicks or ruining a passage that was already in its ideal state. It's a vicious cycle that keeps the troubled writer working harder and harder just to stay in the same place with their manuscript. They have nothing to look forward to, only the imperfections present before them. Once you begin drafting and refining, you must break this cycle if you are ever going to finish your book.

A creator who values their time focuses on the outcome they intend to produce. They want to reach their outcome in the most efficient and effective manner, never sacrificing their vision, so that they may free their time to focus on the next inspiration when it arises. They must not fall in love with an idea and become distracted by the process of planning and crafting. They can learn to use the planning process to keep them engaged in a specific goal, instead of diving into needless busy work.

Further, if an author grows attached to something they have written, merely because it took much effort or emotional activation to write it the way they did, they will not clearly see what ought best be revised or eliminated about it as they edit their work. If they are required to kill portions of what they have birthed for the good of the book's quality, they will lament the loss. It will be difficult to make unbiased decisions about how to optimize the transmission they are intending. The unwillingness to kill one's darlings is a manifestation of the same sunk cost fallacy that prevents people from walking away from their mistakes simply because they have spent a long time making them.

Composition Hurdles

Some people are naturally gifted with fluidity of composition. They can seamlessly articulate whatever appears in mind. Some exceptional writers who can churn out 10,000 words or more in a single day love to boast of their rapid progress. They make casually paced writers feel inadequate for their inability to keep up with such unrealistic standards of output. Yet, these hyper typing writers may be the ones who will never complete a single polished and publishable work, tailored for a meaningful purpose. Ample creative faculty, without discipline or focus, does not result in meaningful creation.

A single refined thought can carry more influence than all the internal ramblings of an unfocused mind over the course of its lifetime. Hundreds of pages, dense with text, mean nothing if not structured in such a way as to entice readers with information that addresses their most burning needs. Meaningful communication satisfies the discontents of its recipients in a sustainable manner. Ejaculating words onto paper and calling it a book accomplishes nothing except serving the author's ego.

People with a message who hate the act of writing may actually be more likely to finish authoring a book than people who love the act of writing. They have set their goal and will find the most efficient way to achieve it. They aren't infatuated by struggle. Writing is just the means to get where they know they must go. They want to finish what they start as quickly as they can, so long as they do not sacrifice the quality they initially set out for. The writer who focuses on the outcome and not the process will walk away with a finished book long before the writer who is in love with their own words.

Of course, it is possible to both love the act of writing and be dedicated to producing finished work. However, the wherewithal to finish what one starts is more valuable for the amateur writer taking their first steps toward authordom. It doesn't matter how excruciating you find writing to be, so long as you have enough incentive to make it through the pain to its magnificent reward. If you also happen to enjoy writing, going back and correcting mistakes or rewriting things from scratch will be all the more easy for you.

Holding the motivation to see a large project through to completion is difficult for people who have never had to delay gratification for months or years before seeing any reward for their efforts. They must adopt a larger time scale perspective than the daily, weekly, or monthly view they are accustomed to. They must find the strength to see the process through the hard times where inspiration and resilience seem lacking. They must know what they are trying to accomplish and hold that purpose in mind every step of the way. Even if they are truly dedicated, the writing and publishing can take much longer than they anticipate for reasons they can't control.

Motivation from Money

The unfortunate truth of selling books is that the majority of self-published authors never make any significant income from their work. They may not even make back the amount they invest in publishing processes like editing, cover design, and promotion. For the self-published author who learns how the market works and can tailor their books to reader demands, each book becomes a new source of significant and sustainable income. The reliable expectation of monetary reward is extra incentive they can use to both finish their work quickly and ensure that it is the best it can be.

For most people, additional income is a useful catalyst for action. Money is universally desired because of its immediate practical function in nearly all aspects of life. Even for the most stoic and detached of us, money is an essential factor to modern living. Because people sacrifice the majority of their waking hours to accumulate and spend money, the idea of being able to break away from this cycle is appealing. As well, an author who is dependent on a regular paycheck will find it harder to invest the time into producing their book than someone who is already financially independent.

Money is a useful means for making the abstract concrete. We all have spent a lifetime learning to assess the value of things by their monetary costs. Specific dollar amounts carry deep emotional weight in our minds. People know what an extra $500 feels like. It's concrete. There's an immediate emotional reward. We cannot react the same to the abstract concept of being a successful author or its many long-term derivatives. Intellectually, we understand that the benefits of authorship will outweigh any incidental dollar amount we receive, but it still doesn't hit us the same way.

If you find yourself delaying the production of your manuscript to accommodate the demands of real life, hold in your mind the idea that your book may be a doorway to sources of new income. Adopting such a mindset is easier after one has already written their first successful book and grown accustomed to seeing hundreds or thousands of dollars every month deposited into their bank account. You can expose yourself to self-published authors who have supplemented their regular income or are living solely on book royalties to serve as your financial muse.

The income opportunities made possible by publishing a book don't end with book royalties from copies sold. There's a trite saying among internet entrepreneurs that "the book is the new business card." It's their way of saying that professionals of a certain caliber of expertise are expected to have authored a book detailing their knowledge or unique approach to what they do. The author can then slap a poorly photoshopped headshot on the cover, pick a generic, hyperbolic title to summarize the theme of the book, and print copies for a couple dollars apiece and give them away or sell them at their networking events and speaking gigs. It's a low-risk and lazy way for them to try to boost their brand authority.

Motivation from Meaning

But maybe you don't care about the money you will make or the boost in public perception you will receive from your book. Perhaps your motivation to write is more spiritual or esoteric than that. When some people surpass a certain level of existential development, they begin to desire a more meaningful life for themselves. The ways they can do this are endless. Each person called toward a meaningful existence pursues a means appropriate to their interests and abilities. Some are physical in nature, such as building houses for the homeless. In such cases, the influence is limited to the direct effects of their physical labor, but their emotional reward is tangible and immediate.

For people who pursue meaning through intellectual and artistic means, such as writing a book, recording a song, or innovating a device or technique, the potential spread of their influence is only subject to the scarcity of their physical mediums. As a writer, the value of your actions does not derive from your fingers tapping away at your keyboard. It is not the same as a builder who creates value by swinging their hammer or pulling their saw. The influence of the paper pages of your book is more than their tangible function as objects to be held and turned.

All meaningful authors write to have an influence upon the minds of their readers. It is the only rational way to measure the effectiveness of information transmission. When someone thinks and acts differently because they have read your book, you will receive an intangible reward far greater than any other consequence of authorship. You will cultivate a sense of purpose in your craft. Your influence will come from the new thought formations your words create in your readers' minds. One intellectually creative act can go on to create influence over and over. There is no practical limit to how far it might go.

Think about a book that has influenced you more than others and stayed with you for years. Recall an author who revealed a profound new perspective or touched your mind in ways no one else ever had. Maybe it was Henry David Thoreau's detached musings on the madness of modern society. It could have been Ayn Rand's heavy-handed ode to free enterprise. Perhaps for you it was the simple wisdom of the present moment offered by Eckhart Tolle. Why did it affect you when you first read it? Why has it stuck in your mind until now?

What creates influence is different for every reader. What people respond to depends on where they are in life and where they are looking to go next. If you have your heart set on becoming an influential author, it's because you believe that somewhere within the substance of your thoughts and experiences is a message with timeless potential. It can reach others the way that your extended mentors reached you through their writing. Believe in this power and hold onto this vision until your book is complete.

Motivation from Authenticity

Unknown authors who write with genuine authenticity and authority will outshine unknown authors who write with ulterior motives. Authenticity is not something an author can fake (at least not for long). No matter how well vanity authors think they can cover them up, their true motivations are bound to seep out at some point within the contents of a full-length book. The more they expose of themselves, the more readers will notice incongruities in their presentation. This is why so many books receive middling-to-negative reviews complaining that the book seemed designed as a giant advertisement for its author—not a heartfelt message meant to improve the lives of readers.

Resist the urge at this early juncture to go for the easy win when thinking about what to write for your book. Don't settle on an approach that seems obvious or derivative of what's already successful. You can stand out from vanity authors by being authentic and clear in your message. If influence is truly your highest purpose, you cannot write to get something from your readers. You can only write to give them something vital that they may not have known they were missing. When you write for the people who need your book's influence, you will do it with the conviction that you have something to say worth reading.

Writing even has many cathartic effects on the psyche of the writer. Once your book exists on the open market, it will liberate mental space within you. You will be able to devote more psychological Real Estate to new ideas after you've crafted a container to hold the old ones. The mind has a way of excusing itself from having to refresh the same information time and again once you've stored it somewhere outside yourself. Through writing out your philosophy and organizing your unspoken knowledge, you will develop a more efficient mind than you had when it was loose in your head. Writing your book in a way that captures your deepest message could be a powerful catalyst for your personal advancement.

What You Dare to Become Known for

Think of the areas of life in which you would like people's respect. On what topics do you wish people would listen to your opinion? Better yet, why does it matter to you that the world takes you seriously here? Influence is power. If you care about something, you should seek influence around it. Your place in society should be one of prestige and importance, but only if you can earn acceptance by your peers in your era.

You know you want to write a book and you probably have a few good ideas about what you know enough to write about. However, do you know what you are comfortable speaking publicly on and aligning your identity with? Authoring a book is a powerful statement about who you are and what you stand for. For first-time authors, narrowing the options according to this new variable will be the most difficult part of the entire publishing process.

Most people cannot easily decide what kind of character they want to be in the eyes of the world. Newbie authors want to tell their entire life story in a single tome or share every valuable thought they've ever had for fear of leaving out a single fact or interesting experience. They regard their books as the only lasting consequence of their life on Earth. It is a testament to their existence, so it must not omit anything of note. To write a book that only captures a portion of their values would be to limit their identity.

As soon as you choose what to say in your book, you collapse all possibilities into a single path. Every word following the first is increasingly limited in the directions it can go. If you struggle to refine all your ideas into a topic viable for your first book, it's time to reframe what your book will be for you. The purpose of your book is not to capture every thought that has ever passed through your head or every detail of your personal history. Its purpose is to curate relevant elements of what you know and have experienced, then arrange them into a factual narrative around a well-defined goal.

Do you know what you care enough about to put your name and face on it, even if all the world may see it? This is easy to answer if you've already committed your life to a professional path. Your trade should be a reflection of your deepest values, filtered through your skills and abilities. If that's the case, you already have a template for your message—or at least one possible message. Turn your experiences and lessons into a guide for others who face similar struggles.

Instead of focusing on yourself, try to see your book from the outside looking in. If the people of the world were to stare into your mind, what is the most valuable message they would find for themselves? The easiest book for you to write will be the one you know the world is ready to read. Then you can compare that to what you know you are able to write.

Future Associations

Still, an author must look beyond the present moment as much as possible if they wish their association with their work to be timeless. What you value now may not be what you always will. Someday, you may come to believe the exact opposite of what you currently do on some very important topics. Once published, your book's influence and your connection to it are hard to make disappear completely. Even if no one buys your book and you remove it from publication, archives of its existence will persist on the internet and used copies may still turn up on eBay.

If your book sells well, people will start talking about it in places and contexts you could not have predicted. Its influence will spill out into the world, leaping between minds, as you will no longer be able to control it. What will happen if the person you are a decade from now no longer wants to be associated with the message you release in the present? Consider the possibility that your religious, political, or philosophical beliefs could evolve with decades of more life experience. Consider that you may enter a line of work that conflicts with the values you want to express now.

The cake, once baked, can never be unbaked. In the age of information, whatever's out there remains out there. This, more than anything, is the reason why you should aim to write beyond momentary market fads or passing personal interests. You are investing into the world's perception of you throughout the remainder of your life. If you are clear about the role you wish to play, choosing the topic and tone of your first book should be no chore. Write something that has no chance of sabotaging your future self.

It may sound like I'm telling you to limit your options to universally inoffensive and mundane subjects like woodworking. I'm not saying that what you write must be perceived as innocuous by all people for fear that you may face social backlash for your unacceptable opinions. What I really mean is to write your message in a way that is consistent with your timeless, internal standards of reason and meaning. It's an awful feeling to look back at one's own life every few years and feel ashamed of the things you used to care about.

Right now, all your interests fall into a gradient of permanent and passing. Some will be with you your entire life. Others will be replaced within the year. A decade from now, will you still feel good that you put all that energy into writing your book about the politics of modern Russia? Or is it just an obsession that has caught your eye for now? Writing your book will contribute a great deal to the course your life will take and the social identity that will stick with you.

Authorial Perception

I'm not exaggerating when I say that becoming a successful author, with thousands of happy readers and recognition for your message, will change your life. Think of how you would like to see it improve from your efforts.

The social effects of authorship cannot be ignored. When people know you have written a book, they will assume many things about you. When they read your book, they will have glimpsed into the workings of your mind. You will begin conversations from an elevated position, as the reader will have already gone on a lengthy journey with you as their guide.

If you have ever lamented that other people couldn't understand you the way you would like, a book offers the opportunity to set the record straight. You can write your own persona into the world through your tailored communication. If you write under a pen name, it will not be long before more people know your made-up label than the name your parents gave you. You will face a rapid social evolution, guided in the direction of your written words.

Should you feel apprehension about what to write for fear of becoming an imposter, search within yourself to discover why you believe your knowledge may be inauthentic. If the new social role your book will place you in clashes with the role you play now, you will resist the evolution. Similarly, people in your life who have grown accustomed to knowing you in one way might not welcome a departure from what they have come to expect of you.

You likely hold many biases about what authors are like. These preconceptions are arbitrary and unfairly limiting. If the image you hold of yourself doesn't match the pattern in your head about what a certain type of author should be like, you will not give yourself permission to write the book you really want. This is a subtle, yet common form of self-sabotage. If you don't have enough knowledge to write the book you want, use the creation process to fill in the gaps.

You don't have to be the perfect embodiment of your words to write a compelling book, just competent and consistent with their place in your life. I will never claim to be the world's leading authority on writing or self-publishing, but I will stand by my passion for the topic and the accuracy of my claims as long as I must. You are allowed to admit the limits of your knowledge or abilities. You are not allowed to pretend perfection, despite what hordes of skeezy internet marketers might tell you.

Noble Intentions

When people listen to what you say, you can change their minds and affect their actions. It follows that you should have a noble reason to want to do this. Narcissism (an arbitrary sense of self-importance) and megalomania (the desire to dominate others) won't cut it if you are going to become an influential author. You must experience a sense of purpose deep within the core of your perpetuating identity related to the expression of your values and ideas.

Of course, there's a fine line between narcissism and just believing strongly enough in something to align your name, face, and public identity with it. It takes maturity to put all of yourself into something and seek recognition for it without losing yourself to the story you tell. We are all actors within the story we are writing about the world. For some people who reach this level of emotional awareness, writing and promoting a book is the obvious next step in the journey of their life.

You likewise must recognize that reality, as it is right now, is inadequate in some way according to your values. The expression of your message has the power to rectify this inadequacy. Whether manifested as hope or pain, the desire to change reality is the impetus for all great creative acts. Identifying and holding your motivation will allow the creative process to come much more easily. It will also make much clearer the appropriate topic to write about because you will know what effect you want your book to have.

Lifetime of Interests

There will never be just one option for what to write about in the domain of nonfiction. If you've been alive long enough to have something worth saying, your experiences are broad and unique enough that they could be arranged into many possible narratives with different outcomes. Even teenagers, with their lesser quantity of experience, may have done things that would shock and enlighten older people. Someone who has spent 50 years working in one industry has acquired unique perspectives that would be valuable to newcomers of that same industry. The broader or more uncommon your thoughts and actions have been, the more options you will have for valid messages to communicate.

When you look at your life through this lens and realize that they are many potential things you could say that would be worth listening to, you face a sudden new burden of choice. The determining factor for which of the many possible topics you could knock out at least a few dozen thousand words on will be which one is most emotionally rewarding for you. Only a fraction of the many moments of your life fall into a category that aligns with some deeper sense of purpose or importance. You will learn to pluck those out of the larger story of your life and arrange them in a complementary fashion.

Every marketer knows the benefits of a product must appear at the forefront of its presentation while its various features take a backseat. Look at your life and message this way. What are the benefits that come from knowing and talking to you? What is the information you find yourself repeating across countless conversations to many interested parties? The details of your life can make for an entertaining part of reinforcing the value of your message, but only if you draw from them to address the needs of the people you speak to.

Cultural Limitations

Whatever you choose to write, do not let your friend's, enemy's, society's, or self-imposed expectations about what you are allowed to do or be stop you from doing and being what you can. Now is the time to the let the truth about you come out in the public eye. Changing your self-conception is the primordial step in your path to change the world by changing the way it thinks. When you change what people think about you, the world around you also changes.

Even in today's educated world, to be able to communicate important things coherently is a power not held by many. To hone this ability is to raise yourself to a higher tier of social interaction and to wield influence. When you understand your message and can transmit it effectively, you will begin to be recognized for such. If you become a competent writer and promote your work well, you will open new doors in all aspects of life as society begins to associate you with your message.

Once your message is out there, you can live with less friction between how you see yourself and how you would like others to see you. In creating harmony between the inner and outer worlds, you will know more peace in your life.

Where Passion, Experience, and Demand Converge

All people, in all conscious moments, are in a struggle to move away from problems and towards solutions. Your words are the fuel that bring them to their desired destination. Train yourself to look at your words through the filter of what they will do for readers and how they will make readers feel. Unsubstantiated appeals to emotions are as flawed a writing strategy as flaccid intellect lacking heart. Make readers think as much as you make them feel.

Always remember that a good book has a defined purpose. Every anecdote, stylistic choice, or inclusion of data should serve that purpose. The hard part for most new authors is deciding what that single purpose should be or being open to modifying that purpose as needed throughout the creative process.

The first time you start thinking seriously about writing a book, adopt the mindset that you will have the opportunity to write every book you ever want over the course of your life. This will take the pressure off you to include every valuable thought that you've ever had. If you take the advice in this book to heart, you will have the skills to write and publish many books in due time. You don't need to worry about screwing up your one big shot to get it right.

When you realize you have all the time in the world and can write any book you want, the problem becomes one of practicality. Now you can ask yourself what the easiest book for you to write will be with the passion and knowledge you presently hold. You will soon be able to cross-reference this information with a more detailed analysis of the marketplace and what you can predict readers will be eager to buy.

All new authors must look past personal biases and early assumptions. They must learn to look at their forthcoming book through the respective lenses of artists, educators, and entrepreneurs. When they can adopt the perspectives of passion, knowledge, and marketplace demand, the right choice for what to write about becomes surprisingly obvious. You will quickly see that there are only so many things that match all three of these criteria for you.

Palpable Passion

It seems obvious that what you choose to write about should be something you have great love or passion for. Every great artist, whatever the medium, expresses their work as an outpouring of real emotions. Your inherent interest in the subject will make the writing and marketing processes significantly more enjoyable for you. You won't feel that you are trading your time for something you hate, at the risk of not receiving the financial reward you anticipate if no one buys the book when it is finally ready.

The problem most people have is that there are many things they care about at least a little. Nearly everyone can list endless interests that can occupy their minds for some time. These are not categorically the same as passions, which have proven to be sustainably engaging over a long period of time. If one does not know of any genuine passions in their life, they ought best to reflect why it is they think they want to write a book at all. From where does this outpouring of desire to communicate stem? Check your vanity at the door.

Firsthand Experience

Secondly, you must know plenty about that which you wish to communicate. Otherwise, you will not be able to populate the full text of a book with your knowledge. An educator excels at passing on the lessons of their trials to others who have not been where they have. This does not mean you need to know 100% of the information on a subject. That's impossible for anyone. You just need enough to have formed a unique, meaningful perspective.

Furthermore, no matter how much you know through study, you should have plenty of firsthand experience on your topic, or at least have access to people who do. It's not enough that you've read a lot of popular books about something. Many other people have done that too. Many of them assume this makes them something approximating an expert. Such people are only recycling other minds' information.

Consuming the knowledge of other people is great. It saves you the trouble of arriving at the same conclusions through long, arduous observation. But you must not stop there. You must apply what you have learned with your own hands, in your own life. Then you will begin to see all the parts of the knowledge that were so hard to put into words. They had to be experienced. Unless you are writing about something that can't be directly experienced, such as ancient history, this is the only way to get the complete picture of your subject.

If you write from a place of secondhand knowledge, it may be apparent by the shallowness of your thoughts. Instead, write in such a way that you impress readers with your attention to details overlooked by general wisdom. Write things that only someone with your unique biases and experiences could say. Write something ordinary people would never think to say. Your next best option is to interview experts whose knowledge has never been published, visit places and practice activities related to your subject, or curate the best bits of existing wisdom into a more convenient format. Written well, books serve the necessary function of documenting direct knowledge and experience during the short window an author is alive to provide them.

To date, the most historically meaningful book I have ever worked on through Identity Publications is *Stories of Elders: What the Greatest Generation Knows about Technology that You Don't* by anthropologist Veronica Kirin. Rather than just share her limited perspective on life before the digital age, 29-year-old Veronica crowdfunded more than $5,000 and drove nearly 12,000 miles around the United States in 2015 to gather the inputs she would need to craft her message.

The purpose of Veronica's journey was to interview 100 people born between 1915 and 1945 who had survived events like the Great Depression, Dust Bowl, and World War II while they were still around to tell their tales. Many of her interviewees were already more than a century old, so she saw her book as a final opportunity to record their firsthand wisdom on topics like technology, social equality, and economy. Juxtaposed by her own Millennial philosophy and experiences, *Stories of Elders* became an authentic series of snapshots about an important time in American history that future generations can use to understand life before the acceleration of modern technology.

Measurable Demand

Finally, whatever you write about, there should be sufficient leverageable demand for it. People need to want it and be willing to pay for it. You must start to think about your work like an entrepreneur, which is the hardest role for many artists and educators to adopt if they've never had to sell anything before. Marketplace demand will translate into financial profitability, which will sustain your ability to continue writing and promoting your message. If you have only passion and experience but no external demand, your writing will be for no one but yourself.

You must know what questions people are actively seeking to answer. You must observe the marketplace and see what kind of content they are already paying for. Analyze what holes exist between demand and availability so that you can fill them with your message.

When you see that every other book on your subject omits certain kinds of information, it may be a good opportunity to be the only one that includes such details. If readers are frequently leaving reviews that complain about a shortcoming of your competition, differentiate yourself by explicitly addressing that issue. If an entire class of readers has been ignored by the tone or focus of other books, you may be in a unique position to write the ultimate guide for their specific needs.

Do not feel that you must force your writing to fit a certain idea once you've decided it's what you want to write about. It is better to see what topic and style of writing come most effortlessly to you. Then you may assess the many ways you can make your natural approach fit into a structure that will work as a popular book in the marketplace. Whatever you write, make your book the best possible version of it. The strategies for how to do this will grow easier for you to cognize as you study the established trends of nonfiction books already available.

When planning the purpose of your book, remember your readers will sacrifice much more than the money it costs to purchase your book. They will spend many hours of their precious time. They will spend their emotions getting involved with the concepts you introduce and the things you make them ponder. The information will linger in their memories, affecting them for potentially years to come. Make sure your message is worth everything they must spend to acquire it.

Without sufficient inspiration, readers will not begin the process of consuming your message. If they begin at all, they may not see it through to completion. They may not give the intake process their full attention, resulting in an underwhelming, partial transmission of your book's most important elements. Emotional inertia will keep your readers in motion, turning pages and finishing chapters until they reach the end of your work. You will optimize their retention and engagement throughout the journey.

Summary of Chapter 2

Writing tens of thousands of words in a structured and eloquent manner is difficult work. If you understand why it's so important to you to complete your book (whether your motivation includes passive income, social recognition, or just a personal sense of purpose), the process will be easier and the result far better.

— — — —

Once a book with your name and face on it exists for sale on the public market, it becomes irrevocably attached to the perception of your identity. You should not bother to create and refine a message that you will not be prepared to stand behind and promote for your foreseeable future. This will require you to introspect about how much you know yourself.

— — — —

To be enjoyable, comprehensive, and successful, your book will need a subject that fits certain defined parameters. You will need to care deeply about your message. You will need to be knowledgeable and experienced in your field. You will need to know that there are many readers who desire to read this kind of message who currently don't have enough options to do so with other books.

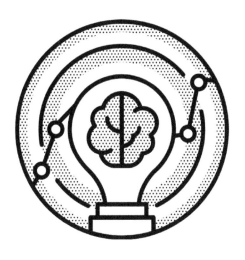

PART 2:
STRATEGY

CHAPTER 3:

The Market Ecosystem around Your Book

Many books have been independently birthed into the world since self-publishing became a technological and economical possibility. Most of these books never sell very well. This has never been truer than now, as the number of wannabe authors seems to increase faster than the number of people who want to read their work. There is a perpetual mismatch between what the market of book buyers demonstrates it is willing to buy and what amateur authors are willing to produce.

Currently, most self-published books are hardly ever read by anyone but their authors' closest friends. No matter how interesting the contents contained within, books published without viable marketing strategies remain buried in relative obscurity for the duration of the authors' lives. Their creators never learn how to attract the right eyes to their words, so their words remain inconsequential. The greater the number of relevant people who buy and read a book, the more influence the words of that book will carry.

Conversely, there is a surprisingly large number of books with poor quality content that still manage to find plenty of readers who are happy to pay for them. The authors and promoters of these books may not be great writers or hold unique insights that make them stand out from everyone else; they have only figured out how to present their work to the right audience in the right manner. They understand the established conventions of the topics they write for, so buyer expectations are easy to appeal to. As such, they do not need to resort to flooding their social media feeds with a variety of pleas for anyone and everyone to buy their book just because they wrote it and they think it's amazing.

Before you begin formulating your plan for your message, research the strengths and weaknesses of the books already written on your subject. You can learn a lot from other authors' public mistakes and victories. Browse your local bookstore or check Amazon.com to see the angles and approaches already present. When you are familiar with what they offer, you can position your message to fill the spaces they've missed. Your book can stand out above them by understanding what has been successful among the conventions and trends of book buyers.

Catering to the needs of the market does not require you to sacrifice your integrity as a communicator. It only means framing your work in the context of what you know people are willing to read.

Category Conventions and Marketplace Trends

Book categories on Amazon and other online retailers have been shaped by what the market shows were the most successful books of yesterday and before. These categories are a response to the ongoing, organic demands of book buyers. When there is too much differentiation within a category, buyers cannot find the type of information they are looking for. The market evolves to accommodate them with newer and finer subcategories. The levels of refinement are only as limited as the specialized demands of readers.

Such is the way that, over time, cookbooks become segregated into subcategories based on specific ingredients, cooking styles, kitchen equipment, and special occasions. The market of cookbook buyers has demonstrated their persistent need for these types of categorization, or else it would be impossible for them to find the exact cookbooks they sought. It would be difficult for someone who doesn't cook to guess what criteria cookbook consumers might use to make their purchasing decisions.

If you want to sell a cookbook, you'll need to understand the way marketplace categories have evolved and the buying priorities of consumers. If you want to sell a self-help book or personal memoir, the principle remains the same. Only the details are different. By understanding the reader expectations of the subject you are writing for, it will be easy to determine how to tailor your message for maximum sales and influence. This is true even if you plan to break those expectations.

Some writing categories are more competitive than others. Some contain high demand and few books, while others the exact opposite. All other things being equal, entering a category with high demand and low competition will improve your book's chances of commercial success over entering one with low demand and high competition.

As well, readers of different subjects practice different general reading habits. The kind of people who read business strategy books may be voracious readers, consuming as many books as they can that might give them a profitable edge as entrepreneurs. For them, even a single new piece of information could be worth a lot of additional revenue. This type of book buyer will assess that $20 spent and the time required to read the book are well worth the rewards generated. So, although business subjects are competitive because many authors write for them, they are also in perpetual demand from readers.

Unconventional Distinction

A specialty cookbook of recipes appropriate for your favorite regional holiday is a different matter. There are many new qualifying factors to consider about the book and its buyers. Such a book might only attract readers from the region its written about, celebrate the holiday of its subject, enjoy the act of cooking, and don't already own another cookbook that serves a similar function. Each new bit of differentiation adds a potential qualifier to the audience, perhaps reducing the total quantity but increasing the intensity of their demand.

Through Identity Publications, I once produced a rather unconventional cookbook called *Intimacy on the Plate: 200+ Aphrodisiac Recipes to Spice Up Your Love Life at Home Tonight* by Olga Petrenko. Due to its nature as a cookbook of recipes containing aphrodisiac ingredients intended to enhance the sex lives of couples, the book only appealed to readers who:

1. Like to read and own books (as with all books).
2. Like to cook (as with all cookbooks).
3. Like to have sex.
4. Have the opportunity to eat and have sex with someone.
5. Like to learn about how foods and herbs affect the human body.
6. Like to experiment with how foods and herbs affect their bodies.

If all these qualities do not apply to you (or someone you know), you have no reason to buy *Intimacy on the Plate*.

Since Amazon has no book subcategories for aphrodisiac cookbooks specifically, we chose to list it as a special occasion cookbook, gastronomical essay, and sexual health and impotency book. Each of these subcategories had plenty of competition from other types of books, but few were directly competing as aphrodisiac cookbooks. Any reader who fit into our narrow range of qualified buyers was likely to purchase *Intimacy on the Plate* instead of or in addition to one of the few other options, such as *Fork Me, Spoon Me: The Sensual Cookbook* by Amy Reiley or *InterCourses: An Aphrodisiac Cookbook* by Martha Hopkins and Randall Lockridge.

Olga Petrenko's aphrodisiac cookbook was further differentiated from its narrow competition due to her Eastern European culinary background, her focus on the science of how the ingredients affect the human libido, and the sheer number of recipes included (about twice as many as the other two direct competitors combined). These factors formed an effective unique value proposition for *Intimacy on the Plate* that worked to drive sales of the book, even though no one had ever heard of Olga or knew of her expertise on sexual health cooking before.

Uncompetitive Categories

As you can imagine, some book categories are scarcely populated at all. You may find that there isn't a single book adequately covering the niche you want to write about. A scarcity of competition is common if you are an expert in a complicated profession that is poorly understood by the public. In this case, it's reasonable that most every shopper looking for a book on your topic may end up buying yours. Without competition, these shoppers won't have many other choices to satiate their information needs. So, even if it's not a perfect match for their specific preferences, they will still buy and read it (assuming there is any reader demand at all).

In such a situation, it may be a long time before you need to worry about another author copying your approach. Even if they do, you will still maintain the first-mover advantage. A lot of traffic will already be going to your book, and you will already have established a positive, authoritative position. You will have effectively monopolized the market for your niche. There are many untapped opportunities for authors who want to write about things that are not represented well in the medium of books.

My friend and accountant, Olivier Wagner, faced a situation like this when he decided to write a book. Olivier specializes in the complicated rules that govern how Americans who live or work in other countries are supposed to file their taxes back home. If you thought typical American tax forms were complicated, you haven't seen anything compared to what American expatriates have to deal with. Not only is the subject complicated, the consequences for misunderstanding it are potentially severe for taxpayers abroad who could end up owing tens of thousands of dollars if they don't structure their lives or businesses optimally to legally reduce their tax burdens. They may also be liable for extreme penalties if they misfile.

While there were already a few books on Amazon addressing subjects like offshore taxes, none were particularly compelling. Most were short, written in a dull tone, and covered only very general filing circumstances. They did not address all the relevant details of the many common reasons that cause Americans to move abroad alone or with their families. They neglected the many possible ways to arrange their income and finances for the lowest tax obligation within the confines of the IRS tax code. Few expat tax books were even available in formats other than for Kindle e-book, such as paperback, hardcover, and audio narration. Still, they were the best option available to readers seeking out this vital information, besides hours of perusing vague blog posts or paying top dollar for private expert advice.

Olivier and I saw an opportunity to capture the lion's share of the book market for people seeking his flavor of expertise. Together, we came up with an outline for what would eventually be titled *U.S. Taxes for Worldly Americans: The Traveling Expat's Guide to Living, Working, and Staying Tax Compliant Abroad*. His book filled the holes in the information matrix, negating the need to read most of the other books on the subject once having read his. I also made sure Olivier included as much of his playful and down-to-earth personality as possible in his writing, despite his initial protests, because I knew the inviting tone would be a welcome change from how his dull competition had written their tax books. From there, it was simply a matter of the two of us designing the presentation of the book and planning a series of targeted promotions to this highly specific audience of hungry readers.

There's nothing preventing another offshore accountant from coming along and writing a book like Olivier's, but it would take a serious investment of time, effort, and capital to do it right. If a competitor's book failed to introduce anything new or improve upon what *U.S. Taxes for Worldly Americans* already did so well, it's unlikely it would gain much traction in the market. Olivier's book has the advantage of a head start and ample publicity in the forms of positive reviews, guest articles, press releases, and word-of-mouth promotion. As well, the number of professionals in a position to write accurately and effectively about this esoteric subject is pretty small to begin with.

Competition Context

It's fine, even necessary, to take inspiration from the writing styles or original thoughts of other authors. You don't have to cross into plagiarism or inauthenticity to do this. It's useful to read the work of your competition and take note of what you like or you don't like about their approaches. You will start to see patterns in what is missing or included in their publications. This will give you a sense of what bears repeating in your work and what new information will make your version of the message superior.

The context provided to you by competing authors can help you determine what information needs to go in your book. You do not even need to read all of them to get a sense of what they offer. The book description and table of contents by themselves might be enough to clue you into facets of their message, showing you what you might have overlooked for your book. You can perform this research in minutes by browsing a library, bookstore, or Amazon's appropriate subcategories. Then you can decide which competing books catch your attention enough to warrant reading.

Context works through both positive and negative correlations. If you see that certain information has been repeated throughout every available resource on your subject, you can interpret it in two ways. Perhaps that information is so vital to understanding what you want to talk about that leaving it out would risk ruining your reader's enjoyment or comprehension. Alternatively, perhaps it is so well-covered by other sources that it bears no repeating. Doing so will just bore readers who picked up your book to get new answers and influence.

Only you can determine what needs to be included to make your book fulfill its purpose. It will depend on the specific audience you know you are writing for and the specific changes you wish to accomplish with the spread of your message. This is not only part of your creative inspiration, but also your market research about what the world already has enough or too much of in the medium of books. Both the best and the worst authors have valuable things to teach you. The notes you make here will directly inform the outline and tone of your work.

Categorical Demand

Hungry audiences are the most reliable early predictor of success for any product in any market. When people want something they can't get, all you must do is provide it for them. You can present sought-after information in a new way, add something no one has heard before, or suggest a new angle to a familiar thing. Then you will earn lasting notoriety within a defined market. Specialization turns competing books into complementary ones—enemies into allies.

Your readers are likely to have read a few other books on the same broad topic before getting to yours. They will likely continue to read any others they find after they finish yours. Unless there is a book that answers every question they might ask on the subject, reading one author's take does not preclude them from reading yours too. Another book is only competing with yours when a buyer who was considering yours chooses another instead. If reading the other book permanently resolves their questions about the subject, they will not return to browse for others. This can occur for readers who are only casually interested in a subject. A single book might be enough to satiate their curiosity.

Readers who want a well-rounded understanding of a topic read every book that appears to address some of their concerns. In such cases, the first book they read will only be a doorway to greater curiosity. Reading one book leads to reading another, and another, and another. Now, readers who might never have heard of you will have developed a strong interest in what you write about. They will seek out unique sources of information. Thus, you will have more sales over time because your competition stoked interest in readers who otherwise would never have read your work. Your book will get more exposure through other books with features like Amazon's "Customers who bought this item also bought" promotion. The pie grows larger and there are more pieces to go around for everyone because it is not a zero-sum game.

Selling Cycles

Not only do different types of books receive varying levels of readership and competition, but they also sell in different cycles and schedules. Some books are topical. There will be a spike in interest when a new trend is introduced to a culture. People rush to learn about something when the hype for it is high. When a subject evolves quickly, readers want constant, up-to-date information about its recent changes. These behavioral trends affect how people buy books on different topics.

Similarly, the market dynamics around a topic might take a turn for the worse. Within a year of publication, a book written about topical things like how to invest in cryptocurrencies or master social media marketing might be totally obsolete. Readers could also simply stop caring about the subject. The technology may have changed, or the hype may have dissipated. Such books must be continually updated (with maybe a new edition each year) or they will be overlooked for more contemporary options that emerge.

Some book topics, by their nature, are seasonal sellers that rise and fall in popularity throughout the year. Others are perennially in demand. No matter the case, you need to understand the psychology of the people who will want to read your book and how all conditions are subject to change.

If your book will make a good Christmas gift, expect an increase in paperback and hardcover sales throughout December. Simultaneously, e-book and audiobook sales might drop because shoppers will be buying physical books to give as gifts to other people. If your book has themes of love and intimacy, late January and early February until Valentine's Day might be when you see the most sales. No matter what you write, there will be countless variables that influence buying behavior on a massive scale. You can't expect your book's performance to be immune to the fluctuations of summertime, tax season, economic recessions, or national tragedies.

Topicality Dynamics

If you are writing your book with the goal of long-term success, consider the changing dynamics of your subject matter. Every book ever written contains some balance of principles and incidentals. Principles describe the unchanging rules of how reality works. Supporting them with examples of how they manifest in a relatable context makes them easier to understand and relate to. Books focused on timeless principles, such as most self-help and personal development books, are more likely to remain popular for decades without decline than books written about fast-changing topical things. Their advice will be as relevant in the decades to come as it is at the time it is written.

You can make your book less likely to go out of fashion by avoiding references that will become dated. In the context of *The Influential Author*, I've made it a point to refrain from referencing specific websites, tools, companies, and resources whenever possible. If I were to tell you where to go to hire freelancers or about the fine print of temporary Amazon policies, parts of this book would become irrelevant shortly after publication. Still, even with the efforts I've taken to minimize transient references, it's possible I will have to release updated versions of this book sometime in the years to come.

If you've read other books about self-publishing, you can confirm that nearly any of them published more than a few years ago are already woefully out of date and of limited utility for the modern author. Not only do the relevant resources change, but the entire industry of self-publishing is undergoing a rapid evolution. It takes a skillful approach to focus on the principles that do not change. Still, some topical, practical advice is useful for readers who need to begin applying the new knowledge you have given them. Temporary tactics and references do not have to be discounted completely.

To get the best of both worlds, the timeless and the topical, I chose to include most references to current resources in this book's back matter appendix. At the end of *The Influential Author*, you will find detailed lists of current resources for many of the tools and services you may need to write, publish, and sell your book (as this book's subtitle suggests). This way, the main content of this book still pertains to principles and strategy, but the reader receives a list of what they need to begin practical implement during or immediately after reading.

I can't predict how readers will receive this book 10 or 50 years after publication, but I know that the bulk of its principled message will still be true. Principles don't change; only their implementation does. You can adopt a similar approach with your book or elect to remove the topical references entirely.

Positioning Your Book in Amazon's Ecosystem

A word of caution that bears repeating here: do not make it your priority to write something only because the market data says it will be easy to sell. You will not craft an authentic message. You will be putting the cart before the horse. Category, keyword, and ranking research are useful when you have a good idea about the book(s) you want to write. You can apply data from the market to refine your idea into something workable.

Category and ranking research can help if you struggle with multiple ideas for books you would like to write but aren't sure where to start. It makes sense to make your first book the one that will be easiest to write and find an audience for. You can work your way up in market penetration difficulty with future publications. If the market data suggests one of your book ideas will receive more demand and less competition than the others, you may take it as a sign to write that one first.

Marketplace Research

To that end, there are many ways to learn the general market conditions and buying habits of different book categories. Using online analytics tools, you can look up the hard statistics on words and phrases searched throughout the year. A large spike or observable pattern in search volume might indicate something important. However, these numbers are not always the best way to understand the habits of book buyers. Just because people are searching certain terms in an all-purpose search engine like Google does not mean they want to read books or pay money to learn about those subjects.

There are lots of reasons people search for things online. They could just be looking for a specific fact to reference. They could be seeking service providers related to the topic. They might prefer blog posts, podcasts, or videos as their preferred medium to learn from. The willingness to purchase a book is not a foregone conclusion. There are tools available now designed to help authors understand the keywords used specifically on Amazon and other book retailers, so they can get only the most relevant data. You can find some of these research tools in the Resources appendix at the end of this book.

You can get more relevant, though less detailed, data about book buying habits by searching keywords and browsing subcategories directly on Amazon. By sticking to the book categories (and not delving into the other areas of what Amazon sells), the results will be more relevant to your goals as a bookseller. What you see there is the same thing all book buyers do when they use Amazon's interface. Use it as though you were browsing for something to purchase.

Kindle Ranking System

Amazon uses an internal ranking system to determine which of its roughly five million e-books published for Kindle are performing the best, according to metrics it has specified and weighted by its own proprietary values. Every e-book is ranked with a number value known as the Amazon Best Seller Rank (ABSR) number. ABSR numbers are constantly in flux, updated every several hours depending on how performance factors for each e-book have changed.

Under the ABSR system, your book can get as high as #1 on all of Kindle (which is highly unlikely without spending tens of thousands of dollars on exposure) or as low as #5,000,000 if it stays on the site for several years without a single sale. If your book gets a modest amount of ongoing sales, it will most likely be ranking somewhere between #100,000 and #1,000,000. Generally speaking, any book that breaks #100,000 and manages to stay there is doing pretty well (especially compared to other self-published books), though this single number fails to take into account other important success factors like paperback and audiobook sales or the amount of time and money spent on marketing to achieve its impressive e-book sales. A Kindle book with an impressive ABSR number can still be losing money if its author or publisher is spending more on ads than they get back in revenues.

ABSR numbers are useful for determining at a glance how a book is performing relative to all others. You can use the ABSR of books similar to yours to learn what is popular and what is stagnant. It will give you valuable input about which categories are most or least competitive, and therefore which will be the ones you can get the most visibility within. You can view the ABSR number of any e-book within the "Product details" section of its Amazon listing, just past the "Editorial reviews" section and before the "Customer reviews."

There are many theories about how Amazon's Kindle store ranking algorithm works. While no one knows the exact equation, it's clear that certain factors have a large influence, such as the number of sales in a given period, how much money each sale is worth (an e-book that sells 100 copies priced at $9.99

is more impressive than an e-book that sells 100 copies priced at 99 cents), and how many verified or unverified positive reviews a book has received.

Additionally, all Kindle e-books on Amazon are ranked on a curve, with preference given to newer books over older ones. The longer a book has been on Amazon, the better it must perform to maintain the same Kindle store ABSR number. If you act fast and have a solid promotional strategy in place immediately upon launching your book, it's easy to get almost any book into the top 10,000 on all of Kindle (and to #1 in at least one subcategory). Sustaining a high ranking for years to come, however, is another matter. A book has to build up a following and increase its sales to keep up the same ranking in correlation with how long it has been in publication.

Amazon's Search Function

Use ABSR in conjunction with Amazon's search feature to get a lay of the land pertaining to what you want to write about. Amazon's search algorithm is designed to show you the books that you, as a consumer, are most likely to buy when you search specific terms. When there is a pattern of shoppers purchasing the same books when they enter phrases on Amazon, those books will show up for other shoppers who search the same phrases. It's Amazon's way of maximizing their revenue.

If you search a phrase like "American Revolution" in Amazon's online bookstore, you'll get a variety of predictable results. Among them are:
- *1776* by David McCullough
- *American Revolutions: A Continental History, 1750-1804* by Alan Taylor
- *The Glorious Cause: The American Revolution, 1763-1789 (Oxford History of the United States)* by Robert Middlekauff
- *How to Read the Constitution and the Declaration of Independence: A Simple Guide to Understanding the Constitution of the United States (Freedom in America Book 1)* by Paul B. Skousen

However, Amazon book search results can also surprise you. At the #1 search result spot for the phrase "American Revolution" (as of the time of this writing), a somewhat surprising result trumps the rest: *Fire and Fury: Inside the Trump White House* by Michael Wolff.

Unlike the other books on the first page of Amazon's search results, *Fire and Fury* is not a book about the war for American independence from England in 1776. It's about controversial, modern-day American president Donald Trump's time in The White House. Most people searching for books on the "American Revolution" are probably not looking to learn about Donald Trump's presidency, yet this book outranks the more relevant titles.

There are many reasons why Wolff's book could be showing up where it does, despite its seeming inappropriateness for the intentions of book searchers. For one thing, it was published just several months ago in January 2018. Because it's still relatively soon after the book's publication date, it may be granted greater visibility by Amazon's algorithm. All other things being equal, a book less than one year old will be shown more often than one that is many years old.

Fire and Fury is extremely topical right now. The Trump presidency is a hot subject of discussion among both supporters and detractors. The book currently has more than 8,000 Amazon user reviews with a 4.3- out of 5-star average rating. It is ranking #7 "most read" on the Amazon charts and around #1,000 ABSR number out of all five million e-books on Kindle (which is considered very good). These factors appear to create a more powerful effect than the specific relevance of the search phrase "American Revolution."

If you search the phrases "American politics," "American government," "American history," or "American president," the book *Fire and Fury* also shows up on the first page of results. Lo and behold, the same applies if you search the word "American" by itself. The book is ranking so strongly for that one word it hardly matters what modifiers you add or phrases you make it part of. In the long run, this high keyword ranking will likely die off. Years from now, it is probable that fewer and fewer people will care about President Trump's present actions.

Your book may never reach the same level of wild popularity as *Fire and Fury*. It's still vital to search a variety of terms related to your subject, as they will reveal reliable habits from book buyers. When you see the focus and tone of books that show up for various phrases, you will get a good sense of where your book will fit into the existing ecosystem.

Kindle Parent Categories

Amazon currently organizes its Kindle store with 31 parent categories to contain all five million of its publications:

1. Arts & Photography
2. Biographies & Memoirs
3. Business & Money
4. Children's eBooks
5. Comics & Graphic Novels
6. Computers & Technology
7. Cookbooks, Food & Wine
8. Crafts, Hobbies & Home
9. Education & Teaching
10. Engineering & Transportation
11. Foreign Languages
12. Health, Fitness & Dieting
13. History
14. Humor & Entertainment
15. Law
16. Lesbian, Gay, Bisexual & Transgender eBooks
17. Literature & Fiction
18. Medical eBooks
19. Mystery, Thriller & Suspense
20. Nonfiction

21. Parenting & Relationships
22. Politics & Social Sciences
23. Reference
24. Religion & Spirituality
25. Romance
26. Science & Math
27. Science Fiction & Fantasy
28. Self-Help
29. Sports & Outdoors
30. Teen & Young Adult
31. Travel

These 31 Amazon parent categories are divided into more than 10,000 subcategories. As the number of books published on Kindle increases (with one new e-book published every minute or about 1,400 per day by some estimates), the categories Amazon uses to organize its content will expand and subdivide (e.g., Nonfiction > Parenting & Relationships > Family Relationships > Divorce).

The way books rank in subcategories fluctuates throughout the day as each book's ABSR number changes, based on how many copies of each book are selling and how long they have been published. By watching which books tend to stay at the top of rankings in certain subcategories, you will get a sense of what readers are looking to buy. Knowing what is and isn't selling will make it much easier to narrow your focus down from all the possible books you think you could write.

Kindle Subcategories

Some books are so large and complex in scope that they have footholds in many categories at some point throughout their hundreds of thousands of words. How do you categorize a book that is a personal memoir covering 20 years of study, during which you learned about tantric sex, ancient religions, and modern culture? Such a book could rightfully fall under many subjects and subcategories.

If that example sounds far-fetched, I encourage you to check out a book I produced and had the task of launching on Amazon, *Venus and Her Lover: Transforming Myth, Sexuality, and Ourselves* by Becca Tzigany. The scope of the book was so large that we chose to split its more than 300,000 words of content into two 7" x 10" 400-page volumes.

The struggle to find the ideal Amazon subcategories for *Venus and Her Lover* was very real. By assessing marketplace competition and browsing habits, we arrived at 14 subcategories just within Amazon's Religion & Spirituality parent category (and several others in the Travel and Parenting & Relationships parent categories) that would be relevant for the book's message:

1. Religion & Spirituality > Earth-Based Religions > Gaia & Earth Energies
2. Religion & Spirituality > New Age > Goddesses
3. Religion & Spirituality > New Age > Reference
4. Religion & Spirituality > Occult > Metaphysical Phenomena
5. Religion & Spirituality > Occult > Spiritualism
6. Religion & Spirituality > Other Religions, Practices & Sacred Texts > Gender & Sexuality
7. Religion & Spirituality > Spirituality > Inspirational > Biography
8. Religion & Spirituality > Spirituality > Inspirational > Conduct of Life
9. Religion & Spirituality > Spirituality > Inspirational > Relationships
10. Religion & Spirituality > Spirituality > Inspirational > Women's Inspirational
11. Religion & Spirituality > Spirituality > Personal Growth > Mysticism
12. Religion & Spirituality > Spirituality > Personal Growth > Spiritual Growth
13. Religion & Spirituality > Spirituality > Personal Growth > Transformational
14. Religion & Spirituality > Spirituality > Women

Once we had narrowed it down to those options, it was a matter of determining which ones would be easiest to rank highly in (hopefully even the #1 spot) and cross-referencing those with the ones most likely to have viable readers browsing through them. Though none of the subcategories was a perfect match, they were close enough to be effective at getting in front of some of the right readers. Fortunately, because Amazon allows authors to list their books in three subcategories, we didn't have to choose just one and hope for the best.

Veronica Kirin's series of interviews in *Stories of Elders: What the Greatest Generation Knows about Technology that You Don't* included topics as broad as how family dynamics have changed, how technology has made many jobs obsolete, and how sickness was dealt with before modern medicine. We were able to curate a list of 15 subcategories within parent categories related to History, Social Sciences, and Technology that had relatively high demand and low competition:

1. History > Americas > United States > 20th Century > 1945 - Present
2. History > Americas > United States > 20th Century > 1950s
3. History > Americas > United States > 20th Century > 1960s
4. History > Americas > United States > 20th Century > Depression
5. History > Historical Study > Social History > Gay & Gender Studies
6. History > Historical Study > Social History > Labor & Workforce
7. History > Historical Study > Social History > Race & Ethnicity
8. History > Science & Medicine > Anthropology
9. Nonfiction > Parenting & Relationships > Aging Parents & Eldercare > Aging
10. Nonfiction > Politics & Social Sciences > Social Sciences > Anthropology > Cultural
11. Nonfiction > Politics & Social Sciences > Social Sciences > Customs & Traditions
12. Nonfiction > Politics & Social Sciences > Social Sciences > Gerontology
13. Nonfiction > Politics & Social Sciences > Social Sciences > Sociology > Social Theory
14. Nonfiction > Science > History & Philosophy
15. Nonfiction > Science > Technology > General & Reference

The best way to position a book (and, therefore, choose the best subcategories to list it in) is to understand the primary motivation readers will have for buying and consuming it. Will they read it to learn about the life of you, the author? Then it's a personal memoir or autobiography. Will they read your book to improve themselves? Then it's a self-help or personal development book. Will they read it to learn about different cultures of the world? Then it's probably a travel or anthropology book.

Granted, book category lines are not always cut so clean, nor are they useful in every situation. Maybe it's obvious what subjects your book invokes, but the way it approaches its subject matter is wildly different from every other book in the same category. Subject conventions apply to more than just the focus of the content. They shape the tone of voice and value judgments of the author.

A New Age self-help book that curses at its readers might not fare well compared to others in the same categories. This type of book is typically defined by the use of positive affirmations and supportive, fluffy wording. Then again, the same book might become a huge hit for defying common practice. Which way the cookie crumbles will depend on some factors you can control (such as just how far you deviate from convention) and some you can't (such as how saturated the market is with the same old script you are stepping away from).

Think about how many New Agers might prefer books that swore at them and used sarcastic humor to get a profound point across. Perhaps many other people who don't identify with New Age conventions would be open to the movement's ideals if only they didn't have to slog through so many goddamn affirmations and hollow turns of phrase.

Following and Defying Category Expectations

Henry Ford, the man most responsible for making private automobiles accessible to common Americans, is often credited as saying that if he had asked his customers what they wanted, they'd have asked for faster horses. This allegorical anecdote illustrates an important principle. People can only desire things that fall within the contextual limitations of what they already know. If you cannot present your message within an established frame of reference, it will likely be ignored. Even worse, it may be scorned.

What if your message is so unconventional, so revolutionary, and so avant-garde that it cannot be categorized? No message is so new that it truly defies convention. Nothing is totally disconnected from everything else. You must come to understand the culture of common knowledge related to your message. The more you know about what is popular and profitable, the easier it will be to position the message of your book for maximum receptivity. If readers can't relate to what you're saying, they're not going to have any interest. This is easy to forget when you're focused on pushing uniqueness in your message without grounding it in the familiar.

Whenever you write about something in a way that has never been done or challenge people's expected conventions, you can excite your readers. Newness, depending on how you present it, invites your audience to learn more. It incites their curiosity. Too much novelty can also overwhelm. The presentation of something foreign sometimes makes people feel intimidated by what they can't follow. They get suspicious and defensive when they must question too much of what they believe or are accustomed to being presented with. Challenging people's conceptions is most effective when you do it in the amount and present it in a style your audience is ready for. The growth of a paradigm is always a voluntary process.

Consider the burden associated with having to convince readers to purchase and read a book on a subject they previously had no known desire to learn about. Learning doesn't work that way, and neither does buying. People must want something. More than that, they must know that they want it. They can't do that until they have a hole dug out for it in their minds. If your message fits no ordinary hole, you will need to bring a shovel.

All subjective evaluations happen against the backdrop of an imagined standard that we inherit from what we experience. If you don't understand the standards your readers use, you might be very confused when reception for your book is not as positive as you'd hoped. You should be tasteful in both how you copy and defy established category practices.

Make no mistake: whatever you write, it must somehow be different than what already exists. Avoid the temptation to mimic the most famous books written on your subject, even if you think you are doing so out of respect or adoration. Those authors have already done it better than you and they hold a massive head start. Writing a book that copies the same voice or promotes the same message can easily be interpreted as lazy or dishonest. Even if you sell some books to people who crave more of that type of content, it will ultimately have a detrimental effect on your author brand.

Besides, you almost certainly won't be the first newbie author already jumping in line to rip off the heavy hitters. Sometimes a book with the right message appears at just the right time on the market. Whenever a book breaks new ground and becomes massively popular, it's sure to inspire many copycats who follow in its wake. New writers attempt to clone these books with their own work, sometimes adding a unique flavor to the mix but often being barely indistinguishable from the source.

4HWW Clones

In 2007, Tim Ferriss wrote *The Four-Hour Work Week: Escape 9-5, Live Anywhere, and Join the New Rich*, a guide to working from a laptop anywhere in the world and getting more done with less time. The book would go on to sell over 1.3 million copies in 35 languages. Despite its generally less-than-perfect reviews, it remains a cultural milestone for digital nomads, perpetual travelers, and efficiency-minded entrepreneurs. It accomplished this because it appeared at the right time with the right message for the right audience, backed by a tactical promotional strategy to ensure it stayed in front of the right eyes.

Since 2007, countless more "how to be a digital nomad and work fewer hours from a laptop anywhere in the world" books have been published to varying levels of success. Some are quite well known, while most others fade into Amazon obscurity for bringing nothing noteworthy to the bookshelf. How many of these *The Four-Hour Work Week* copycats do you recognize?

1. *The Laptop Millionaire: How Anyone Can Escape the 9 to 5 and Make Money Online* (2012) by Mark Anastasi
2. *Click Millionaires: Work Less, Live More with an Internet Business You Love* (2012) by Scott Fox
3. *Travel While You Work: The Ultimate Guide to Running a Business from Anywhere* (2015) by Mish Slade
4. *The 9-to-5 Escape Artist: A Startup Guide for Aspiring Lifestyle Entrepreneurs and Digital Nomads* (2015) by Christy Hovey
5. *Digital Nomads: How to Live, Work and Play Around the World* (2016) by André Gussekloo and Esther Jacobs
6. *Serve No Master: How to Escape the 9-5, Start up an Online Business, Fire Your Boss and Become a Lifestyle Entrepreneur or Digital Nomad* (2016) by Jonathan Green
7. *The Digital Nomad Survival Guide: How to Successfully Travel the World While Working Remotely* (2017) by Peter Knudson and Katherine Conaway
8. *The Art of Financial Freedom: A No-BS, Step-by-Step, Newbie-Friendly Guide to Transition From Your Dead End Job And Join Others Living A Freedom-Centric Laptop Lifestyle: Simple "A-to-Z" Blueprint* (2017) by Stevie Drive
9. *The Suitcase Entrepreneur: Create Freedom in Business and Adventure in Life* (2017) by Natalie Sisson

It would be unfair to assume that none of these books offer anything new on the subject of location-independent entrepreneurship. However, knowing nothing else about the authors or the content of the books, it's extremely difficult to make that determination by what the titles promise in isolation. How should a reader rationally make the choice of which books in the same genre to buy and read without an external factor, such as the recommendation of a friend?

Sometimes an idea's time just comes, and many independent creators are struck with a similar form of inspiration simultaneously. If you happen to have a unique concept in mind for your book and another author beats you to publication (and therefore achieves market dominance) with it, you will have a hard time convincing anyone your inspiration was independent of your competitor's success. A book's unique value should be as obvious as possible from a reader's first impression.

Unlimited Self-Publishing Gurus

Books about marketing and self-publishing for authors suffer from a similar but even worse fate, ironically enough. A quick Amazon search will bring up dozens of titles that promise to help amateur authors write and self-publish their work, often in a matter of just weeks. There is enough demand on the subject of writing and self-publishing that authors can continue to pump out their own versions of the same how-to book. One of the purposes of *The Influential Author* is to subvert these tired conventions, but even with this goal in mind I cannot avoid repeating some of the same information as the many others who have come before me in this domain.

Most of the copycat books on writing and self-publishing rarely sell more than one copy per day. They almost all have fewer than a few dozen positive reviews. This is an odd state of affairs for books that promise to help you market your own books and making a living as a self-published author. Many of these books about publishing are not even available in paperback or hardcover format, and even fewer so as audio narration. Wouldn't you expect their authors, who are supposed to be experts on the process, to have taken advantage of all publishing avenues?

The redundancy among self-publishing books is stupefying. Judging by the titles and subtitles of the following 25 books, how much differentiation or uniqueness do you expect to find in each of them? Are you willing to pay $10 to $20 to own a paperback copy of each of these? Or do you think one or two of them might tell you most of what you need to know before diminishing returns kick in with the rest? Do you trust that those written in 2012 or 2013 will be as up-to-date and relevant as ones written in 2018 or after?

1. *A Detailed Guide to Self-Publishing with Amazon and Other Online Booksellers: How to Print-on-Demand with CreateSpace & Make eBooks for Kindle & Other eReaders* (2012) by Chris McMullen

2. *Createspace and Kindle Self-Publishing Masterclass - Second Edition: The Step-by-Step Author's Guide to Writing, Publishing and Marketing Your Books on Amazon* (2013) by Rick Smith

3. *Book Publishing Instructions: A Step-by-Step Guide to Publishing Your Book as a Paperback and eBook* (2013) by Jeremy Myers

4. *30-Day Author: Develop a Daily Writing Habit and Write Your Book in 30 Days (or Less) (Wordslinger)* (2015) by Kevin Tumlinson

5. *How to Write: A Bestselling Book in 21 Days* (2015) by Ernst Jones

6. *How to Publish Books on Amazon & Sell A Million Copies Using Kindle, Print & Audio Book* (2015) by Glenn Langohr

7. *Self Publishing Mastery: How To Write A #1 Bestseller, Build A Brand, Dominate Your Niche & Outperform Your Competitors* (2016) by Justin Chua

8. *Kindle Bestseller Publishing: Write a Bestseller in 30 Days! (Beginner Internet Marketing Series Book 5)* (2016) by Gundi Gabrielle

9. *Publish, Help People, Get Paid: How to Transform Your Life Experience into Ethical Income (Self Publishing, Book Marketing, Information Products, Building an Author Platform, Author Tips, and More)* (2016) by Joey Lott

10. *You Must Write a Book: Boost Your Brand, Get More Business, and Become the Go-To Expert* (2016) by Honoree Corder

11. *Published.: The Proven Path From Blank Page to Published Author* (2016) by Chandler Bolt

12. *The Holy Grail of Book Publishing: All your questions answered - 3 Volume set - A bestselling author's complete manual to self-publishing and marketing your book* (2016) by Mimi Emmanuel

13. *The Easy 9-Step System to Your First Book in 30 Days: The Complete Beginner's Guide to Become an Authority Author in Weeks!* (2017) by Nuno Almeida

14. *Write Your Book on the Side: How to Write and Publish Your First Nonfiction Kindle Book While Working a Full-Time Job (Even if You Don't Have a Lot of Time and Don't Know Where to Start)* (2017) by Hassan Osman

15. *How to Self-Publish for Under $100: The Step-by-Step Handbook to Publishing Your Book Without Breaking the Bank* (2017) by Cinquanta Cox-Smith

16. *14 Steps to Self-Publishing a Book* (2017) by Mike Kowis

17. *Self-Publishing on Amazon 2017: No publisher? No Agent? No Problem!* (2017) by Dr. Andrew Williams

18. *The Author Startup: A Radical Approach To Rapidly Writing and Self-Publishing Your Book On Amazon (Self-Publishing Success Series 1)* (2017) by Ray Brehm

19. *KINDLE PUBLISHING: How To Build A Successful Self-Publishing Business With Amazon Kindle and Createspace. A Detailed, Step-By-Step Guide To The Entire Process (Kindle Publishing Series Book 1)* (2017) by Delfim Alvaro

20. *Book Launch Formula: How To Write, Publish, and Market Your First Nonfiction Book Around Your Full Time Schedule. Become an Authority, Build Your Brand & Create a Passive Income* (2017) by Justin Ledford

21. *Let's Get Digital: How To Self-Publish, And Why You Should (Let's Get Publishing Book 1)* (2018) by David Gaughran

22. *Five Keys to Successful Nonfiction Writing: How I Write One Book per Month* (2018) by Matthew Robert Payne

23. *How to Publish a Book on Amazon in 2018: Real Advice from Someone Who's Doing it Well (Work from Home Series: Book 5)* (2018) by Sam Kerns

24. *Publish. Promote. Profit.: The New Rules of Writing, Marketing & Making Money with a Book* (2018) by Rob Kosberg

And finally...

25. *The Influential Author: How and Why to Write, Publish, and Sell Nonfiction Books that Matter* (2019) by Gregory V. Diehl

By now, you are beginning to realize the absolute necessity of making your book stand out among its competition. Like it or not, it's going to take you longer than 30 days to do it right. If you are going to find any success in your book's market, learn to be strategically different. Then, present your message in such a way that the difference is undeniable.

With so much competition from other books, many of which are indistinguishable from one another, it's vital you understand what will make readers pick one book over another. How do we, as shoppers, arrive at the decisions for what we will take home from the store or add to our online shopping carts? Are you self-aware enough to notice these factors in your own buying habits? You can study the psychology behind human purchasing behavior every time you shop.

Although we are not always consciously aware of their influence, the choice of which books we purchase or leave behind often comes down to just a few dominant variables. There could even be a single, accidental quality that flips the brain into "purchase mode" that the writer or publisher of a book is blissfully unaware of. Maybe it's the author's age or appearance. Maybe it's something about how they phrased their title or arranged their cover. All these writers see is that their book is selling, and that's enough for them.

The Familiarity Heuristic

One big selection factor in all products, not just books, is familiarity. Readers will be far more likely to purchase your book if they recognize its title or cover (or the name of its author) when they come across it while shopping. The familiarity heuristic makes us unconsciously prefer things we know to things we don't know. It's the opposite of our tendency to get captivated by things shiny and new, which is its own marketing hack. When we can't assert the cognitive effort to assess novel things, we fall back on whatever is already in our minds.

Even if a shopper has not heard of a book, they may still hold some brand recognition for its author. If you have read earlier works from Stephen King or John Grisham, you might be willing to risk your money on an unknown title from them. You'll have little concern about whether you will get your money's worth from the transaction. As the eventual author of many books and other creative or educational products, you'll see the opportunity to build this brand recognition too.

If you already have recognition in other mediums (such as a blog, podcast, or YouTube channel), it can spill over to your books too. However, cross-medium success is not guaranteed. The half million subscribers to a comedy video channel featuring three-minute satire clips might have no interest in reading a book of the same gimmick dragged out for 250 pages. If people are attracted to your personality in another format, they might not like how you present yourself in a book. There are new limitations to the medium. The contextual overtones of your message might be lost, leading to confusion or offense with what garnered you favor in audio or video. But if readers already know they love your style of writing (even if it's on an unrelated subject), they might not hesitate to purchase your book.

Cross-medium brand recognition can even work against you. There are plenty of book browsers who might decide not to buy something because they recognize its author from a medium that seems incompatible with serious authorship. Ironically, the same content published by someone unknown might sell better than if published by someone known for something unrelated. In the former case, there are no biased preconceptions to overcome. When was the last time you felt compelled to read a novel authored by a famous Hollywood actor? The cynical assumption is that they must just be trying to bank on their already famous name by hiring a ghostwriter to create another revenue stream for them (as opposed having actual talent and passion for the craft).

Unique Value Signifiers

Even when shoppers have no previous exposure to a book or its author, other factors can lead them to make a buying decision upon mere moments of analysis. When you look at other books like yours, can you easily determine what is unique about them? Can you tell what the experience of reading them is going to be like and what kind of information you will receive? How do the title, subtitle, cover, description, and author photo and bio accomplish this?

The odds are pretty good that you had never heard of me, author Gregory V. Diehl, before purchasing and reading this far into *The Influential Author*. Most likely, you were seeking answers to questions about authoring and publishing that you thought *The Influential Author* would answer better than the deluge of other self-publishing books. You got this positive impression from the meaningful title, the thoughtful cover design, the detailed book description, and positive reader reviews specifically pointing out what the book did well that no others did. You may have also been recommended it from a friend, which is a form of promotion that can instantly override all skepticism about a book.

If this was the case with you, you probably didn't worry much about the fame, background, or qualifications of the person who wrote the book, so long as the title, description, opening sections, and public reader response demonstrated that you would find the information you sought.

Start thinking now about how to engage a small audience intimately, addressing their strongest concerns much better than books written for large, broad readership. Readers won't care that they don't recognize your name or know your credentials, so long as they believe your book contains the answers they have been seeking. In finding the answers that they could not find elsewhere, your readers will grow to like and trust you. They will praise you for organic reasons, without prompting. This is how you will create an impressive and lasting marketplace position, whether for just the first amazing book or all others that follow.

Summary of Chapter 3

Understanding how book buyers perceive their options and navigate categories of topics is essential to planning the purpose, structure, and presentation of your message. Different types of readers, times of the year, and changing social trends can all have a major effect on what and how people buy and read.

— — — —

Amazon and other online book retailers use complex categorical hierarchies and detailed search functionalities to organize and rank their millions of offerings by what they know will most likely appeal to what shoppers are looking for. By learning how these systems work, you can spot opportunities in the market and prepare for your book to gain visibility before you even begin writing.

— — — —

Shoppers and readers will judge your book through the context of other books like it. You have to determine when it is wise to conform to the common practices of your genre or do something radically different. By engaging a certain type of reader more intimately than other books do and standing out from the crowd, your book will begin to build a following.

CHAPTER 4:

Designing the Meaning of Your Message

A book is more than a collection of useful ideas. It's a journey from a low point of understanding to a higher one. Your role as author is to guide readers along a path to where you want them to be with the superior knowledge you hold. You can only do that if you know where they are when they begin the journey, what is missing from their current paradigm, and the best way to introduce them to what they may not have even known they were missing.

Many experts take their knowledge for granted. Their unconscious competence might make them great performers in their fields, but it doesn't make it easy for them to teach others what they know. Being socially acknowledged as an authority makes it easy to stop questioning how they know what they know. If you are going to place new knowledge in other minds, you will have to remember the steps you took to get where you are, which might require many hours of reflection upon your intellectual journey.

If you have reached a state of unconscious competence, it means you have forgotten what it was like not to know the things you are now an expert on. Your knowledge has transcended the need for verbalization in your mind. You act without thinking about why. But thorough education requires explicit, verbalized exposition. Just try explaining your knowledge to someone completely foreign to your field (preferably a curious child who won't be shy about asking questions) and see how often they get lost or need you to backtrack in your analysis.

In the coming months of writing, you are going to attempt to make conscious and explicit what was once unconscious and implicit within you. You are going to gain a greater understanding of how your mind processes important information. You may even identify major gaps or errors in your understanding that need correcting before you can continue drafting. By teaching others what you know, you will learn it better than you knew it before. By writing out your unspoken knowledge, you will apply dedicated order to the experience life has given you.

Look at the information that populates your life. Look at the conversations in which you often find yourself. These things don't just happen out of habit. There's a reason you keep coming back to the same stories and discussions. Structuring the content of your book will eliminate much of the idle chatter in your mind. Polishing your message will simplify how you demonstrate your knowledge to people who seek your input.

Take time to ponder your intended meaning before you invest your time writing sentences, paragraphs, and chapters indiscriminately. You will soon realize why outlining your work is philosophically necessary, not just a practical approach to make writing your rough draft easier.

Focus, Scope, and Resolution

Any meaningful piece of writing maintains a definite focus, and this goes doubly so for books published with a retail price. Writing with pride and passion implies that you care about your content and how it will affect your readers. Your book's focus needs to be substantial enough to fill its chapters, and not so condensed that you need to skip over crucial components. Different types of messages carry different focuses and intended outcomes.

Written works of a philosophical nature open up the way readers think to a larger context than before. They guide people to ask new questions. They don't just offer easy or functional answers. The purpose is to leave the reader pondering the many possible answers and potential meaning of what the message has revealed.

Works of an informational nature do the very opposite: they provide answers to specific questions readers have when they begin the journey. The goal is to move from a wide, open, and aimless approach into sharply delineated categories of information. They exist to make readers' conceptual maps smaller and more detailed, zooming in from the broad overview they had when they began.

Another way to think about the focus dichotomy is through the frame of problems and solutions. When someone knows the nature of their problem, they naturally seek out the most appropriate answers they can find. When a person runs out of pressing problems, their idle boredom naturally leads them to find others worth taking on. This is the eternal cycle of a human psyche. As an educator and philosopher, you facilitate motion through the different stages of the psychological cycle.

Ask yourself now: is the primary purpose of your book to offer answers or instigate questions? Or is it some combination of both? Whenever one need is satiated, it opens to door to a higher level of thinking than the questioner had before. Through stacking consecutive layers of questions and corresponding answers throughout your book's chapters, you will create a path to a higher state of understanding about things previously unfathomed. To do this well, you'll need to research the questions commonly associated with your field (especially if their answers are not easy to find elsewhere) and plan your content around them.

Liberating Vital Information

In the age of information, it might surprise you to realize how much vital information is not accessible to the public. There are many high-dollar professions built around helping normal people with urgent and complex processes that require a special kind of expertise. To get reliable answers to some questions, you might have to pay hundreds of dollars to a consultant or licensed specialist in the area of health, law, or finance (such as the case with my friend Olivier Wagner, the expat tax accountant turned author). While a book doesn't completely replace the live, personal advice of hiring a professional, it can liberate sacred information previously kept behind closed doors.

A good example of liberating exclusive information is the Identity Publications' book I produced called *Get Bail, Leave Jail: What Every American Needs to Know about Hiring a Bondsman and Getting Released before Trial* by Sean Plotkin. You've probably never thought about what you should do if you ever get arrested and find yourself locked in a jail cell, accused of a serious crime and awaiting trial. The bail bond process, which is an integral part of America's criminal justice system, is not something most people have accurate or detailed knowledge of. The consequences of their ignorance are compounded when they or someone they love are dealing with an emergency situation that requires immediate action.

The author of *Get Bail, Leave Jail* saw the lack of common knowledge about bail bond processes as an opportunity to brand himself and his bail bond agency as reputable sources of information and assistance in what many people consider to be a controversial profession. Because Sean Plotkin's is the first book to adequately cover all the bail-related issues that can arise from the moment someone is arrested to the time their bond is exonerated in court, it has taken this important and misunderstood industry out of obscurity and into the public light for the low cost of $9.99 for the e-book and $19.99 for the paperback. That's quite a bargain compared to the alternatives of spending dozens of hours trying to find the right information yourself from free sources, paying hundreds or thousands of dollars in consulting fees from experts or facing the legal consequences of your ignorance behind bars.

Next, you'll need to decide the level of magnification and resolution you are going to apply to your topic. An infinite number of books can be written on increasingly refined, yet related, subtopics belonging to the same parent category. You can take the stance that your reader is a total newcomer and only needs a basic overview of concepts (the "Intro to" or "101" approach). You can challenge the established wisdom on a complex but well-known subject by bringing it into an esoteric domain that only a few experts on the planet will even be capable of understanding.

You can also take a common subject but talk about it from a perspective that only applies to a rare and specific kind of person (instead of "social media marketing," write about "increasing Facebook ad conversion rates for stay-at-home dads in the aerospace industry"). Plenty of types of people need to understand social media marketing, but not all of them need to improve their Facebook ad conversion rates, and certainly, most of them aren't involved in the complexities of working for the aerospace industry from home. Your options are only as limited as your imagination and your ability to find enough people to pay for what you write about (so maybe rethink that one about the aerospace dads until there's an employment boom in the industry).

Informational vs. Philosophical

Informational books are easy to spot by their titles, which typically denote the focus and resolution of the problems they solve:

- *The 1-Page Marketing Plan: Get New Customers, Make More Money, And Stand Out From The Crowd* by Allan Dib
- *The 22 Immutable Laws of Branding: How to Build a Product or Service into a World-Class Brand* by Al and Laura Ries
- *Cryptoassets: The Innovative Investor's Guide to Bitcoin and Beyond* by Chris Burniske and Jack Tatar

- *Good Prose: The Art of Nonfiction* by Richard Todd and Tracy Kidder
- *How to Be Invisible: Protect Your Home, Your Children, Your Assets, and Your Life* by J. J. Luna
- *Never Split the Difference: Negotiating As If Your Life Depended On It* by Chris Voss and Tahl Raz

These are the kinds of instructional guides readers will turn to when they know they have holes in their understanding of a subject that matters to them. The information they are missing likely prevents them from being able to do something they care about as effectively as they would like to. These books take something the reader knows they don't know enough about and give them more things to know.

What issues are you attempting to solve for your readers? Why haven't they been able to solve those problems until now? What will make your book their best hope for resolution? It will have to do something that no other solution has offered them. The better you understand the nature of the problem, the obstacles to overcoming it, and the approaches other authors offer, the more unique and effective your information will be. That means happier readers, marketing that speaks to the right people, and more sales sustained for the long-term future.

Philosophically oriented books take subjects readers think they understand and increase their awareness of how much they don't yet know. The more one learns about a subject, the more they see of what else they can learn about it, such as with the examples presented here:

- *12 Rules for Life: An Antidote to Chaos* by Jordan B. Peterson
- *The Art of War* by Sun Tzu
- *As a Man Thinketh* by James Allen
- *The Book of Five Rings: A Classic Text on the Japanese Way of the Sword* by Miyamoto Musashi
- *Destination Earth: A New Philosophy of Travel by a World-Traveler* by Nicos Hadjicostis

- *The Four Agreements: A Practical Guide to Personal Freedom (A Toltec Wisdom Book)* by Don Miguel Ruiz
- *Man's Search for Meaning* by Viktor E. Frankl
- *A New Earth: Awakening to Your Life's Purpose* by Eckhart Tolle
- *Start with Why: How Great Leaders Inspire Everyone to Take Action* by Simon Sinek

To me, the greatest books weave both philosophy and instruction into a dance of refining awareness. That is the standard I have set for the purpose of *The Influential Author,* not being content merely to talk about the philosophy of meaningful communication or the practical steps to publishing a book. One should give context and meaning to the other.

Whatever you write, it must accomplish at least one of two things:
1. Inform the reader of something useful to their goals.
2. Engage their emotions.

Every sentence you create must follow these guidelines. If it doesn't, why even bother to write it? Why should a reader bother to digest it? Fail to follow these principles and you will end up with substanceless, filler content: words that do nothing more than take up space on a page and waste everyone's time. When readers enjoy the process of learning, they will welcome new ideas and lust for the expansion of their knowledge. Indeed, the success of all forms of education depends upon the quality of entertainment they provide.

This doesn't mean you can't repeat yourself at all. Some repetition is unavoidable in early drafts when you aren't certain in exactly what form and order things will ultimately be presented. A certain amount of reminding the reader of important data or tying new concepts into previously established ones is vital to retention, but only so long as you can find new forms in which to present it and keep it fresh in mind. Simply restating yourself ceases to entertain, causing the audience to cease to care. It will also make your book run longer than it needs to be to get its message across in its ideal form.

Scope and Length

Determining the ideal length of your book requires you to think about its focus, its resolution, and how it will appear in the eyes of readers once it is published, including the typical page count they have come to expect from other books on your subject. An extremely long book (compared to category conventions) can come across as either intimidating or impressive. An extremely short book can appear reader-friendly or underwhelming. The word count, once formatted according to the author's preferences for font size and page size (known by publisher's as the trim size), will roughly determine the total number of pages in a book.

There's no definitive answer to how long a book should be, no matter its subject. Having experimented with many sizes, shapes, and types of books, I can only suggest a few guidelines. To receive the full social and financial benefits publishing a book offers, aim for a minimum of 30,000 words (which works out to about 125 pages in a 6" x 9" book with typical book font sizes). Anything less than that is more of a glorified pamphlet than a real book. You'll know the psychological difference if you take a variety of short and long books off your shelf and pay attention to how each one feels in your hand and the impression it makes in your mind. Think about how you want your book to affect people when they hold it.

A shorter book can still deliver enormous, concentrated value, but it does not take on the same qualities and appearances book buyers expect when they hand over their money for a professional publication. Except in rare circumstances, you will not be able to charge as much money for your book and it will not impress people as much to acknowledge you as its author. On the other hand, a bible-sized nonfiction book (or, really, anything more than about 400 pages or 100,000 words in length) might seem like a more in-depth study than casual readers are willing to take on.

This chapter of *The Influential Author* contains just over 8,200 words, contributing to a total of about 130,000 words in the entire book. That's quite a bit longer than most of the popular books on Amazon about self-publishing (two to five times their length, in fact). This length was not planned from the beginning of my drafting. It was arrived at organically as I outlined, drafted, revised, and expanded my vision for what the book should contain. Once a few chapters had been written and I had detailed notes on the rest, I realized this length would be necessary to contain everything essential I had to say and accomplish the book's purpose. Its extended length will also help it stand out to writers looking for a deeper and more complete guide.

I've worked on books that were better suited for lengths between 30,000 and 40,000 words. Their subject matter and purpose made it more reader-friendly if people could quickly skim through to find exactly the information they needed on a specific topic (such as the case with the bail bond and tax books I produced). Expanding the word count with throat clearing or philosophical waxing would have changed the fundamental functions of the books, diluting their effectiveness for readers seeking conciseness and precision. Their relatively short length was still long enough to be taken seriously, but handy enough to carry around and reference as needed.

If you are not clear in your goal for your book from the time you start writing, its scope may shift and grow beyond anticipation. Endless rounds of editing and rewriting will ensue as you realize you aren't covering everything you want to. This is particularly a danger if you believe your book must include every valuable thought you've ever had or tell the story of your entire life. Believing your first book is your only shot to communicate what matters to you leads to a desperate state of content overstuffing. The influence of your book will be defined by its limits.

I faced a difficult time wrapping up the content of my upcoming personal development book, *The Exceptional Individual*. Its scope kept expanding as I drafted and revised it, well beyond what I anticipated when I began writing it more than two years ago. Originally, the book was addressed to intellectually gifted young adults struggling to find a healthy role to play in society. With nearly 50,000 words written and edited, I submitted my rough draft to beta readers and began making preparations for its Amazon launch.

Only upon reading the beta reader feedback did I realize *The Exceptional Individual* wasn't reaching as far as it needed to. I had prematurely set its destination and approached it from a limited perspective for the sake of easy audience targeting. There was still much more I had to say on the subject of self-actualization for people with exceptional traits. So, I decided to spend a few months rewriting portions of the draft, attempting to deepen its influence and meaning until it addressed all people seeking an unconventional set of rules to live by that would enable them to find greater happiness and purpose.

Those "few months" I appointed to perform the necessary alterations extended to more than a year. I kept finding more sections of the book that could be refined, deleted, or expanded to match my improved vision. Despite the relatively short length of the book, *The Exceptional Individual* ended up taking far longer than any other I've worked on, including the one you are reading now that contains more than double the word count.

If I had been able to begin the book with the scope and focus I ended up with, the writing and editing processes would have been much faster. My outline and tone would have been optimized for my purpose from the start. Only through constantly revising my original vision was I able to arrive at the superior version I finished with. I didn't really know what type of book I was trying to write until I had nearly finished writing the wrong one.

In this particular case, that's the path I had to take to arrive at *The Exceptional Individual*'s destiny. You may have to adapt to similar twists and turns in your own authorship journey, or you may have a much clearer vision from the start about the purpose and scope of your message. Just be willing to question where you are going and the best way to get there, no matter how much work you've already put into your book. To keep taking the wrong path will only move you further and further from your destination.

Educational Structure and Flow

Every author with a message of worth must learn how to make their meaning flow with ease and consistency for their readers. It is not a simple thing to be able to explain how things work in just the right order, at just the right time, and in just the right amount of detail so as not to omit something important or overwhelm anyone. The distance between teacher and student is frequently too great. The gap is hard to cross without getting lost along the way.

The process of taking seemingly unrelated patches of knowledge and weaving them together through logical connections is known as intellectual integration. When an author skips steps in the progression from their basic premises to their grand conclusions, the knowledge is not integrated and requires the reader to hold many unconnected ideas in their mind at once. The reader cannot check the new system of information for internal validity on their own. They must place too much trust in the unsupported assertions of the author as a dogmatic authority whose word is law.

If an author tends to sidebar into tangents unrelated to the logical progression of the book's message, the reader will become inundated with extraneous information. They won't have appropriate spaces to keep it all within the structure they are supposed to be building by following the author on the intellectual journey laid out in their words. The perfect message is just as long as it needs to be, and not any longer.

If adding information would detract from the purpose of the message, leave it out. If omitting information would take away from the reader's ability to derive the intended meaning, put it in. Every idea should be exactly what it needs and be and go in exactly the right place in the narrative you are crafting, which depends on what concepts have to be understood before others. Every point made should flow from the one before it into the one following it. The breakdown of your book's chapters will depend on the order your information needs to be presented in if it is to be understood by your readers.

Organizational Approach

You can think of individual chapters as categories of concepts related to your book's subject. How is your reader most likely to segregate and structure their thoughts? How do you categorize your own information here? If you were writing a book about the history and production of coffee beans, two obvious ways to classify the totality of your information would be either by time period or by part of the world (or a combination of both).

You might have chapters on coffee bean cultivation practices in modern day Africa, the Americas, Southeast Asia, and India. You might trace the journey of the coffea genus of plants from its origins in East Africa, beginning in the 1400s up to Yemen, before spreading to Persia, and Turkey, then throughout Europe and eventually becoming most prominent in Brazil. Such a book would be quite different than one that categorized its information through chapters on espressos, cappuccinos, lattes, and americanos.

If your book is meant to be more biographical in tone and focus, the most obvious way to structure it would be chronologically. Simply divide the important events of a person's life by the rough ages at which they occurred. This, of course, is still subject to your interpretation as the author of what is considered important and similar enough to be grouped together within the same subsection or category. There are more than 20 books on Amazon documenting and discussing the life of Napoleon Bonaparte. It's hard to imagine each one addresses the same information in the same order. Each author applies a filter and countless invisible judgment calls within the narrative they design.

For the series of interviews conducted within *Stories of Elders: What the Greatest Generation Knows about Technology that You Don't* by Veronica Kirin, the author/interviewer could have dedicated a chapter to each interview in the order they occurred. Instead, she chose to break up the chapters by the topics of things discussed, viewing the entire series of 100 interviews as a cohesive whole and picking out observations as they pertained to categories of experience like Communication, War, Poverty, and Medicine. Her structure serviced readers interested foremost in specific domains of progress, instead of the specific individuals interviewed to whom readers have no previous exposure.

If you are writing from your own life experiences, your memoir is probably meant to make a grand point about what some selection of your life experiences has taught you about something you consider important. Readers don't want to hear your whole life story unless you have achieved something of historical importance. You can make the focus of your message the conclusions you reached, backtracking to the various events that instigated, supported, and developed the philosophy you espouse.

Such is the way I organized my travel memoir and personal development book, *Travel as Transformation: Conquer the Limits of Culture to Discover Your Own Identity*. My travel experiences within it are loosely chronological, but the chapters are named and defined by categories of realizations I had while traversing the globe for a decade. The focus is the effects the experiences had on my personal development. I used chapter names like The Ordinary World, Call to Adventure, Departure from the Known, and Trials and Challenges, which also alluded to Joseph Campbell's classic hero's journey monomyth structure. I found this to be a unique and compelling way to frame travel compared to using the names of countries or the years in which my travel experiences occurred.

If your book's focus is practical matters and giving advice to people who don't know what to do about a specific set of problems, structure your chapters by the order, prominence, and/or severity of their issues. In *Get*

Bail, Leave Jail, I advised author Sean Plotkin to make his first chapter a breakdown of the basic functions of the bail bond process in America so that the terms and processes described in the rest of the book would make sense in context. The second chapter contained advice on the first steps someone should take if they or someone they know has been arrested and needs to be bailed out of jail.

From there, the chapters of *Get Bail, Leave Jail* covered the fundamentals of finding the right bondsman, how their working relationship with them would go, seeing a bond go through to trial and exoneration, and even what happens if a defendant goes on the run and bounty hunters are called to bring them in. Each chapter was designed to be able to taken on its own if a reader was in a position where its advice would suit their immediate concerns, but also as a complementary whole for readers starting from total ignorance about bail bonds and arrest.

While drafting *The Influential Author*, it was relatively easy to brainstorm everything I would need to include in the book. However, the extended length made it difficult to know the right places to put them all, how to separate them from each other or link them together, and how much space to devote to each. There had to be consistency and order throughout. Once I had seven major sections to contain each general portion of the book process starting with pre-drafting conception and ending with post-publication rumination, I found a way to logically break each section in half—two chapters per section, making 14 total.

As I was writing each chapter, I realized further partitioning would be needed to keep all the information I was presenting in mind. With an overhead view of the content I had written for each chapter, I found an effective way to divide each of the 14 chapters into three subheadings of approximately 1,500 to 4,000 words each, making 42 total subsections. Beta reader testing helped confirm that this breaking down of the book's ample content made it easier for readers to understand and retain it all, while also giving them convenient places to start and end reading in short and convenient sessions if they should desire it.

Reader Motivation

Your readers might approach your book thinking they already know a great deal about your subject. They may have already read other introductory books that outline its basic tenets or cover a different specialty than you intend to. Any previous exposure will bias their interpretation of your work. As an educator, you must bridge the gap between the condition readers come to you in and the condition you want to bring them to.

It should, therefore, be clear that the most important role of a good teacher is to ignite curiosity in the people they are teaching. All people have some level of natural inclination to seek new information about the things they care about. The transmission of new concepts depends on it. Without curiosity's activation, new information will be lost among internal noise and automatic defenses to foreign concepts. You must work with your readers' natures, not against them.

To that end, the function of a nonfiction book description, preface, and introduction are to prep your reader for why they should care about what will be covered in the book. They are your opportunity to set the tone and objective of the book on your terms so that your readers will not have false expectations or overlook the significance of your words. They should stoke curiosity by revealing the motivation and importance behind the book itself. Knowing where everything is going and how it is going to get there makes a big difference in a reader's retention and evaluation of what they read.

No matter what you write about, expanding paradigms is a laborious process. Only the people who want the outcome you intend for them will even begin reading. Fewer still of those will make it all the way through your message. You must bait their emotions with the reward of the outcome of your lessons. You must remind them, at all portions of your text, why they

89

are bothering to consume what you have offered. You must stimulate their emotions at the right intervals, a task many nonfiction writers overlook. This will carry them through the stress of mental expansion.

There are many ways to provide motivations for readers' investment. The most direct is the promise of a practical reward for adopting the principles you espouse. It's also often a good strategy to begin your work with a series of questions that prompt curiosity about your readers' current state of ignorance. When readers know they have a problem, they will naturally want to solve it.

In the preface to *The Influential Author*, I chose an approach that combines simple questions with the promise of practical reward for answering them. Read it again:

Many books on self-publishing proclaim that everyone has a book in them. They promote the false notion that anyone can become a successful author with hardly any effort. Such all-inclusive declarations are nonsense.

To write a book, one must invest hundreds of hours into strategizing, writing, and rewriting. To write a good book, one must become an exemplary communicator, using words as tools for a purpose. To become a respected author, one must have a purpose worth fulfilling and not be shy about promoting it.

To write a book is not the path for everyone, but it may be the path for you. The process is a challenge, but if you are determined to put in the necessary work, it is possible to find success as an independently published nonfiction author.

A nonfiction book with a valuable message can feed a specific type of hunger held by thousands of readers for generations to come. It can be a medium of information that adds longevity to the most valuable products of its author's life, even long after they are gone.

If you think you desire to write and publish, you must ask yourself what your book will do that no other book already does. You must inquire about your reasons behind your desire and whether they are strong enough to bring order out of the chaos of your still-unprocessed thoughts.

These opening paragraphs are meant to state the problem with the current state of ideas about independent authorship and self-publishing. For readers with interest in such things, the preface should promote curiosity, especially as they begin to realize that their current knowledge is lacking. The tone of the rest of the book is clearly implied, letting them know what reading the rest of the hundreds of pages will be like. The rewards of completing the journey are also obvious.

Then the preface follows with these questions and explanations for the importance of each of them:

- *"Is the content of your book unique?"*
- *"Are your tone and presentation more effective than other authors'?"*
- *"Why are you inspired to bring your message to the world?"*
- *"Who needs to read your message and why?"*
- *"Will you still desire to write your book if it makes no money?"*
- *"How will your book change people?"*
- *"How will your book entertain readers?"*
- *"Are you prepared to earnestly promote your book?"*

Hopefully, after reading these questions and pondering over them, you are now thinking about your manuscript or writing aspirations in a different light.

Most people who begin reading *The Influential Author* have probably never applied the standards I outline here to their work. No one has explained to them the importance of seeing their message this way. They should be concerned, intrigued, and enthusiastic enough to proceed with the rest of the book and receive the full intended value. If they are not, it means that either I have not done a good job of preparing them for my message or they are simply not the right kind of person to read it.

You can apply a similar approach to your message, no matter what the subject and intended tone are. You only need to think like a good educator about the goal of the information your book provides.

Then, you need to think like a marketer. You need to understand how to present the most vital and interesting parts of your "product" (your message) upfront so as to capture the attention of new readers and make them want to complete the "sale" (reading the whole book). Both roles, educator and marketer, are based on empathy: the ability to understand something familiar from a stranger's unfamiliar perspective.

Knowledge Structures

Unconsciously competent people can easily flow into a state of optimal performance in their chosen field. Their adeptness has become a type of second nature, nearly indistinguishable from basic instinct. They cannot analyze what they know or how they know it until they counter-intuitively complement their silent proficiency with conscious competence.

Until you've explicitly spelled out each logical step in your hierarchy of knowledge, it's difficult to see what you might be assuming to be true without confirmation. Writing out every pertinent detail makes it impossible to overlook your blind spots any longer. You may even realize that something you long assumed accurate simply doesn't hold up. It's much better to have these realizations during the writing process while you can still modify your views than after you have publicly published something you cannot support (although, as you'll learn once you publish, some readers will find fault with anything).

Know that your knowledge is more than a collection of facts. It is the deliberate and consistent structure within which you organize those facts. In passing your knowledge to another party, you are replicating that structure, brick by brick, within the space they have willingly allotted you in their mind. The stages of construction that reflect your understanding will appear in the outline of your text. Reflect on them now to prepare for a concise and effective writing process.

Always ask what unstated assumptions must be true for your cherished conclusions to stand. Determine what truths a reader must have already accepted to reach the same end you have. If you present only conclusions, relying on your status as an authority for your readers to believe you, you will have failed as a teacher. Walk your readers through the steps between where they are when they begin the journey and where you would like them to arrive. Knowing the steps of this journey will make outlining and subsequently populating your book's sections and chapters straightforward and logical.

When you know what mental place your readers ought to be in when they begin consuming your work, you will have a clearer idea of the kind of person who is best suited to read it. Is your book a beginner's guide to something? Is its purpose only to introduce the foundational concepts to a broad topic? Or is it meant to take people with functional knowledge to a higher level of specialty and proficiency?

If your message is something that you can adequately cover with a series of steps or instructions, you might consider your book a "complete" or "how to" guide to some specific domain of life. In this case, your book probably won't be extremely long. It will consist of a short introduction to concepts a newcomer might not understand, followed by their options for practical actions they can take to achieve their goals.

The Right Types of Readers

How your book affects a person's philosophy or actions is a difficult thing to measure or control. The outcome depends on the reader's subjective interpretation, their life experiences, and other factors you cannot always know or influence. How many times has a friend raved about how good they thought a book or movie was, but when you followed their endorsement and checked it out yourself you couldn't see what they did? With enough exposure, your message will come to receive every type of feedback imaginable. Murphy's law applies here. Every reaction that can happen will happen, from the very best to the very worst. You can think ahead now about what kind of person will have what type of reaction and plan your book around this projection.

If you understand the unique reasons why your book deserves to exist, it should be easy to envision who those reasons most apply to and who their value would be lost on. The correlation works in both directions. If you know who you are writing for, it will be simpler to write for that person's needs. You won't deliberate as much over exact phrasings, or the type of information that needs to be included or omitted. You will just tell your audience what you know they need to hear because you will know who your audience is and what they want. If you know who you are writing for, you won't care so much when the wrong type of person doesn't like it.

It won't matter how good a writer you are or how much money you put into marketing if you present your message to the wrong people. If readers don't see an obvious connection in your message to their pressing needs, they will likely give up on reading it. If they manage to make it all the way through it, they will be unhappy with the experience. Unhappy readers lead to negative word-of-mouth publicity and public reviews, killing your success before it's even begun. While you can't prevent the wrong people from getting their hands on it completely, you can set up the presentation and promotion of your book to minimize their interest.

That being said, do not limit yourself to solely your own perspective when trying to understand your message. Like all creators, you suffer from some degree of self-bias. You are too close to your message to understand how outsiders who do not share your personal history and insider perspective will perceive it. Even your inner circle of friends and colleagues suffers from the same weakness because they know you too well. They cannot be neutral about your work because they have already glimpsed inside the mind that created it. You will solve this problem by reaching out beyond your comfortable social limits.

Throughout the refinement stages of your manuscript, you will learn to appreciate the feedback of blind beta readers who have no previous exposure or expectations beyond what's contained within the message itself. In presenting and promoting your work, you will test every creative choice among samples of your ideal readers to determine, as objectively as possible, what will perform well and what will not. This will give you insight into the most appealing elements of your work that you may have overlooked. It will also enlighten you to some fundamental flaws that you would not have seen on your own.

Targeting Factors

Targeting your nonfiction book for the right readers does not have to be complicated or require boring market research. It may not matter whether your readers are 20 or 60 years old. It may not make much difference if they are men or women, how much money they make, or whether they prefer smooth jazz to hip-hop music. What matters is that they want to learn what you are trying to teach and that their style of learning is in line with your style of teaching.

The message you are reading right now is intended for people who have something important to say and want to become commercially successful nonfiction authors. From the content and tone of my message, it's easy to derive a lot of information about the type of reader who gets the most from it. I can predict certain truths about the ideal type of reader for *The Influential Author*:

- They may have read other books on nonfiction writing or self-publishing and are now sick of receiving the same vague, inflated advice not relevant to their situation or goals.
- They may be professionals in a unique or complex industry that is sorely misunderstood by its patrons.
- They may have lived an unconventional life and are now determined to share what their experiences have taught them.
- They may be content creators within another medium like blogging or podcasting who want to transfer their success to a new, long-form written medium with greater authority.
- They may be lifelong artists or intellectuals who have been desperate for a way to monetize their mental and emotional abilities for a while.
- They are people who have some entrepreneurial experience (or at least an entrepreneurial personality).
- They have strong desires to communicate meaningful information and see the results of their message.
- They have the patience necessary to sit and write for dozens or hundreds of accumulated hours.
- They are in positions to gain from the social identity that comes with being published authors on their chosen topics.
- They have the work ethic needed to bring their intended messages to fruition as clear and cohesive books.

If you belong to all or most of these categories, it scarcely matters to me your age, the part of the world you are from, your marital status, or your annual salary. You will be in a position to get the full intended value of my words here. You will also be likely to be satisfied with the time and money you had to invest into consuming my message, and therefore more likely to leave me a positive review on Amazon or promote me to your social network of like-minded people who also stand to gain the same things you are gaining right now.

The audience targeting factors that matter for you will be unique to your message, but understanding your ideal reader will help in more ways than you might imagine. If you know what your reader stands to gain and their frame of mind going into your book, it will inform your choice for title and subtitle, cover art, book description, and every marketing tactic you employ. Unlike most vanity authors who cannot see beyond their own limited perspective, you must step outside yourself to find the ideal framing device for your work.

Audience Competition

When you look at books similar to yours that have found commercial success, the intended audience for each should be clear. There should be some overlap between them, but also a uniqueness to each one. The tone of the description, the specific information covered, the keywords featured in the title and subtitle, and the colors and imagery used in the cover design all play a role in segregating buyers into categories of specific interest or disinterest. Try to reverse engineer the approaches used by your most prominent competition. Your goal is not to copy them, but to learn from their success and try something new with the same principles.

Capitalize on other authors' strengths only so much as is appropriate for your message. Do not copy them to the point of betraying yourself. Authenticity lies at the core of influential authorship. The purpose of studying present market availability is to learn how to display your message as you actually intend it, while also meeting the cultural expectations of your audience. Successful transmission happens in the middle ground between what you want to say and what other people want to hear.

If you make the mistake of mimicking another successful book, your schemes will backfire. You cannot possibly maintain authenticity when you copy another person's approach. Their voice and their purpose are not your own. Furthermore, as previously stated, your competition has a head start on you. They published earlier than you, built a sustainable audience, and created a long-running reputation of reader satisfaction. If you have no unique merits on which your message will stand, you will create many unnecessary obstacles on the path to marketplace success.

Do not make the mistake of thinking the appeal of your message will be limited to just one, clearly delineated group of readers. Different people will have their own reasons for being interested in a subject. You might assume your primary readership will be consumers planning to make a purchase for something related to what you write about, but what if they are students studying for a class tangential to your subject. How will their reading motivations be different? What about professionals working in a related field? Train yourself to look at your work through every relevant lens of evaluation.

Personality Appeal

Have you thought about what you want the personality of your book to be? This will factor heavily into how different audiences perceive its value. Your book's personality should be some facet of your natural demeanor. Otherwise, you will be inauthentic. When you think about your subject, what kind of emotions do you experience? Does teaching others how to play chess make you excited, pensive, or melodramatic? All of these are valid personality options to display. The book that promises to make you laugh, cry, get mad, or question everything you thought you knew about the names of different opening chess moves is sure to stand out against a sea of generic "how to play chess" books.

Many books with fantastic content and hundreds of hours behind their creation remain forever invisible and unappreciated. Their authors and publishers do not understand how to display them in appealing and accurate ways to the right people. If you've ever paid to see a movie based on a misleading trailer (or decided not to see one because the trailer was so bad) you understand how this works. Everything readers see about your book before they open the pages is the window dressing that makes everything inside accessible. Before you even begin drafting, you should think about what impression you want your book to create in order to attract the right readers and satisfy their expectations.

All readers choose the books they will buy based on what they perceive their reading options to be. There is now a greater variety of books than ever before. There are also more readers for whom the increasing number of books are written. When readers find more choice about what books to spend their limited money and reading hours on, their book choices get more refined. The longer this trend continues, the more important it will be to communicate a unique angle for your book from the first impression. It's the only way to stand out from the crowd. Try not to let the pressure get to you.

Summary of Chapter 4

There are infinite ways to write about a subject. Once you broadly know what you want to write about, you have to decide what part of that topic you are going to focus on, how far your coverage of it is going to extend, and what level of fine detail you are going to get into.

— — — —

After you've decided the depth and angle of information to be covered in your book, you'll need to be able to arrange your ideas into a sequential and logically consistent educational structure. If you take your knowledge for granted, you may omit details or skip steps that are required for a newcomer to achieve the same level of understanding as you after reading your book.

— — — —

No matter what you write, readers are liable to interpret it in any number of ways you did not intend. You can make efforts to tailor the right types of interpretations by making your book appeal only to readers who will receive the type and amount of value you intended by writing it. You do this by having something unique to say and saying it with a unique style.

PART 3:

CREATION

CHAPTER 5:

The Qualities and Conditions of a Writer

It should be clear by now that not every message deserves to be made into a book. Not everyone's life story needs to be shared with the world. That doesn't stop thousands of new authors from attempting to spread their messages every year though. Without a traditional publisher as gatekeeper, plenty of self-absorbed, low-influence writing makes it to the digital shelves of Amazon, diluting the quality of reading options available to consumers.

If you are going to fulfill your destiny as a publicly lauded author of a meaningful message, you will need to hone your verbal abilities and endurance. Writing well is a skill set that results from a combination of natural ability and practiced acumen. You do not need to conduct an extensive study of English grammar or the history of literature to develop the skills necessary to write your book. You only need to set the stage for your organized ideas to make their way onto the page in a clear manner with minimal resistance.

There is no single correct way to do this. It will take some experimentation to find the ideal combination of factors for your mind, message, and lifestyle, which is the hardest part of adopting a serious writing habit for many people. Most of us were trained in public schooling as children to treat writing as a chore or obligation, applying it only for purposes in which we had no intrinsic investment. We wrote only because we had to under threats of punishment and scorn. That is the mentality we now must reverse and begin to look at writing as a discipline we choose to pursue for our own reasons.

Your motivation will also affect how you approach the task of drafting. If you still seek validation through authorship, it will lead to a style of writing that comes across as arrogant and lacking self-awareness. If the primary motive behind your writing is to demonstrate your skill with the written word, you will seem over-the-top and pedantic to casual readers. Your incentive for undergoing the trials of extensive drafting should be to reflect the important things you know and believe, with many other viable goals (such as making money, growing your brand, or stroking your ego) as secondary.

Now is the best time to become the type of person capable of writing a meaningful book for all the right reasons. If you take the tasks ahead seriously, they will lead to major changes in the way you view yourself, your abilities, and your purpose for communicating in any form. Your first responsibility is to manufacture the internal and external conditions that will allow you to tap into the best parts of yourself—the only parts that are capable of surpassing and growing from the struggles that await you.

Navigating Writer's Block and Creative Inspiration

You may not think of yourself as a writer, but chances are you write a lot more than you think you do. If someone told you to develop the discipline to write thousands of words a day for your book, the task might seem a more substantial burden than you could manage. Similarly, the idea of committing oneself to walk three miles every day, while not impossible, is beyond the comfortable imaginings of most non-athletes with already busy schedules. Yet, plenty of sources indicate that an average person unknowingly walks about three miles (approximately 6,000 average-stride steps) in the course of a normal day. It is the same with writing.

If you use email, social media, and text messages, your mind is already accustomed to the demands of random transmutation from thought to text. You just don't notice writing when it happens spontaneously and you're not deliberating over what you are going to say. A prompt is placed before you by your conversation partner, and your brain rapidly generates the most appropriate response. Or else, you have a need emerge within you, a question that needs addressing or a sudden burst of inspiration, and you reach out to someone with a vital articulation.

Over the course of an ordinary text-based conversation, you might inadvertently write over 1,000 words in chunks as small as a few words at a time or lengthy paragraphs of more than 100 words each. How this happens and in exactly what quantity is different for each person's lifestyle and technological prowess, but it's easy to see how you are more capable of creating large amounts of written text every day than you think. An average person walks almost 100 miles in one month of their ordinary life without ever thinking about it. How many words do you think you have written in the last month of your life without stopping to notice it?

The necessary task is to funnel your natural writing habits toward your book's first draft. Part of the reason you did the heavy lifting of thinking about the purpose, philosophy, and structure of your message before the outlining stage is so that you can now switch into a psychological state of producing written output. Because you won't have to spend much time thinking about what to write, you can just tend to writing what fulfills the purpose you have set for yourself. Now you will take the seeds of cultivated ideas and expand them to their logical ends.

What stops people from writing often has little to do with the physical act itself. Most people have more of a thinking problem than a writing problem. Writing is hard for them because it forces them to become better thinkers. If you want your book to be effective and the writing process expedient, you must become so good at thinking that you can communicate to people who don't necessarily think as well as you do. You must be able to do this without deliberating over every sentence that leaves your head.

It seems a cruel irony that destruction often comes more fluently to the mind than creation. We can identify and pluck out parts of what exists, erasing or modifying them in just moments. Our brains are built for rapid and efficient error correction, a consequence of conscious judgment. When we have nothing to work with, a blank canvas with unlimited possibilities, our brains are prone to quickly faltering. The burden of choice is too onerous. From nothing, anything is possible. The effort required to determine which single thing is worth the effort to bring into being out of infinite potential things is too massive for most minds.

This is the primary source of the malady called analysis paralysis. The mind cannot so easily arrive at new constructs as it can pick out which finite things are wrong with old ones. Everyone, including you, is a critic; few people are creators. So, you must seed your critical mind with something to work on, to modify, stretch, or reduce. You will accomplish this by laying the groundwork for all your vital ideas in an evolving outline before and throughout the writing process. This way, you will never be at a loss for words or inspiration.

Writing a little bit is easy. As noted, almost everyone writes a little every day. Writing a lot, pages and pages on end, is emotionally taxing and creatively draining. If you have not already honed the skill of churning out thousands of words per day in a readable fashion, you are going to learn some difficult lessons about your productive abilities as an author. Writer's block does not have to prevent you from proceeding with your book at a reasonable pace and enjoying the process, though. Even if you only manage to write a few hundred words a day, but they are words that serve the purpose of your message, you will eventually arrive at your goal.

Your waking mind is always outputting attention in some form. Writer's block occurs when you force the flow of your attention in a direction other than where it naturally wants to go. If you fight against the momentum of your consciousness, it will crash as an idle and festering rut. You won't be able to accomplish anything, no matter how hard you try. Look for where your attention wants to go. Track the trajectory of that momentum to persuade it toward your goals, such as finishing a chapter of your book's first draft. Rerouting attention requires the selective negation of ideas, not the spontaneous emergence of something from nothing. It is a process of psychological alchemy: the changing of one form of awareness into another.

Ignore any writer who claims there is one secret weapon to effectively destroy writer's block and other forms of creative stagnation. Such a claim is as ridiculous as the claim that there is a single perfect diet, hobby, or career for all people, despite our myriad differences. All writers are different. You must prepare your body and mind for optimal creation, the circumstances of which are unique to every individual. Learn how you work best by modifying and testing the many variables that influence your creative flow under different writing conditions.

Personal Writing Environment

Whatever your creative habits are, do not fight your fickle brain. Do everything you can to give it what it wants if you expect heavy production from it. There will always be elements working against you that you cannot control; address the elements you can so they won't impede your progress. There may be new environmental factors you discover that have an enormous influence on your ability to write fast or well. For you, it could be a roaring fireplace, a sandy beach, the trickle of a water fountain, the chatter of restaurant patrons, or the cheesy dialogue of daytime soap operas playing on your television in the next room over.

Long sessions of meaningful writing come when circumstances allow for them, but such conditions are different for each writer. Some writers thrive in a serene lakeside cabin, miles away from civilization. Others need the hustle and whirr of a busy café. Drowning out all other noise with headphones and heavy metal might be the ideal catalyst for you. You won't know until you've paid attention to how you respond to different types of stimuli across controlled experiments.

One of my favorite (and not entirely uncommon) muses is the presence of a feline, so I have developed the habit of taking stray cats off the street and into my temporary apartments as I travel around the world. They pay for their stay with the inspirational effects of their behavior.

It seems clear that about 80% of my ability to think (and therefore write) depends on only a few basic variables. I know I can't be even a little hungry or thirsty, which is complicated by the fact that I have a fast metabolism and often get so caught up in my writing that I forget to eat or drink for several hours. Then I fall into a mental fog and cannot continue until I have fed and rehydrated. Knowing this weakness in myself, I make it a point to never be without ample food and water in my vicinity when I write.

Sonic Landscape

Another gamechanger for creativity might be the various sounds present in an author's writing environment. My mind is particularly attuned to the nuances of noise and music. It has trouble developing the latent inhibition required to block out car horns, foot traffic, or the tonal disharmony of the human world. Hearing the universe in high definition can keep my attention on a leash. However, give me the wind moving through the trees or the hum of forest insects, and I'll have the ideal sonic canvas to write to.

Music has its own motivating influence too. I keep a playlist of music and a pair of audiophile-quality headphones on hand to cover up the sounds I cannot control. The style of music that catalyzes creativity is different for every writer. For me, it's driving rhythm, complex instrumental harmonies, and narrative musical flow. I owe a lot of my output as a writer to the music of popular film score composer Hans Zimmer. His overproduced melodies and unconventional instrumentation almost never fail to put me in a productive mood.

Bodily Mechanics

Different days require different types of physical positioning and movement if I am expected to produce any worthwhile writing. If I'm sitting at a table or desk, I bob my leg in synchronicity with the speed of my thoughts. I take short, frequent breaks, sometimes as often as every paragraph, to get up from my work and pace for several minutes around the room. Walking correlates with creative thinking for me. Still, sometimes staying in bed all day is the ideal creative posture. I listen to what my body tells me at the time I intend to be productive, ignoring conventional wisdom about what the daily habits of a writer should look like. This is the wisdom that years of trial and error have provided me, though you might find yourself to be the type of writer who needs an exclusive and dedicated writing space.

Even something as simple as the interface of the computer I write on affects my production. Some writers refuse to work on anything other than their favorite typewriter or mechanical computer keyboard. Alternate between different devices during your writing sessions. See if you notice patterns in how the words come to you on one interface versus another. It could be the size of the screen, the amount of resistance to the keys, or even the font typed in. Maybe you function better with pen and paper, though such a burden I can hardly imagine.

Psychic Stimulation

If you have a particularly active mind, you may suffer from boredom while writing or editing that detracts from the quality of your work. Against conventional advice, you can combine your writing time with other activities that will stimulate your creative faculties as you grind through the tedious parts of creation. Being slightly distracted can help you mimic the state of mind a reader might be in when they consume your published work. People rarely read in a vacuum. Why should anyone write in one?

You can watch a movie with a plot that doesn't require your full attention (maybe a mindless action flick or a simple buddy comedy) while you chip away at your partially completed manuscript. You can have guests over to discuss your work as you write. I will frequently listen to podcasts or audiobooks while I write, sometimes ones on the same subject I am writing about. I don't see this as multitasking, but as providing my unconventional mind the precise stimulation it needs to remain productive. For many writers, however, listening to one conversation while engineering another proves too mentally taxing to accomplish either.

Human Interaction

Take time to cultivate a social order that supports your writing habits. What that social order looks like will be different for every writer, as no two people need the same social influence to operate at their best. If discussing the latest developments and overall vision of your work with a trusted circle helps you flesh out your ideas and produce content faster, make sure you have the right people in your life. If you try to have these types of interactions with people who have no interest in or appreciation for what you are trying to accomplish, your social efforts may backfire and only hurt your productive capabilities.

Being around the right kind of people to aid your writing might mean spending most of your time in isolation. It might mean avoiding people you normally like in your life but who interrupt your creative flow for some reason. It might mean learning to talk about your writing in a way that invites constructive criticism and suggestion, not binary, one-note approval or rejection. When you make the switch from non-writer to writer, you may not receive much support from your peers who can't seem to understand why you now spend your evenings and weekends alone, at home, passing up opportunities for normal social behavior to slave away on something they can't see any visible progress on. You must press on, one way or another.

Everyone knows the stereotype of the amateur novelist who talks without end about the book they are writing and how great it will be when it's done, hardly ever making any actual progress on it. For some writers, talking about what they want to do provides the same sense of reward as actually doing it would, therefore negating their emotional incentive to produce. Such writers have their motivation in the wrong place, having fallen in love with the idea of being a writer and not the purpose of the role itself.

Creation Prioritization

The timing and order of creation matter too for writing without obstacle. If you hit a block in one section, consult your outline and move on to the parts of the book that seem most interesting in moments of obstruction. Your excitement will carry you through the early stages of writer's block, so give your excitement whatever it seems to want. Fickle grinding through the finer details of your message comes later, once you've said most of what needs to be said about all your major points. Do not write what you do not feel like writing until you feel like writing it.

Quality creation cannot be forced or micromanaged. Give yourself freedom from this pressure to produce by always having multiple options for your creative energy to flow to whenever it needs a new direction. If you get caught up in the minutia too soon, it will slow your momentum. Your task is to cultivate your creative forces and aim them where they are best suited to go. You are to get out of your own way and let creation happen, which may not have anything to do with setting daily word count goals or anything like that.

Emotional Ammunition

Learn to use every emotion, each of which has a unique motivating influence on human behavior. You can harness your passion, in whatever emotional form it takes, to carry you through the most arduous portions of the writing process. You won't necessarily enjoy all the time you spend writing. Along with the joy of expression, there may be times when sadness or anger become useful motivators for writing. It all depends on what kind of person you are and the nature of your ideas (and the consequences of completing your book). Find the emotion that drives your creative process.

The first book I authored and published was *Brand Identity Breakthrough: How to Craft Your Company's Unique Story to Make Your Products Irresistible*, a guide to effective communication for companies and solo entrepreneurs. The final edit of the book ran roughly 65,000 words, which, at the tender age of 27, was a far greater quantity of words than I'd written about a single topic before. It was not an easy task to organize the content and oversee the launch and marketing of the book on my own with no experience in authorship or publishing.

Before that point in my life, I didn't even think of myself as a writer. My professional background was in various forms of education, sales, and marketing. I saw myself, foremost, as a good explainer of things. I never particularly enjoyed the process of writing. I needed to find motivation stronger than solely my passion for entrepreneurship if I wanted to get my book done in a timely manner. Otherwise, I would likely have spent years waiting for inspiration to strike.

Due to circumstances beyond my control, I found the inspiration needed to finish writing and launching *Brand Identity Breakthrough* to moderate success in just a few months. This quick pace was possible because I was fueled by more than mere enthusiasm for seeing my first book in print. Instead, I called upon ample reserves of anger and a desire for vengeance to propel my writing.

For you see, my first book came about as the result of professional fraud committed by a woman and her assisted self-publishing company who I had hired to help produce the book and make it a bestseller on Amazon. I had met her through a trendy online entrepreneur and digital marketer community, which I now realize probably should have been my first reason to be cautious of her moral and professional credibility. Digital author labs like the one belonging to the woman I hired are notorious for finding hopeful, wannabe authors and making big promises about being able to launch them into self-publishing stardom through hacky promotional tactics and cheap third-party outsourcing. It's embarrassing now to look back on the encounter and recognize how naïve I was to mistake this woman's overpromises and eagerness to work with me as a sign of professional and moral caliber.

First, the woman I hired to help create and launch *Brand Identity Breakthrough* enthusiastically told me I should expect to see a return on my $5,000 investment within the yearly quarter that we began working together. That should have been my first red flag, as even getting the first draft of the book written in that time would have been an impressive feat, let alone all the editing, beta reading, design work, market testing, and pre-launch promotional outreach I now knew would be necessary to ensure a successful launch. On top of that, I would have to wait for the book to sell enough copies or for its existence to lead to enough new sources of revenue that I would make more than $5,000. "Within the quarter" was the manipulative promise of a hack who had no experience with the amount of work it would take to get a good book done.

Second, every time I showed hesitation about proceeding with the publishing plan being pushed on me, the woman I hired responded by rapidly piling on more vague services that sounded impressive but would be difficult to quantify and evaluate the worth of. Now that I am familiar with what it actually takes to make a self-published book successful (regardless of whether it ever reaches bestseller status on Amazon), I can look back on what she promised me and recognize that almost none of it made sense with the price or timeline she gave me. It was far too cheap and quick to be done even for someone with ample experience in this space.

This irresponsible woman took advantage of my newness to self-publishing. She exploited our mutual online community connections and was helpful enough in the beginning to build trust with me. I would learn approximately nine months after investing the five grand with her that the woman who took my money had no ability or intention to deliver what I had paid her for. When her fraud was revealed and it became apparent I had no hope of recovering my money, I had a difficult emotional choice to make. I could accept defeat, cutting my financial losses and moving on with the harsh lessons I had learned, or I could finish the book myself and use my background in sales to figure out how to give it a successful launch on Amazon.

At that stage, my moral outrage at having been conned was stronger than my desire to be an author, so I applied that outrage to my production. I finished *Brand Identity Breakthrough* because I felt a karmic obligation to fulfill the work my adversary had set my expectations on receiving. My sense of injustice, which might have left someone with a different personality feeling idle and disenfranchised, became the fire to finish what my fraudster could not. My negative emotions became powerful muses. Perhaps your inspiration will come from the last place you expect and from emotions you would never have considered. Perhaps you will need to explore new lifestyles and activities that spurn your fickle creative muse.

Psychologists have a concept called the Zeigarnik effect. It states that people are more likely to remember and be motivated to complete tasks they actively perceive as unfinished. "The advantage of remembrance" is put into play in every movie with a revenge plot, for example. The protagonist will often keep a physical memento of a wrong that was committed against them by the antagonist, such as a piece of jewelry once worn by a murdered loved one. This practice reminds them of their unfinished business. Their anger gives them focus and makes them stronger.

If you view the writing of your book as an open-ended journey with no clearly defined goal, you will approach it differently than if you viewed it as a defined task with strong reasons for quick completion.

Consciousness Tampering

One stereotype of writers is their dependence on mind-altering chemical substances to find their muse or cultivate the wherewithal to hack out thousands of words each day. Robert Louis Stevenson, famously, churned out *The Strange Case of Dr. Jekyll and Mr. Hyde* flying off the rails of cocaine for six days in the 1880s. Stephen King too was addicted to cocaine for many of his most prolific writing years. Ayn Rand relied on Benzedrine, a form of speed, to write the more than half a million words of *Atlas Shrugged*, her magnum opus. John Keats' poetry was at least partially inspired by a love of opium. Aldous Huxley credits mescaline for opening his mind enough to write *The Doors of Perception*.

You may already know through personal experience the potentially powerful effects certain chemicals offer the mind's creative and productive capabilities. You may alternatively be the kind of person who detests the idea of this form of assisted creative "cheating." No matter your feelings about the many forms of legal and illegal drugs, the truth is we are always altering our minds through every innocuous substance we introduce to our bodies. The food we eat affects our thoughts and mood. The quality of the air we breathe matters. Every emotion you feel, from love to lust to hatred, is the result of a powerful chemical concoction coursing through your brain.

It's easy to let yourself be biased by social stigma, but many taboo substances in the United States, whether natural or synthesized, are used openly in other parts of the world or have been popular throughout eras of history. Even many of the common substances in your diet could rightfully be considered mind-altering drugs. Every dark chocolate lover knows the signature feeling of bliss that comes when they consume enough of it. This is because cacao beans contain theobromine and phenylethylamine, compounds that produce joy and the sensation of falling in love. Yet, few people consider chocolate a drug in the same way they would heroin or LSD.

Caffeine, alcohol, and nicotine, though legal and socially approved, have been demonstrated to be as addictive, unhealthy, and mind-altering as some notorious and illegal drugs. Yet, the stereotype of authors slaving over their typewriters with a mug, bottle, or cigarette in hand to mitigate the stress of creation persists in our cultures. These various vices may assist in the creative process for authors who know their own persuasions well. If you've never introduced these compounds to your body and witnessed how they affect you, you cannot necessarily assume the same about yourself. On the other hand, you may already know from negative personal experience that these types of substances affect your creative consciousness poorly or become too habit forming for you to use responsibly.

It doesn't matter if what works to bring out the writer in you follows conventional writing advice or not. If you are trying to look and act like what society has told you a writer is, you will never produce anything authentic. Pay attention to your faults, quirks, strengths, and flow. Depending on how much control you have over the constituents of your lifestyle, you will soon arrange your life to optimize your thoughts and writing. You can only do this when you have made writing a priority, which will only happen when you understand how you work best.

Learning to Write with Clarity and Conciseness

A lot of great writing begins as a collection of individual thoughts or general statements that are later expanded and elaborated upon to form a cohesive train of thought and a complete narrative representing the paradigm of the writer. So long as each thought makes sense in isolation, it is possible to find a creative way to unify them into a structure of knowledge. Alternatively, if your sentences come from nothing and are only present to look or sound nice, you will have no solid material with which to build your knowledge house.

Sometimes you don't know what you're trying to say until you're most of the way through saying it. Sometimes you don't know how a sentence is going to end until you've started it. Trying to have it all planned out in minute detail before you begin is a flawed approach to creation. You should have an idea where you are going but remain flexible on how you will get there. The path will present many unanticipated bends and opportunities that require you to improvise. Be confident in your ability to adapt.

Your thought streams will come to surprise you as you draft. Let them. Whatever comes out of you, make it your goal to have it be the best possible version of it. Do not sacrifice the quality of your words to meet your preexisting expectations of what you thought you were writing. The goal is always slightly moving, approximating more and more the eventual finished state of your book. If your goal is fixed, you limit its creative possibilities and prematurely nullify much of its potential value. On the opposite extreme, if your approach is too malleable, you risk its scope expanding beyond your control and you never being satisfied with it.

To write in such a way that will not inhibit or negate any emergent opportunities, you may follow this basic sequence of creation:
1. Get your basic ideas down as coherent sentences.
2. Arrange your coherent ideas in the appropriate logical/ chronological order.
3. Refine their wording and style to capture the most appropriate version of your voice for the content.
4. Remove any unnecessary repetition in your word choices or meaning as well as extraneous details.

Intentional Redundancy

It is not wise to write with the assumption that your readers will absorb and retain 100% of your words and meaning. A reader consumes a book at their own discretion. Try as you might to control the flow of information precisely, there is no way you can force any of your readers to go through your book at a consistent pace and in the correct order. You cannot make them pay detailed attention to each sentence and recall what came before or interpret every word as intended. Your perfectly crafted message exists only in theory until you test it under real-world reader conditions.

Some readers in the real world skim long passages of text. They jump between chapters throughout the beginning, middle, and end of a book. They rarely devote their full attention to what they are doing. Hence, you can predict that there will almost always be some loss of efficiency in the transmission of your knowledge. While you can predict some level of information runoff, what you cannot predict is exactly what information will be lost and in precisely what manner. The loss is unique to each reader and read-through.

Too easily, writers with advanced knowledge on a subject forget what it was like to gaze upon their subject from the outside with no prior experience. They write for someone who holds a perspective similar to their own because everything makes sense to them as they have chosen to present it (largely defeating the purpose of reading it in the first place). Proper retention in an uninformed mind requires a certain amount of simplification and redundancy in the presentation of information. Even at the expense of conciseness, slightly too much information is infinitely better than slightly too little (as anyone who has tried to assemble furniture according to the minimalistic instructions provided by IKEA will know). With a scarcity of detail, the reader might miss a critical piece of data necessary to interpret the rest.

For clarity's sake, get used to repeating the most important principles of the knowledge you are trying to convey at strategic intervals throughout your work. Repetition drives an important point home. Callbacks to earlier sections of your book give readers the opportunity to mentally retrace what they have learned so far from what they have read. Hints to what is coming later prepare the mind to allocate space and give more significant meaning to what might seem like insignificant details now. Putting new information into mental practice as soon as possible is vital to retention.

You must also restate the context of what you write about as often as you can without making your message feel redundant and clunky. If a reader jumps ahead of your intended order to the middle of a chapter or returns to reading after a long break, how many sentences will they have to read before they can understand again the context of what you are discussing? Look for opportunities to rephrase sentences in such a way that their complete meaning is explicit or can at least be inferred without much effort. Cater to the laziness of your readers. Do not make them jump across gaps in your presentation or work to connect concepts that have no apparent relationship to a newcomer to your subject.

Language Unit Breakdown

When can you say that your book is done? When every word is exactly the right word, constituting exactly the right sentences, which in turn make up the exact right paragraphs, themselves the building blocks of the subsections that divide your chapters. It's simple in principle, but meticulous and maddening in actual practice. Though you will need to apply many rounds of editing and revision to all parts of your rough draft, you can minimize unnecessary labor by getting things as right as possible the first time around.

Begin with an understanding of what each written unit of information accomplishes in its own right.

A **word** represents a concept (nouns and verbs), the modification of a concept (articles, adjectives, and adverbs), or a relationship between concepts (prepositions). Words, like currency, exist because people have collectively agreed through common usage that they mean something. When a concept is prevalent and important enough within a subculture or society, it organically gets assigned its own phonetic and written label.

Everyone has experienced the frustration of wanting to express a concept for which there is no established word in English, forcing them to rely on lengthy descriptions to create an accurate portrayal in the mind of their conversation partner. You can test this by looking up words in other languages that describe concepts for which there is no concise equivalent in English. This is one reason we often borrow foreign words instead of inventing new English words that mean the same thing.

A **sentence** is a completed thought, representing new meaning created through changes to the categorization of the concepts applied within it. It's no accident that according to the hard rules of English grammar a complete sentence must contain a noun and a verb, otherwise known as subjects and predicates (so called because the function is to assert or "predicate" something about the subject).

With every sentence you write, you make a claim about an aspect of reality. You tell your reader, in one form or another, that x does y. It's a phenomenal amount of responsibility. When no single word exists to represent the concept you want to communicate, you must rely on one or more sentences to describe the necessary novel assertions about concepts already established in the lexicon.

A **paragraph** is a small collection of thoughts linking a continuous series of categorical changes to a set of related concepts. If you break up your paragraphs effectively, it will be easy to rearrange the order in which they appear, cutting and pasting as you wish, without losing the ability to comprehend the context and meaning of each one taken on its own. The topic of a paragraph should be made clear and its sentences made to lead into one another causally and stylistically.

With self-contained paragraphs, you have the luxury of experimenting with the manner of their sequence and inclusion. You may even decide to move whole paragraphs or groups of paragraphs to other sections of your book, hardly having to rewrite a single word to retain the same meaning. In that way, your writing efforts are rarely wasted, only repurposed depending on how well they serve your message as you have presented them.

A **subsection** is a collection of related paragraphs that form stepping-stones to comprehension about a specific facet of the chapter they constitute. Each subsection is an encapsulated monologue, generally taking no more than several minutes for the reader to complete. Each can be introduced with a descriptive subheading or presented without label. The subheading for this subsection is "Drafting Your Message with Clarity," which is the second of three within Chapter 5: The Qualities and Conditions of a Writer of the book *The Influential Author*.

A **chapter**, then, can be thought of as a collection of conversations about one aspect of the topic of the book itself. The names and purposes of chapters can either be decided before creating any content for them or after enough subsections have been written to make the purpose of their coverage clear.

Beyond chapters, there exists the context of the book as a whole. The title, cover design, and every bit of external marketing has exposed the reader to unconscious expectations and set their minds to intake its message in a certain way. Everything that comes before or after any given chapter affects the overall reception of the book.

Reader Reading Habits

Readers who feel confident about their familiarity with the subject of your book are liable to jump ahead to specific chapters that the table of contents indicates contain information they are looking for. They assume they already have the prerequisite details to skip what they predict will be redundant passages. Your readers may or may not be correct in this assumption. If you write your book in an original and personal manner, there should be no other way for your readers to have arrived at the same information in the same way that you except them to when they read your words exactly as presented. Even the chapters covering seemingly familiar ground should offer unique insight that is worth the cost of acquisition.

You might think that the layers of meaning begin and end within the covers of your book, but they extend into realms you cannot extrapolate. Every person who starts or finishes reading your book does so within the context of their own life experiences. Over this aspect of interpretation, an author has no control. You can only do your best to prepare every portion of your message to guard against the likelihood of misinterpretation. But no matter how beautifully you write or with what precision you delineate your knowledge, your book may reach a multitude of people who hold a great variety of preferences, biases, and personalities that affect the context of your message.

How, then, can you as a writer even begin to construct a clear message without remaking the universe itself from the atom up? How can you draw conclusions not dependent on all your readers having had a specific set of prior life experiences to understand? Unless you are writing for refined specialists within a narrow niche of study, almost any assumptions you make about your readers will be unreliable. So, learn to explain your knowledge in ways that are almost universally accessible, depending only upon awareness of the most basic prerequisites of your subject matter.

Start picturing what concepts you would have to introduce to someone's mind before they could have a meaningful conversation with you about your area of expertise. You cannot do this perfectly for everyone, because each reader will be starting at a different level of pre-existing knowledge when they open your book. But you can describe concepts using terms that you can expect the general populace of your target demographic to know according to accepted premises. New words and causal relationships can be explained in a clear context along the way.

There are many things I've had to assume about what the people who will become readers of *The Influential Author* know and want before they see my work. Many people interested in nonfiction self-publishing are not good candidates for my message because their pre-existing knowledge or expectations do not align with my specific approach. They may want simple, brief, and step-by-step instructions for writing their book and uploading it to Amazon. They may not agree with my opening assertions about the importance of books and the spread of influential ideas as the primary catalyst for social progress.

Rather than try to cater to people who lack the basic characteristics required to get the value and meaning I intend (which would force me to sacrifice clarity for everyone else), I simply write with the preconception that the wrong people will not be the ones to pick up my book and begin reading. Or, the wrong people might start reading my book, realize it isn't working for them, and then wisely put it back on the shelf. To write with the wrong people in mind or set my target too broadly would make it impossible to advance the subject to any meaningful degree.

Communication Shortcuts

Still, you cannot assume everything about what your reader knows at the start of your book. You will need to be somewhat inclusive in your wording. Analogies and metaphors, for example, are shortcuts communicators can use to speed up the transfer of complex information to unfamiliar minds.

A skilled explainer makes comparisons to familiar structures present in the minds of their readers. Metaphors make the unknown seem to work the same as the known, instantly removing the veil of obscurity before it. When new information takes a similar shape to old information, it loses its fearful and intimidating qualities.

You may have noticed some of the verbal shortcuts I've used throughout this book so far, such as comparing writing a lot of words every day to unknowingly walking a long distance over a period of time. My purpose in using these kinds of comparisons is not to make me sound smarter or wittier, but to incite imagery that will be familiar to most readers. They are part of my attempt to make potentially tricky or esoteric topics accessible. A higher amount of information is transferred in a smaller amount of space without sacrificing accuracy or engagement.

Comparisons are most effective when their meaning is creative but clear. If you try to force the same clichéd expressions into every conceivable situation, you will counteract the purpose of the analogy by obscuring the intended meaning. Any phrasing that is used too often takes on a multitude of new contextual interpretations you cannot control. Metaphors and idiomatic expressions run the risk of dragging writing down due to overuse or antiquity. Only use clever sayings when they improve the transmission of meaning.

Many words and phrases, though having specific meanings, have been misused so long that a general audience may not understand what you intend to communicate when you use them unless you make the meaning explicit in the context of your book. Nowadays, calling someone a Nazi anywhere outside of Germany likely isn't a claim to their participation in the National Socialist German Workers' Party. It could be a serious allegation of racism or other forms of bigotry. It could be a superficial complaint of a person's stubborn adherence to archaic rules (such as the notorious "grammar Nazi," whose passion for the proper rules of English fundamentals is a burden on every speaker or writer who cares more for transmission than tradition). Without explicit distinction, a modern "Nazi" could be nearly any disliked acquaintance or authority, from your least favorite grade-school teacher to a *Star Wars* stormtrooper.

The range of accepted meanings for this once clear word is so vast that any writer using it runs a significant risk of offensive misinterpretation. If you find yourself falling into the trap of regurgitating words and phrases out of habit and repeated exposure, you are not consciously thinking about your communication. You are not thinking about your original ideas and the mental state of your reader. Like so many other struggling writers, you do not actually have a writing problem; you have a thinking and feeling problem.

We, as writers, often feel obliged to inject fancy phrasing or evocative imagery into our otherwise dull and direct passages. The risk of trying to excite our readers is the potential loss of accurate meaning, especially in nonfiction where there's less room for interpretation on the part of the reader. Context will determine whether your creative language will improve or obfuscate your message. You either need to get so good at describing the artistic images you want to use that they successfully deepen your readers' emotional investment or cut them out entirely.

It's okay not to be a poet or a painter of ideas. If you start with clarity, poetry can more easily be added in later than if you approach things the other way around. So, if at all in doubt, make it your priority to be simple without being boring.

Discovering Your Personal Style and Creative Voice

What is the personality you want readers to associate with you as the author of the message of the book you are writing? Sometimes complex, formal language is what you need to create the effect you intend. Other times, it is more appropriate to fill your writing with colloquialisms and informalities, so long as they capture your authentic voice. Finding the balance between the straightforward and the creative is all a part of learning to write as yourself.

If everything ever written was optimized solely for conciseness and clarity, there would be little to no differentiation between authors. Instead, we use a language where the same 26 letters can be and have been combined into endless, unpredictable permutations. The factories of wordly creation, the brains of writers, each develop their own signature patterns that can be found even across topic and genre. As every painting is in some ways a self-portrait, every piece of writing is likewise an autobiography.

For many new authors, the hardest part of writing is simply learning to sound like themselves instead of someone else—to use the words and phrases that accurately represent their meaning and personality on paper. Meaningful writing should never become an exercise in presenting yourself as something different or better than what you really are. If you try to overstep the vocabulary and style you have become accustomed to using in real life, you will overlook the context and connotation of the fancy new words you have suddenly introduced to your repertoire. To an astute reader, you will seem phony or underqualified to be writing your own book.

Your voice must belong to you, and it must not be forced. Write like the ideal version of yourself, even if that means utilizing pretentious diction and breaking what you perceive to be conventional writing rules (at least for now). Write like yourself, even if it means keeping things simple and grounded, just like a casual conversation with you.

If you find yourself feeling anxious over the choice of every single word or phrase, you have let general writing advice invade your mind and stifle your creativity. You are worried about what the "correct" way to phrase something is supposed to be. You are trying too hard to sound like yourself, which itself is a paradox. You are just unconsciously emulating the habits of other writers. Yourself is who you are when you stop trying to be someone else.

The personality of your voice should remain mostly consistent throughout your message unless there is a clear reason for changing it up. Inconsistency is one of the biggest signs of an immature writer who has not yet developed control of their expressions. Scattered tones can even create the impression that a book has multiple authors, negating readers' ability to feel like they are developing an intimate connection with one person. Later, when you revise your work, you will take the time to spot the inconsistencies in your voicing and refine them until they match the standards of your authorial brand.

When you tap into the intrinsic motivation you hold for your subject, it will make it easier for you to bypass any bad writing habits you might have cultivated, breaking your cultural inertia. Then you will start to communicate like yourself, not a consolidation of influences from grade school to adulthood floating around in your head. This is the beginning of writing with your authentic voice. You will no longer feel the unconscious need to copy other writers. Your phrasings will be your own because they will convey your real personality and intended meaning. Just remember why you are writing and let the appropriate emotions take hold of you.

Keep your intended meaning in mind any time you sit down to write. It's easy to get lost in the deluge of paragraphs, chapters, and endless pages unless you are mentally and emotionally dedicated to constructing a message. When you can clearly see what you mean to convey, you will naturally search for the ideal phrasings to represent it. The psychological investment here is substantial but the reward of prose that is both original and authentic is worth it. Like any other skill that seems complicated at first, this principled approach to communication will grow more comfortable.

Through self-conditioning, you won't have to try hard to achieve the rapid transmutation of ideas into words. You will reach a point of unconscious competence over your conscious articulations, just as you likely already hold a similar type of invisible adeptness over the knowledge you write about. Refining your work then mostly becomes a process of assessing your individual phrasings through the context of the whole of your work. You can pick and choose among many valid, original ways to express the same idea.

Language Rules and Guidelines

In written English, there are hard rules and soft guidelines. The hard rules are necessary for the essential cohesion of the language, as the laws of physics are needed for the cohesion of the physical universe. The way you conjugate your verbs should always agree in tense and quantity with the subject performing them, or else your meaning becomes incomprehensible. Adverbs should modify verbs and adjectives, not nouns. Without some semblance of universal consistency, all potential for meaning breaks down.

Within those hard rules, however, there is enormous potential for creative variability. The soft guidelines of English can be disobeyed, with style, by someone who understands why they exist and, therefore, when they need no longer apply. A writer who throws all caution to the wind though and invents his own rules and guidelines as he goes becomes incomprehensible. Stylistic guidelines apply to things like certain situations of when to use commas, how many sentences to put into a paragraph, and when to overload a subject with hyperbolic adjectives and adverbs.

In your quest to become a respected author, do not get confused about the outcome you are seeking. Remember that the goal of a good writer is not to master the language they use. That is only one possible byproduct of becoming an excellent communicator. The pursuit of a meaningful writer is to learn to use language in the way that best suits their message, which has nothing to do with other possible writing goals. There is a galaxy of difference in the mentalities of a grammarian and a communicator, possibly more so in English than any other world language.

When you take upon yourself the goal of proper English, you set yourself up to force your thoughts and expressions to fit within the archaic molds of language bureaucrats who enforce rules for the sake of rules. You let stiff-minded

128

grammarians dictate how your message ought to flow. The hard rules of language have their place (and I will discuss them in Chapter 8: Proofreading, Pedantry, and Punctuation), but they should not be so highly regarded in your mind as to stifle your creative voice before it has even formed.

With the writing goals of clarity, creativity, beauty, and engagement, you will wield language as a tool to build paradigms and replicate experiences. You will be its master, not its servant. Without these goals, any semblance of personality or artistry can get lost in the mold, so you begin to sound exactly like every other "proper" writer.

Language is a capsule for emotion and idea delivery. The test that matters is that your words are interpreted by your readers the way you intend. However you accomplish that is, more or less, irrelevant. Bad habits, the kind we all pick up in the course of casual speech and writing, only matter when they impede your ability to communicate clearly. If your message is important to you, you have all the incentive you need to improve your written communication abilities on your own terms.

You already know that clear thinking leads to clear writing. It should also delight you to learn that the correlation works in both directions. The more clearly you can write and speak, the more clearly you can think, which in turn will reflect further upon your communication abilities in a wonderfully constructive repeating cycle.

Anti-Conciseness

The common writing guideline of conciseness states that excellent written communication should be as brief as it can be without sacrificing any of its meaning. This is a parallel of the principle of parsimony, Occam's Razor, which insists on eliminating unnecessary details from any analysis and supporting the answer that has the fewest number of unknowns.

George Orwell captured the essence of conciseness in two of his most cited rules for writing, stating: "If it is possible to cut a word out, always cut it out." and "Never use a long word where a short one will do." Orwell's range of conditions for acceptable inclusion is left open to interpretation, though surely we can all agree the phrasing of his rule is superior to a long-winded alternative like: "Don't use a big word when a singularly unloquacious and diminutive linguistic expression will satisfactorily accomplish the contemporary necessity."

Who decides when it is possible (or wise) to cut out a word or a phrase from a sentence? For that matter, to cut out whole sentences, paragraphs, or sections? The overuse of big, boisterous words can seem repugnant, but where is the line that separates effective stylings from filler phrasings? Experienced editors can provide vital guidance about curtailing overindulgent style, but their advice should not be taken as gospel. While the reader is the only one in control of what they will read, only the writer has the final say in how the use of language accomplishes their goals. This is where the author's personality begins to shine, and they write in such a way that no other author would or could.

Meaning appears in many layers, the most overlooked of which is often aesthetic beauty, the part of language that evokes emotions to surround its intellectual content. Writing that is too heavily edited, stripped of all its "unnecessary words," has lost its emotional overtones. Without explicit or implied imagery, any form of writing can become dull and hollow. In that state of reduction, reading becomes a chore. Much of the author's meaning disappears. Personality is gone. The human part of the interaction no longer matters. The information exists in a vacuum.

None of this is meant to imply that you can just write however you want and expect everything to be fine. Language that is too flowery and beautiful runs the risk of diluting its precision. Its meaning becomes vague because it only makes its reader feel its associated emotions, not think about its associated ideas. When readers are too comfortable with the material, they don't challenge themselves. All forms of paradigm expansion require willingly subjecting oneself to growth and change. The pleasant feelings that come from reading should be presented as a reward for traversing the journey and a buffer against the loss of interest.

Orwell ends his list of writing guidelines with the wise caveat to "Break any of these rules sooner than say anything barbarous." He understood that accurate transmission was more important than convention and that even his own advice should not be taken dogmatically. Author Neil Gaiman echoes a similar sentiment at the conclusion of his eight rules for writing well: "The main rule of writing is that if you do it with enough assurance and confidence, you're allowed to do whatever you like." I couldn't concur more.

Worth More with Feeling

What remains when you stop trying to sound like a writer is what you can consider to be your authentic voice. It will still require a great deal of honing and revision before it is ready for public release, but such opportunities to refine spontaneous communication are part of the beauty of writing. Your written self is you on your best day under tailored communication circumstances. With practice, it will come as naturally to you as any other skill which once seemed foreign but now occurs daily without second-guessing. You only need allow yourself to forget the social narrative you picked up about what kind of people were qualified to be writers and the obscene amounts of training they would have to endure.

Emotions flow within a spectrum of peak experiences. You have the power to summon these experiences in the minds of your readers and combine them in any manner that fits your purposes as a communicator. If humor provides the ideal context through which to transmit the practical elements of your message, you can make your reader laugh at regular intervals. If darker emotions, such as anger or intimidation, serve your purpose better, you can determine the most tasteful way to employ them without betraying the authenticity of your message. The same contextual principles apply to intimacy, joy, and sorrow. All are shades through which to color the information of your message.

How you make your readers feel as they are reading your message is how they will remember you long after they are done. Such is the power of infusing narrative flow into nonfictional works. Stories are how we package information, making it easy to recall and relive for years to come. Narrative allows a series of events or a progression of information to become an archetype for the mind. By tapping into the right combination of emotions in just the right sequence, your message will enter that sacred, long-term vault in your reader's mind.

While it is essential that you articulate the measurable, practical influence that reading your book will have ("after reading this book, you will be able to..."), promises of emotional experiences are even more important to lasting value transfer. Emotions tap into the core of why readers will choose to learn the information your book contains. The grander the meaning behind your words, the more taxing the process can be upon the learner. Emotional lubrication, applied in the right context and quantity, eases the consumption of difficult information.

For better or worse, self-publishing eliminates the convolution a book traditionally had to make it through to get in front of the public eye. Taking charge of your own evolution as a writer simplifies what has been traditionally required to become a quality author. The only metrics that matter by the time your words hit the shelves is that you communicate the meaning you intend and your readers don't lose interest along the way.

Summary of Chapter 5

To write your book in an efficient and effective manner, you will need to organize your time and environment to allow for optimal emotional navigation. If environmental factors persistently draw your attention away from crafting your message, it will be a long time before you can get even the first draft of your book on paper. You must develop the focus and endurance of a writer for either short bursts or extended stretches, and you can only do this by understanding your unique creative nature.

— — — —

For your book to have the transformational impact you desire, your readers must be able to understand the way you phrase your knowledge. Each sentence and paragraph must not demand too much of their cognitive abilities, as they will be devoting those to integrating the concepts you have taken great effort to articulate for them. You must always be clear without sacrificing accuracy or utility.

— — — —

Beyond clarity, your writing should have its own personality that (for better or worse) readers can recognize as yours. If you attempt to make your message sound like it could have come from anyone because you fear turning off any readers who might not appreciate your stylistic additions, your writing will be forgettable and dull. You must find the ideal way to capture yourself on the page.

CHAPTER 6:

Writing Your First Draft

I rather dislike the term "rough draft." It implies a compartmentalized approach to creation, one wherein your first pass is just practice and doesn't really count. Naturally then, what comes after the rough draft in this simplified model is a crowning accomplishment of perfect words and phrases. I don't take such a neat view of the drafting process. The mind has separate faculties for creative output and destructive modification. These distinct but related voices are in a chronic battle over the words on the page. If you can unite them, you will eventually arrive at something ready to be put into print.

You won't write your entire book from start to finish without stopping for revision. You probably won't even get through a whole chapter in one go. Most likely, you will find it less stressful and more productive to tackle the independent subsections that go into your chapters in a patchwork order—creating, revising, and rearranging each one as the whole vision becomes clearer. Establishing and amending content will blend together almost seamlessly, differentiated only by the proportion of making new material or changing old material at any given time. But every author must start somewhere and every author has a different set of methods.

It's impossible to predict from the outset how long it will take to write your book. It depends on many factors that you do not know at that early juncture. You may know from past writing experience that you can comfortably write a few thousand words a day if left to your own devices.

But do you know for certain how long your book needs to be to serve its ideal function? And do you know that you will be able to keep up your daily ideal writing pace when confronted with a complex and incomplete outline that demands deep, critical thinking and revision?

The book drafting process is not as simple as sitting at a keyboard and tapping away at it until your message is complete. Every new sentence you write exists within the context of every sentence before it and those you anticipate will come after. Every new section must be written with the perspective of everything around it, which can be extremely difficult to do when your text runs so long that you cannot quickly skim across for a visual reminder of what has been covered or left out. You may need to break your draft up into many separate documents to keep the length of each one manageable as its total word count expands.

As difficult as drafting can be, it's far from the end of the journey. Many first-time authors assume the most time-consuming part of the process will be writing the first draft, but endless rounds of editing, revising, and rewriting can grow to unpredictable proportions. The refinement process that comes after you have articulated the most important tenets of your message will be shorter and easier if you know from the beginning what you are trying to say and the most efficient way to say it. That is why the first step after you have figured out the philosophy and strategy behind your message will be to craft its essential outline, which you will, in turn, populate with the necessary information.

The Structure of a Nonfiction Book

Nonfiction books have evolved over centuries of publication to follow many standard practices in presentation and structure. If you aren't an avid reader, you will not be familiar with most of these standards on a conscious level, but you will probably still notice something is off about a book that does not adopt them. You may be wondering why it's necessary to load up so much front matter at the beginning of your book or how a book's preface differs from its introduction. Regardless, each book convention that remains in use today serves a purpose.

Although you should probably design your book to follow what traditional publishers have done for decades, it remains within your artistic license to ignore these traditions and present your book however you want. If you choose to go against convention, there is a risk of alienating your readers. The more astute ones might recognize that you have broken the structural standards of conventional publishing houses and interpret it as a sign of unprofessionalism. Such readers will dismiss you as an amateur self-published author whose message is not worthy of serious consideration.

Even casual readers who do not know how books are supposed to work might feel that something is wrong and not know why. Their feeling of displacement will taint their initial and ongoing impressions of your message, from the moment they pluck it from a bookshelf or flip through its pages. You have much more to gain by following the conventions of your medium than by being avant-garde and trying to reinvent nonfiction publishing, at least for your first book.

There are three main parts of a nonfiction book:

1. Front Matter

Like an appetizer before the main course, the front matter of book prepares readers for what is to come. It includes things like the table of contents, dedication, copyright information, foreword, and preface. These pages exist to tell readers what the book is about, why it is written, and why it's worth their time and money to read it. They will also contain copyright information, ISBN, publishing details, and statements to guarantee the author's rights and avoid the possibility of litigation.

What's included in a book's front matter (and the order in which it appears) can change from book to book. Some authors prefer to place certain elements that are traditionally present in the front matter after the main content as part of the book's back matter instead, such as acknowledgments to people who aided in the book's preparation. Some conventions are more appropriate for specific styles and topics than others (you may choose to forego the inclusion of a foreword or an epigraph, for example, if you don't want to feel like you are diluting the message of your book with someone else's words).

2.   Body Matter

After the front matter comes the book's body matter, which you might otherwise think of as its main content. The body matter traditionally contains an introduction, different chapters or units of the book, and a conclusion to bring the message together.

3.   Back Matter

After the main text comes the back matter, where the reader finds the afterword, author biography, and possibly other supplementary material like an appendix, glossary, bibliography, further resources, and notes. The back matter of the book is also the ideal place to ask readers for their feedback. You can mention how valuable their reviews on Amazon.com and other platforms are.

Front Matter

Title Page

A book's title page is the first thing the reader sees, immediately presenting them with vital attribution information, such as the names of the author, editor, translator, illustrator, and publisher, as well as the year of publication, publisher location, perhaps an image relevant to the book, and, of course, the title and subtitle of the book. Many of these details can go on the copyright page instead of or in addition to the title page.

Some books will start with a half-title page (also somewhat humorously known as a bastard title page), which just contains the title and subtitle, followed by a full title page with the full publication details.

Copyright Page (Colophon)

A book's copyright page contains legal protection information about the title of the book. At minimum, it should include the word "copyright," the copyright symbol (©), the copyright year, the author's name, the statement that all rights are reserved, and the book's ISBN information. More a formality than anything else, the following expanded sentence is also often included to make explicit exactly what protections apply to the book's content.

"No part of this publication may be reproduced, distributed, or transmitted in any form or by any means, including photocopying, recording, or other electronic or mechanical methods, without the prior written permission of the publisher, except in the case of brief quotations embodied in critical reviews and certain other noncommercial uses permitted by copyright law."

Before publishing, you will need to purchase and assign an International Standard Book Number (ISBN) to each distinct print edition of your work and, in some cases, audio and electronic editions too. This 13-digit number appears on each edition's copyright page. ISBNs are recognized around the world as unique signifiers for different versions of books. They are required for sales and distribution in most situations. If you decide to change publishers or overhaul your book's content years after release and create a second or third edition, you'll need to assign it a new ISBN if you want to follow the official ISBN guidelines. However, you can keep using the same ISBN if all you do is change the cover design or correct a few typos.

The copyright page also includes credits for illustration, production, editing, as well as the book's Library of Congress Control Number and edition number. Publishers will usually also list their name, contact information, and address with the instructions to contact them for permissions to use copyrighted material from the book or order in bulk quantities at wholesale prices.

The copyright page appears on the left-hand page immediately after the title page.

Dedication

Books are traditionally dedicated to someone who played a significant role in the author's life in a manner related to the subject of the book or who otherwise supported its creation. To whom you choose to dedicate your book (if anyone) is your decision. You can even use the dedication as an opportunity to make a statement about something important or show off your personality by dedicating it to an inanimate object, a place, a pet, or an abstract concept and infusing it with wit or sarcasm.

Whatever you do, remember that your book's dedication is a lasting statement about you and the inspiration behind your message. Try not to make the mistake I did when I dedicated my book *Travel as Transformation: Conquer the Limits of Culture to Discover Your Own Identity* to the woman I loved at the time and who was a major inspiration for me during the writing process. Only a year after the book was published, our relationship fell apart when I learned she had been cheating on me. These revelations gave me some pause about continuing to credit her as the inspiration for my second book.

Though I felt compelled to alter the book's dedication, I didn't want to completely rewrite my personal history and pretend she had not been part of the creative process when I wrote it. So, I kept her name in the dedication but changed the wording in the book's later editions to bestow her with a different type of credit. It's still embarrassing for me to open those early editions of my work and be forced to remember how naïve I was about the person I thought I was writing for and because of.

The changed dedication worked out to fit nicely though with the book's themes of growth through challenge and discovering your identity by losing the things most sacred to you. The original dedication for *Travel as Transformation* was: *"For Anastasia, who showed me I'm not the only one like this."* In subsequent revisions, it became: *"For Anastasia, who gave me my final test of identity."*

Quote (Epigraph)

You may want to use a page in your book's front matter to include a quote or passage from someone that holds significant meaning about the themes and purpose of your message. It can be a witty saying, a poem, a song lyric, or whatever you want. For maximum influence, make it something that sets the appropriate mood for the reader, as if to show them that someone famous and wise echoes thoughts that support the propositions you make throughout your book. This is another way of creating an impression of endorsement by association. If someone well-respected thinks the same way you do, it elevates you closer to their level.

Of course, you're not limited to including quotes only in your book's front matter. Many authors choose to begin or end each chapter or section of their books with a relevant quote. For this book, I decided to include several quotes from seemingly unrelated sources throughout history (including Isaac Newton, John F. Kennedy, and William S. Burroughs) that capture philosophical and sociological themes that are important to the purpose of *The Influential Author*.

Table of Contents

The table of contents outlines different parts of the book, such as chapters, subheadings, and other sections. It allows the reader to begin the book with an overhead view of the intellectual and emotional journey they are about to go on, which will make the information more accessible and retainable as they encounter it. The table of contents also makes it easier to jump ahead to sections that contain specific information the reader is looking for, reread parts that bear repeating, or find their place after taking a break from reading.

You can even format your table of contents to include the subsections that appear within each chapter (such as I have done with the table of contents for *The Influential Author*), providing easier navigation and a better understanding of the message before a reader begins.

Foreword (not "Forward")

Traditionally, the author of a book does not write their own foreword. Its purpose is for someone who is well known and respected in the area the author has written about to add their input and bring credibility to the message. Their perspective helps readers understand the importance of what the author is going to tell them throughout the book. The foreword validates the expertise of the author so that readers will give more weight to their opinions. If someone eminent lends their name and endorsement to a book, it may even attract their followers and impress book browsers who recognize them. Readers who have never heard of you may choose to purchase your book solely because of the person who wrote the foreword.

If you don't already personally know someone who would make a good candidate to write the foreword to your book, don't be shy about looking up the email address of an appropriate party and reaching out to them with a proposition. If they aren't extremely busy and wouldn't object to any of the implications of the content of your book, they might be excited by the idea of being included in what could be a hugely successful publication. Just make it clear to them in your outreach why you specifically want them to write the foreword and the benefits doing so might confer to them.

Preface

A preface is a short introduction by the author of a book that sets expectations for what is to come. Its purpose is to explain the motivation behind why the book needed to exist and what drove the author to create it. The author can also address the specific type of people who will benefit most from reading their book. By explaining the scope and limits of what's included in the book, readers will not be disappointed by what they find in its main content.

The role of the preface should not be overlooked. Besides the back cover or inside flap description, the preface is one of the first things prospective readers skim through when deciding if a book will give them the experience they are looking for. The preface will even be visible as part of the first several pages that shoppers can preview before purchasing through Amazon's "Look Inside" feature for e-books and physical books.

However, some readers have developed the habit of skipping past parts of a book's front matter, such as the foreword and preface, because they don't understand that these parts might be vital to their reading experience and comprehension. To negate the possibility of your readers missing any essential information, you can give a more important-sounding title to your preface.

For *The Influential Author*, I called my preface "Questions to Help You Get the Most from This Book." A name like this creates curiosity and incentive to see what I went out of my way to put before the book's main content. You might be worried that you won't get as much from the chapters that follow if you don't take time to think about what I am asking.

Think of your preface as a copywritten sales pitch to the reader about your book. Make it short, consumable, and straight to the point. Don't be shy about hitting upon the problems and pain points that have driven the reader to seek out new information. Make it clear that your book offers the solutions they have been seeking in a unique and compelling way.

Body Matter

Introduction
In the introduction, the author explains the background, goals, and organization of their book (which is why I labeled mine "Introduction to This Book's Structure and Purpose"). The introduction is the perfect place to set up the premises the readers will need to understand the chapters to

come. The introduction may be included in either the front matter or the body matter, depending on the preferences of the author.

A book's introduction is not just a rehash of the preface. While the preface may be easy to skip, the introduction is more integral to understanding the message. Without it, the reader might approach the first chapter and each one thereafter with a totally inappropriate state of mind. Without the right expectations, they will be quite disappointed with the book. If you have any instructions on how readers should consume the information in your book, the introduction is an excellent place to give them.

In the introduction, you can also lightly promote your background and credentials. The more your readers know about you, the more context they will have for your bias, values, and position. That way, even if they don't agree with everything you write, they will at least understand where you are coming from. It will make them appreciate the fresh perspective you offer, no matter how unconventional or unexpected.

Although you might reasonably assume that it is wisest to write your introduction before anything else in your book, the opposite sometimes works out better. To write a good introduction, you need a complete understanding of what it's supposed to be introducing, which might not be possible until you've written most or all of the main content of the book. This is just one example of making the most of a non-linear approach to writing long-form content like a book.

Main Chapters
A nonfiction book should be divided into self-contained chapters designed by the author to address the independent components of their message. Readers should be able to consume the totality of the message in portions that stand on their own as complete transmissions of concepts, each one contributing something quantifiable and epistemologically relevant to the whole. Your book outline will help you determine what chapters are necessary to get your message across effectively.

As you outline the structure of your book, you will set up the division and order of your chapters by the metric of what will optimize reader engagement, comprehension, and retention. Subdividing your knowledge can be as simple or as complicated as you make it, as concepts are fluid and arbitrarily delineated.

The subject of a club sandwich might be optimally broken down into concepts of bread, mayonnaise, lettuce leaves, tomatoes, bacon, turkey, and toothpicks for the casual gastronomist to be able to prepare at home. However, that is not the only way to conceive of a club sandwich. An organic chemist might care more about the concepts of the molecular structure that differentiates poultry from grain. A physicist might care more about the concepts of heating and slicing the sandwich. A historian might care more about the concept of the Union Club of New York City, where the club sandwich originated in 1889. An etymologist might want to know about the concept of the fourth Earl of Sandwich, an 18th-century English nobleman, from whom sandwiches derive their name.

You will not necessarily write your main chapters in the order they appear in your outline. As well, you may even end up changing the order of your chapters or move major points around between them during the initial drafting process or subsequent revisions. If you try to force yourself to adhere to a strictly linear creation process (e.g., not letting yourself begin writing chapters two or three until you've finished chapter one), your progress will be slow and your ideas stifled. The beauty of being in the creator's seat is that you have an overhead and behind-the-scenes view of everything the consumer usually only sees the result of. You are the master of this universe.

Conclusion

A conclusion in a nonfiction book performs the inverse function of an introduction. Instead of summarizing the premises behind the meaning of the main content to come, it comments on the importance and logical consequences of what was covered. The conclusion connects the book's concepts to the whole of reality, establishing their place in the pantheon of the human story. If the reader is left asking any form of "So what?" at the end a book's final chapter, the conclusion is a good place to reiterate any meaningful points that may have been overlooked across the chapters and plant seeds of ideas for what the reader should do with the knowledge they now hold.

It's okay to be a bit redundant in your conclusion, so long as it is concise and clear why you are repeating specific information. For marketing and branding purposes, it's also a good idea for your readers to leave your book with a favorable impression of you and happy memories of the reading experience. The conclusion is your last chance to set those impressions in their minds before they run off to leave a public review or tell their friends how good or bad your book was.

Back Matter

Afterword (not "Afterward")
A nonfiction book's afterword serves a much similar function to its foreword, except that for personal or stylistic reasons the author has chosen to place it at the end of the main content instead of the beginning. Sometimes an afterword makes an excellent addendum to a new edition of a previously published book, touching upon further information that has come to light in recent times, more background information about the author or the book's creation and reception, or a prediction about the book's future. The afterword is most often written by someone other than the author and probably not the same person who wrote the foreword (if any).

Afterwords are not necessary to improve the content of most nonfiction books, so it's probably best for you not to include one in the first edition of your first book unless you have a clear and specific reason for doing so.

Appendices
Appendices are the best place to list reference information that would not be appropriate within the meat of the book's main chapters. If you mention

online tools in your message and suggest readers check out other sources of information, an appendix is a good place to spell out precisely what they should do and where to find what they need.

The information contained in appendices is not fundamental to understanding the message of the book. It's also information that could become dated and irrelevant soon after publication. 10 years later, current resources might not still be available or advisable. By separating these things from the main content of the book, you won't cheapen or date your (more or less) timeless message.

Nonfiction appendices sometimes include quick reference guides (FAQs) pertaining to the central questions asked about the book's subject, further reading or online resources, a brief history or timeline of historical events relevant to the topic, endnotes, and diagrams or other charts to illustrate essential concepts.

Glossary

A glossary includes the definitions of operative vocabulary as used in the context of the book, presented in alphabetical order. Specialized branches of knowledge require vocabulary most people are not used to hearing in casual conversation.

It's also possible that you have used words in your book with connotations not often shared by other speakers or writers. Not knowing the precise meaning of your terms as you intend them to be understood can detract from your readers' ability to grasp your message. If you've applied a particular purpose or association to a word within the context of your book, you should spell it out both when introducing it in the body matter and again in the back matter glossary for easy reference.

Bibliography/References

Certain types of books will be greatly improved by citing sources that support claims they make about scientific facts or historical occurrences.

You can use superscript numbers to refer to more detail in footnotes on the page or in a dedicated section of your book's back matter.

A bibliography lists the sources the author used to research the topic of their book (even if there are no specific references to them in the text). A traditional bibliography includes titles, author names, and publication information. Some annotated bibliographies will also include descriptions of the sources and how they were used. Another purpose of the bibliography is to provide references to readers who want to learn more about the subject.

Index

An index is an alphabetical list of essential reference subjects accompanied by the page numbers where they are discussed throughout the book. Note that traditionally an index is not the same as merely listing page numbers where specific terms are found, but also where the meaning implied by the term is discussed. If the same word or phrase appears with an irrelevant contextual meaning, it should not be part of the index (or have its own separate entry).

An index is handy for the type of book where readers may need to often jump around to different sections and locate specific pieces of information. Finding an integral term will lead them where they need to go much faster than the table of contents, which typically only lists section and chapter headings. The terms indexed may include important places, events, or famous names.

Acknowledgments

In the acknowledgments of a book, the author mentions the people who contributed in some way to the creation of the book, either consciously or not. These people may include friends, family, professionals, and mentors. Some authors prefer to put the acknowledgments in the front matter, after the dedication, to signify how valuable these people have been for the book.

If you have worked with unpaid beta readers, this is a great place to give them shout-outs for their hours of volunteering to make your writing better.

Author Bio

The author's biography includes relevant information about the writer of the book. It may be a page, a paragraph, or even a sentence, depending on what you think is essential to get across. An author bio usually includes a brief background of personal experience, professional accolades, or credentials relevant to your message, and other accomplishments in writing and other careers. If you are writing your book to promote a business or a service you offer, your biography is the best place to briefly expand on that and direct readers to check out more of what you offer.

You can include your email address and links to all your social media accounts in your bio, so readers will have ways to connect with you and check out other books you have written.

Tactical Outlining and Drafting

There's a common false dichotomy promoted by writers who believe they must fall into one of two camps: "plotters" (those who see everything in advance and need to know what they are going to write before they begin) and "pantsers" (those who fly by the seats of their pants and make it all up as they go along).

Both extreme writing approaches have their merits and their limits. Both mentalities are necessary in some portion to write something worthwhile. Any finished work of art is the result of many cycles of creation and destruction, careful plans that reach great heights before suddenly pivoting into unpredictable directions. Before you know it, the house you thought you were building might need a portion of it knocked down to make room for something better.

The purpose of outlining (both before and while you draft) is to compose an organized and consistent narrative that will remain intact through the length of your book. A finished book, consisting of tens of thousands of words, is a complex beast of information. An outline serves as a map to help you find your way through the process of birthing the beast, which will, in turn, make the reading experience more enjoyable and coherent for your audience.

Without a map to remind yourself of what you are supposed to be writing, it's easy to inadvertently repeat yourself, go off message, or confuse your meaning. An outline serves as a schematic to understand the story you're trying to tell and how best to tell it. When you have directions to follow and milestones to pass, it's easier to monitor the progress you are making. You will also be able to divide up your time, switching between different segments as you find it appropriate to do so during the drafting process.

There's a potential dark side to outlines, though. If too rigorously followed, outlines restrict the creative flow of writers. They can trap ideas in corners instead of letting them roam free to wherever they might go. To get the best of both approaches, make it your goal to maintain a fluid outline that grows and evolves with the content of the book and the inspiration of your mind. Creation begets creativity. The more ideas you bring to light on the page, the more you will see what more can be brought. To ignore new inspiration simply because you didn't consider it when you first drafted the plan for your book would be foolish.

Only you know your own writing faculties and preferences. Unless you have plenty of experience in other writing mediums, your first nonfiction book is probably not the place to start blind freewriting with the hope that it eventually turns into something usable. You need some level of clarity and focus to be effective with your articulations. When crafted in a way that complements how you think and operate, adaptable outlining strikes the crucial balance between ordered limits and chaotic creation.

If you already have the main elements of your message planned, you'll have the freedom to explore them in greater detail as you begin drafting. With a clear direction for your writing to take, you can write with more purpose. Writer's block will be easier to manage because you will have a menu of subsections to write and already written material that needs editing. You will always have something in front of you that needs working on, and you will not be lost about what to do. If you have only a general idea of what you'd like your book to say, the message will likely get lost or diluted along the way.

The hard part of choosing where your message begins and ends is the fear of leaving something vital out. An overly ambitious writer believes that by selecting a defined (and therefore limited) narrative for their thoughts, they won't be able to include everything they want to say.

Authors who cannot envision the structure of their book from the outset should start by jotting down notes on everything they know they want to say. With the benefit of the detached perspective this offers, they can rearrange the concepts into a logical order until an unbroken chain of understanding emerges. The author will soon see what is missing from their paradigm and what is superfluous to it. Break down the crucial elements of your message, lay them out in a logical order, and formulate how your book ought best to include them.

Conceptual Development

In the process of evolving your outline, you will probably change the placement of your subsections many times. You may split what you presumed to be one independent topic into many. These are essential steps to arriving at a message that conveys the information you desire in its ideal fashion. Cohesiveness from start to finish is one of the primary factors by which readers will evaluate the professional quality and practical value of your book. When you look at a section you have written that does not fit the structure of your narrative, you must choose to eliminate it or expand the scope of the narrative to include it. Either side of the road works for different reasons. Staying caught in the middle may get you run over.

There is also an important philosophical reason to begin drafting with an outline of your intended content. An outline is a litmus test for ensuring your idea has the potential to be developed into a full-blown book, not merely a series of interesting scribblings or a glorified pamphlet about your favorite subject. If you don't take the trouble to organize your knowledge, it's easy to prematurely assume you know enough to write a cohesive book. You may also have so much information floating, unorganized in your mind that it is enough to fill several volumes. But that quantity of information, however vast, is useless so long as it remains formless and abstract. Organization gives meaning to data and makes it accessible.

If you cannot organize your knowledge into its simplest form on paper, you have little chance of ever expanding it into hundreds of pages in a way that makes sense to uninitiated minds. Through the process of constructing an outline, you could even decide that the premise of your book needs more ideating before you begin writing it out. Coming to this realization will prevent you from wasting countless hours fleshing out a half-formed message or scrapping a good-but-premature idea altogether. Your outline will show you what parts of your paradigm are not yet ready for transmission and what you need to do to be prepared to write your book.

You may have heard that many successful authors famously do not use outlines when they write. It is valid for some people in some situations to use this approach, but these are generally the cases of people knowing the rules of writing so well that they can safely break them. For some authors, their writing is specifically intended to be loose, wandering, and countercultural. That is probably not a goal you share (at least, not at this stage of your writing career). Customers are more amenable to spending money when they aren't confused about what they are buying. The same applies to their enjoyment of the book as a whole. Clarity correlates to comprehension.

When you think of your book like a journey, you will begin to see that, like any good journey, there are distinct phases of plot progression and development. No matter your subject, you will need to lay the foundation for the bold arguments you are going to make in the message. Many talented and intelligent people cannot write well or explain their knowledge to other people because they do not know how to take their expertise down to common levels. And so, many valuable ideas remain utterly inaccessible to most of the world's people who might benefit from them beyond measure.

Human beings are not very good at retaining information when it is presented randomly or without respect to changing emotional states. The mind cannot survive bombardment of facts and feelings because it cannot keep them all in memory or compile them into a meaningful arrangement. Information without structure is chaos. Structure is the difference between noise and music, though both are composed of the same elemental sounds. Structure cuts out what is redundant or irrelevant and arranges ideas in an order that is adequate for an unfamiliar mind to consume with minimal data loss or emotional strain. The value of your ideas only matters if you can structure them to make their value accessible.

Supporting Arguments

Your outline is the minimum viable structure for your book, the branches from which all the many twigs and leaves will emerge in their own unusual ways. The outline is where you address what must be known before anything else can be. Divide your knowledge into categories. Structure them in a logical sequence so that the information of each builds upon the information of all previous ones. Within each knowledge category, you have the opportunity to list stories, proofs, and other forms of elaboration that support the primary points you are trying to make.

Everything you write is an argument and a claim of some kind. You cannot share what you know without making an assertion. Large assertions require equally large support to be accepted. At all times, you are both convincing your readers why what you say is true and simultaneously why it matters that it is true. Your outline is the perfect place to ensure you have ample ammunition of both varieties before you even begin drafting the primary content. Any claim you make in your book without some type of convincing demonstration is liable to be discarded by at least some portion of your readers just as quickly as it was made.

Your outline should provide answers to what you believe and why it matters within the context of your book's purpose. If you are writing with an intellectual or scholarly focus, your supporting arguments may come in the form of citations to research and laws demonstrated by historical figures. If you are asking your readers to trust your personal expertise and want them to engage with your personality, you might use specific anecdotes from your personal life or professional experience that show how you know what you are claiming and give the reader confidence in your opinions. You can appeal to current events, the works of other published authors, or verifiable assertions that will create a body of interrelated arguments that at least appear internally consistent. It all depends on the effect you are trying to have on your audience and what they will consider valid support.

To get to this part of *The Influential Author* where I am able to talk about outlining, there were several foundational concepts it was necessary to cover in the introduction and preceding sections of the internal structure of this book. Appropriately, the two sections before this one on Creation are entitled Philosophy and Strategy. Without the philosophical and strategic underpinnings of meaningful communication, the things I write now or after this might be lost on readers. From that starting place, I could ease readers into the tenets of transforming their thoughts into the written word and setting their message up for success on the market. Now readers have context for why outlines matter. Now my words might actually mean something and provoke new action.

Once you've got the blueprint for your book in a manageable and comprehensible form, you're free to focus on writing content that will connect with your audience. Your focus may now shift toward creating meaningful prose and brainstorming additional ways to captivate readers' attention more fully.

Initial Drafting

Do not, as so many new authors do, make the mistake of feeling you need to save your best material for another project. You only need to ask yourself if what you are inspired to say as you work on your draft is relevant to the purpose of the book you are creating right now. If it is not, write it anyway until you have exhausted your inspiration. Stash it somewhere safe so you can access when the right time arrives.

Drafting is a repetitive process. The first iteration you write of any section will not be what ends up in your book. Your words will undergo many changes in strategy and style in the untold revisions to come. You will repeat yourself, find new inspiration, and scrap many valid ideas you once were determined to include. Passages that at first seemed to fit best at the end of your book will suddenly feel necessary in its introduction or middle chapters. Entire conversations will be lost to the scythe of self-reflection. You cannot avoid this back-and-forth process. You can only prepare for it from the outset of writing.

So that you do not begin with false expectations and suffer inevitable disappointment with your writing, it is useful to conceive of the first draft of any portion of your book as a mere seed of what it will become. The seed contains the idea, an approximation of the principle you want to communicate. The seed may not seem very impressive at first. By putting your thoughts down on paper, you plant it and give it a chance to grow and bear fruit. Your first draft is the foundation for what will eventually be your final draft. Keep this perspective as you create it, or you may suffer the dissatisfaction that accompanies inflated standards.

Your first draft will likely be longer than what finally ends up in print. After the initial acts of creation, a lot of your progress will come in the form of eliminating unnecessary material. Books go through countless rounds of editing before they're ready for publication. Give yourself permission to make your first draft as exhaustive as possible. Even if you think you're going to cut a section out, write it anyway. You might realize later that you can put that section somewhere else in the outline or tweak it to make it work. Your focus at this juncture is to create content related to your topics and subtopics. Dig deep into your brain to discover everything you have to say about each point. Then you will know when you have said too much or further research is required to have enough that is worth saying.

Intangible Progress

Although tempting, you cannot track your writing progress by word count alone. What good is it to write 10,000 words in a day if most of those words are unusable for your purposes? Real progress comes in many forms, not all of them clearly visible or quantifiable. Do not force your productivity to fit the popular conceptions of how life as a writer works. Instead, open your eyes to the many distinct ways you can contribute to the advancement of your book, including but not limited to conducting competitive research, cultivating creative inspiration, or refining your vision.

There's a parable about Italian High Renaissance sculptor Michelangelo that demonstrates the intangible and often misleading nature of creative work. Having little appreciation for the artistic genius of his son, Michelangelo's father would forbid him from working with his hands like a manual laborer. So, he learned to work with his mind instead. When he began to work on what would become the famous Statue of David, Michelangelo spent months just staring at an 18-foot block of marble, never touching it with his hands. When asked when he would finally begin working on the statue, Michelangelo responded that he already was working. To Michelangelo, the bulk of the labor took place internally, well before his hands ever contacted the marble.

Imagine a scenario instead wherein Michelangelo had measured his progress toward the completion of David by the number of swings of his hammer upon his chisel against the marble. Hitting the marble an arbitrary number of times has no relevant bearing on how close it will be to matching the artistic vision that is the Statue of David. There were, however, a minimum number of hammer strikes necessary to form the featureless block of marble into the art it became. It is the same with writing or any other creative endeavor. Your book will require a minimum number of words to be considered complete and true to your artistic vision, but it is folly to quantify your progress solely in terms of how many words you have written.

A day spent in silent reflection over the toughest parts of your message is progress. Bringing forth from the ether the perfect paragraph after hours of deliberation about how to connect two independent sections is also progress. Browsing for inspiration from other artists, if done with conscious intention, can be progress. Even recreation or relaxation in manners unrelated to your writing is progress, so long as it ultimately contributes to the completion of your book. Take a break and play video games or go to the gym for an hour. If that's what it takes to jumpstart your author brain, do not be so vain as to let the assumed judgment of other writers stop you from doing what you must.

As it is with much of life, the mindset you maintain about your writing is more critical to your success than the specific actions you take or the order in which you take them. Writing and editing your book is an intellectual and emotional journey. It's a spiritual one too if that's your persuasion. You must be willing to take the journey and change yourself along the way. There will be times that writing will feel like mindless grinding, chipping away at uninteresting portions of your message that require little creative input but must get written one way or another. Knowing that these tedious parts are contributing to the fulfillment of your vision will make the monotony bearable.

Overhead Perspective

With a thorough outline, you can jump back and forth between independent sections according to the order in which you feel most comfortable and inspired to write them. Use this to your advantage. Nothing will stifle your creative progress faster than forcing yourself to write your book in the order of its structure. You don't have to stay stuck on the first chapter until it is exactly right. If you are in a rut, move ahead to any portion of the book which you feel ready to work on, even if it's just a few sentences at a time that you can later elaborate on. Your outline is the map that will keep your expanding patchwork message organized.

You cannot build a house until you have good bricks to work with. You will write sentences and paragraphs that seem perfect in isolation, but you don't know what to do with them in the context of the whole book. The beauty of writing in a digital word processor is that you can rearrange large swaths of text however you want. Place these independent chunks in the rough order you know they should appear according to the blueprint of your outline. You will water their development drop by drop until they resemble the garden you envision.

In rearranging the bits of information on the screen in front of you, you will find exciting ways to combine them and create new meaning. Seemingly unconnected sentences might work better when merged into the same paragraph or placed in sequence. Worry about the quality of your communications before you try to address if things are being presented in the right order or style. A viable thought or series of thoughts can always be reordered and repurposed later when you have greater clarity for your book's vision. Empty sentiments and fluffy phrases are just the Styrofoam around your goods.

There is no limit to the changes you can make at any stage of drafting. There will be a lot of reworking to come, so it's wise not to become too attached to any particular combination of words early on. A single, cohesive paragraph about the subject of the 12th chapter of your book may later grow into a fully developed subsection. You can move from a single sentence describing each intellectual step in your book, to a single paragraph, to several paragraphs, until you've arrived at every necessary subheading within each chapter. You will continue to water and prune each block of information as you review your text from an omniscient, bird's-eye view of the bigger picture.

Nontraditional Methods to Expedite Your Drafting

Even if you know the full scope of what you want to say in your book, you still face the arduous task of churning out the many thousands of words that will communicate your ideas in a readable format. For a speedy typist who does not need to stop and reflect on their message throughout the writing process, this takes dozens of concentrated hours. For average typists who also need ample time to plan out and frequently revise their work, writing a book constitutes of a large enough time burden to prevent most prospective authors from ever completing their manuscripts.

Writing for extended periods incurs a high cognitive stress load. Most people cannot just dive into profound writing without preparation or difficulty. Any writer can get distracted by the chaos of a regular day or unexpected emergency. Many people are lucky to find even one uninterrupted hour each day where they are still competent enough to write after the obligations of work, family, and society have taken their toll. By that time, most people just want to unwind or go to bed and prepare for the toils of the following day, not turn their brains inside out looking for verbal gold.

Acknowledging this, it is in every writer's best interest to expedite the drafting process in whatever ways they can. There are many ways to jumpstart or shortcut the laborious process of manually drafting your content. The efficient communicator uses whatever tools they can to wring as much output as possible from every calorie of input.

Prewritten Material

If the topic of your book is one you have been involved with for a while, there may be things you've already written that would be relevant for inclusion. Articles, blogs, social media posts, or even personal journals may contain ample written content you could add to or lightly adapt for your book. With some minor tweaking, old material can be made to appear new and a seamless fit for your outline. In most cases, it takes considerably less effort to edit and expand something old than to manifest something new.

Once you've completed your outline, it is a good time to dig through whatever archives of previously written material you may have. Take stock of all the writing you have ever done on the subject of your book and cross reference it with what your outline requires. You have a tentative list of chapters and key points to work with. Use these as a rubric by which to organize whatever you have written, even the pieces that at first seem irrelevant or out of context. Determine which chapters or subsections you could fit at least some passages from your old work into. There's nothing to stop you from slicing up your writing and reorganizing the various paragraphs into the new structure of your book outline.

If you're a blogger, you've probably already categorized your posts according to distinct tags and topics. If you're working with handwritten content or personal journals, create a system to organize it by topics, such as different colored highlighters, sticky tabs, or just notes in the margin. You can then sort through the old and decide where you might best plug it into the new. Pick out the appropriate paragraphs and paste them (or manually type them) into your book outline under the right heading. You don't need to expand on your old content right away. Getting it all organized now will make it far easier to finalize for publication. So long as the seed of the idea is captured, your writing load will become much lighter.

If your work has been published in any public medium, you'll want to rewrite large portions of it or at least "spin" it by swapping out every few words for synonyms so the piece appears to be original. This is important for many reasons, one of which is the way that Google and other search engines index what they consider to be unique content. If blocks of text show up in the same way across multiple websites, it will negatively affect how they are ranked. This may not seem like a big issue in a published book, but part of your promotion will involve sharing portions of your book across different websites in the hopes that they rank well for the public eye and drive traffic to your book itself (and thus increase your sales).

Self-plagiarism is another issue. Publishing one's own work in a new context without explaining its previous use is widely considered unfair to readers expecting new material when they purchase a book unless otherwise cited up front. In some circumstances, self-plagiarism can even be construed as copyright infringement. If someone previously paid you for exclusive rights to publish your work, they own it. You will probably not be able to reuse it without their written permission. You can contact the person who bought the rights to your writing, but the chances are that it will be easier just to rework the old content into something new. It will save you and your buyer a lot of time and grief trying to figure out the ins-and-outs of quotation, attribution, and compensation.

Though it might seem a tedious burden to rewrite what you've already suffered through the process of creating, you probably won't want it to be the same even under the best of circumstances. Your perspective and purpose should have evolved since the time you originally wrote the old piece. See this as an opportunity to challenge yourself and come up with better ways of explaining your points. You will create something better than the original if you are willing to grow.

You may be surprised at how much viable material you have to work with when you take stock of all the writing you have done across the years. You may see that you already have tens of thousands of words, making up half or more of the total desired length of your book (or even several books' worth of material). You'll now need to perform extensive organization, shortening, and expansion of your content, according to the needs of the book. Editing your existing work should be more comfortable than crafting new content. You will already be familiar with the train of thought. The bulk of the creative work will already have been done by your past self.

Most of your old work might prove to be unusable, and that's okay. Maybe now you're writing for a different audience. Perhaps some concepts have been covered earlier in your draft and need not be repeated. A few short sentences or a paragraph here or there might have captured a perfect idea you wish to replicate and expand in your book. Copy these useful portions into a separate document and spend as much time as you need to develop the ideas fully. You might only get two or three more sentences out of it, or you might get entire chapters. Even if a whole piece is usable, you'll probably need to add some introductory content that makes it fit the context of your book. You must frame it within what comes before and after.

Just as you can dip into the products of your past self for inspiration, there's no reason you can't creatively borrow the work of other writers. Browsing passages from similar works alongside your own is a clever hack to keep you focused on the message you are trying to craft and make it easier to stay creative when you run into a rough patch of drafting. Read the best articles or books on your topic, then think about how you would have made them better if you had written them yourself. Look for what they are missing and what questions readers might be left with.

No matter what you read, you should be able to come up with new ideas for filling the holes left by your predecessors. Use those ideas to make your book stand out. No matter how great the best books in your genre, there are none that could not be made more explicit, complete, accessible, or optimized for a different focus. All artists borrow/steal from others to some extent. Writers are no different. Great writers, like inventors, know how to start with another person's ideas and turn them into something that is uniquely their own.

Selective Ghostwriting

If you are a good manager of skilled workers, it is possible for you to arrange your book's production in such a manner that much of the writing grind is handled by professional writers you hire to bring your vision closer to fruition. With a thorough outline, you have the liberty to employ one or more competent ghostwriters to produce the first pass of your book's content. The task will then fall on you to edit and arrange what your ghostwriters create in a fashion that still holds true to your original message and is consistent with your authentic voice. So long as you are still the one making the creative decisions and guiding the pen of your ghostwriters, your book will remain in line with your vision.

Before you hire ghostwriters, consider once again what you want from your book. Your goals will help you narrow down what qualities to look for. You'll need to give your ghostwriters detailed, accurate instructions about what you want them to do. Just telling them to write a few chapters about your book's subject isn't sufficient. Providing samples of your writing will help your ghostwriters understand the tone you want, as will details about the target audience and purpose of the book. You should also be able to tell them the approximate word count you want for each section they work on for you.

When you work with ghostwriters, you're the director of the operation. The ghostwriter is there to make sure your ideas come out cohesive, readable, and marketable. They cannot read your mind, so their output can only be as good as the guidance you provide. If you do not have a clear vision for your book, you cannot expect hired guns to make strategic or creative decisions for you, any more than the director of a movie should expect the actors in a scene to know how they should perform without a script or direction. The responsibility to make the book fulfill its destiny is yours alone.

A multiple-ghostwriter approach is helpful if your book covers a wide berth of information, each requiring different areas of specialization. Ghostwriters who have some personal experience with the topics or tools discussed will produce better quality work in less time. They won't have to research concepts foreign to them, so their writing will flow more naturally. Break the book up into chapters or subchapters before you start searching for ghostwriters. Write a short synopsis or outline for each subsection. You will hand these off to the ghostwriters who seem most appropriate for each one.

Your ghostwriters will research and draft that section according to the tone and length you have specified. When your ghostwriters return their finished passages to you, it will be relatively easy for you to reduce, alter, or expand them to match your intentions. It's unlikely that even the best ghostwriters will capture your voice and intentions perfectly without the need for addition or revision, so keep your expectations flexible. No writer can be better at being you than you can. Even if you end up changing half of what your ghostwriters deliver, you will see how much easier it is to work with something already written than to create it all from scratch. Ghostwriters take a tremendous burden off your shoulders by breaking through the inertia of a blank page.

Some sections of your book will be easier to farm out to hired help than others. Single out the portions that rely on information that can be researched by anyone with internet access and common knowledge. The parts of your manuscript that depend on your personal experience, opinion, or specialized expertise will be more difficult to delegate and receive usable results.

You will finish the book faster by having more than one writer working on different chapters concurrently. This is a tactic favored by authors with managerial experience. They like to play to their strengths, as they should. Managers will need to bring their team's respective works together, editing and rearranging them as necessary to unite their message in the finished draft of the book. When you hire a ghostwriter, you're not absolving yourself of work. You're just trading one type of labor for another. Now instead of writing, you are managing and editing someone else who writes for you.

Whenever I've been employed in the capacity of a ghostwriter, it has been my conscious goal not to allow my strong voice and opinions to overshadow the message and personality I glean from working with the authors who hire me. Even if your ghostwriters were multifaceted enough to outline, write, edit, and proofread the entire text of your book for you, it would no longer be "your" book. You would have contributed nothing to its message, thus defeating the purpose of producing it in the first place beyond vanity or royalties. The partial approach to ghostwriters that I advocate here leaves you in creative control, which is necessary to the integrity of your work.

Spoken-Word Transcription

Another way to ameliorate your writing burden is to talk instead of type. Most people can spontaneously speak more easily than they can spontaneously write. An average writer types about 40 words per minute but speaks more than three times as fast at a rate of 130 words per minute (almost 10,000 words per hour if uninterrupted). People are just wired in such a way that thoughts prefer to transmute that way. If you struggle to get words on paper through writing, dictating at least part of your book out loud may be the solution.

Dictation used to require hiring a transcriber to follow the speaker around with pen and paper, rapidly jotting down everything they said. Nowadays, laptops and smartphones are equipped with microphones with which anyone can record themselves and send the file off to a remote transcriptionist. The transcriptionist then returns the complete, editable document of text from the recording.

Dictation software has also reached a level of accuracy that, while far from perfect, is good enough to be a viable alternative to human transcriptionists. However, even the best dictation software often transcribes a voice incorrectly. You may waste precious time fixing incorrect dictation. Dictation software also has a notoriously difficult time with punctuation. It requires you to speak words like "comma" and "period" in a slow, measured manner that is a severe drag for people who like to talk spontaneously.

When you have your transcribed text in hand, it will require a fair amount of editing to be useful in your draft. The way we speak is different than the way we write, and what works for one does not always work for the other. Ordinary people talk in sentence fragments. They don't conjugate verbs consistently. They insert unnecessary filler words when they can't think of exactly what to say. Despite all this, dictation can still be a decent way to get the base content of your book in front of your eyes so you can modify it into something better.

There's an erroneous sentiment among some types of readers that listening to audiobooks does not count the same as reading the same books in written format. A parallel judgment exists for those who dictate their writing instead of doing it all by hand, mainly from writers who take pride in the struggle of the process. As a practical author whose focus is on the delivery of an important message, you can ignore this form of social posturing from other writers (most of whom will never publish anything anyway).

The simplest way to proceed with dictation is to look over every point made in your outline and record yourself talking as much as you can about each of those things. You can cover many thousands of words with only the minor effort of reiterating conversations you've likely already had many times in your life.

For many people though, it's not easy to keep talking and cover all the pertinent details on their own. They need prompting from an external source. You may choose to partner with someone interested in (but not necessarily familiar with) your subject to interview you during the dictation process. Your partner can play the part of the curious reader, prompting you when more elaboration is necessary or introducing questions you would have overlooked if just recounting the information as you have come to understand it. Your interviewer will tell you when to be more specific or to explain the reasoning behind the information you present.

Many people have a hard time talking about themselves, though some others seem to have too easy a time doing it. Your message may benefit from relatable personal anecdotes from your life that demonstrate the principles you talk about or help the reader understand why you think the way you do. Instead of trying to cram your whole life into the book, a curious conversation partner can help you determine which of your personal stories are interesting and relevant enough to include without coming across as vain or self-obsessed.

Do whatever it takes to get your words out. Drafting is just the first step in acquiring the words that will next need to be revised and arranged, again and again, until they begin to approximate the best possible version of your message.

Summary of Chapter 6

Professionally published books have many traditional rules about structure and layout that should be more or less followed if you want readers to retain your message and take it seriously. Every element of front matter, body matter, and back matter plays an important role in your book and should not be changed or omitted without good reason. The negative effects of doing so may be subconscious but still real.

— — — —

Beginning with a cohesive outline that breaks the main points of your message into sections, chapters, and subsections will make it much easier for you to populate the first draft of your book rapidly. You just need to keep expanding each point until they are each complete enough that you can modify and rearrange them as needed. A good outline also makes it easier to write in a nonlinear order, jumping around as needed depending on what is simplest or most interesting for you to work on next.

— — — —

There are many nontraditional means by which you can expand your word count and expedite your drafting that do not require you to sit and write for hours on end. By reusing prewritten content, hiring ghostwriters, or dictating your content, you can significantly alleviate your writing burden. You just need to be prepared to adapt and edit the content to fit the specific voice and needs of your book.

PART 4:
REFINEMENT

CHAPTER 7:

Effectively Editing Your Message

A finished work of art is the result of many alternating cycles of creation and destruction. It is finding the balance between these two forces: the light and the dark, structure and chaos. Anything that does not serve a book's purpose must be modified or eliminated, no matter the author's creative bias.

Despite the many hours you've already put into crafting your message, there is much work to be done before it is ready to be published. Now it's time to edit, rework, proofread, and finalize your content so that it reflects the meaning you intend the best it can. By the time you have finished the final chapters of the initial draft of your book, you should have new insight into what you wrote when you began. Knowing what content comes in the later parts of your draft should affect your understanding of what needs to be present in the earlier parts. All portions of a message must work as a cohesive unit if the communication is to be as effective as it can be, but accomplishing this is not psychologically easy for most writers.

The unwillingness to change one's own mind is why many writers dread the process of revision far more than the process of drafting. Like all other areas of life, once a person has invested part of themselves into something, they have a hard time letting go. They don't look at the value of the thing objectively, only through the filter of what they've sacrificed to get it. They forget that those sunken costs have no bearing on how a reader will perceive their message. The reader knows nothing of a book's creative history. They

171

only know that it is either giving them what they want or that it isn't... that they are either happy with the experience or they aren't.

Revision is not an afterthought or a quick pass across your first draft to clean it up for public eyes. It is a series of heated arguments with your past self to determine the value of your expressions. Taken to its extreme, the process is enough to drive a weak-minded writer a little mad. There are only so many times you can revisit the same phrasings, tweaking little things about order, flow, and word choice before the experience negatively affects your emotions. To be a great editor, you must learn to be a very good companion to yourself. You must offer your mind the space it needs to recuperate and prepare for another round of refinement.

Figuring out where to begin and how to approach revision can be more difficult than figuring out what to write about in the first place. The process is not as simple as starting with page one and fixing errors as you go until you reach the end. At times, I stare at pages of my rough work, wondering what it was supposed to be for when I wrote it or what next to do with it. Some days I revise like a sculptor, arranging all sides of clay mash into something gradually resembling a defined figure. Other times, I am a surgeon, slicing out and inserting precise wording to make a segment of my draft work exactly as it should before moving on to polish any remaining rough spots. These processes can show up differently for any given writer on any given day.

If for some reason you feel compelled to skimp on editing or proofreading the content of your book, you will sooner or later regret it. You may end up printing and selling many books, only to discover months later that there have been slews of typos and gaping omissions in your text. Every reader who will have paid good money because they were intrigued enough to look at your message will have received a damaged shell of it. If you are writing your book to build a positive brand image for yourself, you will accomplish the very opposite through the associations of laziness and incomprehensibility your rushed book creates.

If your unedited book remains on the market for long, you will receive negative public reviews that damage your reputation and sacrifice future sales. It doesn't matter if you have a great message with powerful argumentation and valuable implications. Typographical errors, unnecessary repetition, or confused structure will shake your readers' confidence in you and your message. Polish is one of the surest signs of worth. It implies the message was important enough to go over again and again to optimize every little detail.

The only way to know that the seemingly endless revision to your book is done is if you look at every word of it and cannot think of a way to improve any of them. Until you reach that point, every change you make will be in service to approaching that impossible ideal. You will probably never get there, at least not without suffering through an incredible diminishment of returns on the time and thought energy invested into each additional change. If, however, you can get your manuscript to a point where the minor problems don't keep you up at night or threaten your readers' experience, you might come to accept that good enough is good enough.

Types and Functions of Editing

There is no universally right or wrong way to edit your work (just as there is no objectively best way to write the first draft). There are only conventions that have proven useful for the way most writers compose their work and most readers consume it. It is up to you to determine what you believe is crucial to the process of optimizing your message. Each round of editing takes time and talent, which translates to money spent if you decide to employ professionals for the task instead of handling it yourself.

Developmental Editing

Developmental editing has the function of looking at a draft as a complete entity to determine if it has all the parts it needs to tell the message it intends. It also considers whether those parts are all in the correct order to make the most epistemological sense. It is a strict evaluation of what is working or not working about what you have written. It addresses abstract issues, like the clarity of the author's intent, the logical consistency of the information, chapter and section length or density, and suitability for its target audience. This is the sculpting portion of the editing process.

A good developmental editor can tell you from the beginning of your draft whether it is clear what they are supposed to be learning, in what order, and what the emotional experience of reading will be like. They get this information from the table of contents, the introduction, and reminders throughout each chapter of where the reader currently is and where they are going. These navigational waypoints add clarity to the flow of the book's message.

Think of a developmental editor like a script doctor for a movie: an outsider who comes in to make sure the narrative and themes of the movie are all presented where they will be most effective for the viewing audience. Developmental editing is the first type of editing traditional authors submit their books to, for it is the structure through which all other valuable details will be made available. If the structure is broken, it won't matter how good the individual words, sentences, or paragraphs are. No one will read them, or they won't make sense in the book's context.

A developmental editor will:
- Check if your book accomplishes all the things it sets out to do in its introduction and early chapters.
- See if there is consistency in length, breadth, and depth of coverage for the many subjects that make up your manuscript. They know that readers will feel cheated and you will appear lazy if some sections are long and detailed, while others are short and vague.
- Assess the overall structure of the book's chapters and subsections.
- Contemplate ways to make the purpose of the book more specific, unique, or compelling.

Line Editing

Line editing is typically the second phase of book editing. It refines the editing process down to the level of individual sentences. As the name suggests, line editing involves going through your draft with meticulousness, on a line-by-line basis. It should primarily be performed once you are confident that your draft is basically in the right order and won't require major sections to be removed or rewritten. Otherwise, you might expend many hours of effort perfecting parts of your draft that won't even make it into the final cut anyway. Now is the time for the surgeon to enter with scalpel in hand.

Through line editing, many individual words or phrases can be deleted without subtracting from the meaning of a sentence. Or else, sentences and paragraphs might be made clearer by being expanded to include more detail. Perhaps this is where you start to notice that you have a habit of using the same words and phrases in close proximity or that you substitute a lot of specific nouns with vague pronouns. All these little changes make a huge difference to how clear and enjoyable reading your book will be.

One reason new authors find the drafting process so frustrating is they attempt to perform line editing at the same time they draft. They stop after every sentence or paragraph to assess if every word used is the best possible word it could be. They get neurotic about all the other ways they could have said the same thing and how their choice of voicing will be interpreted by readers. Their lack of confidence drives them crazy and delays their drafting. Only an experienced and cognitively flexible writer can pull off such rapid adjustment to their work in real time. For most, it is wiser to separate the drafting and revising processes and let some time pass between them. The time needed may range from a few days to several months, depending on the writer and their work.

As you commence with the first rounds of line editing, you may be flabbergasted to find that nearly every sentence in your draft can be made somehow clearer or more engaging. Do not be frustrated by this revelation. This is the purpose of line editing and part of what separates amateur authors from real pros. Only a dedicated communicator has the wherewithal to go through every inch of their message (several times if necessary) to make it all as good as it possibly can be. You will be rewarded for your endurance with a book that is treated by its readers the same as ones written by famous authors and published through traditional publishing houses.

A line editor will:
- Ensure you're using words in the ways that will best connect with your audience and convey the meaning you intend.
- Fix run-on sentences by splitting them in two or three distinct statements.
- Monitor the tone and emotions you want to be associated with your message.
- Suggest ways to spice up key sentences with descriptive language and quotable phrasing.
- Swap out oft-repeated words for synonyms to reduce the mental fatigue of linguistic repetition.
- Help bolster any arguments lacking detail or support.

If you work with a professional line editor, make sure it is one you can trust to understand your intentions. You should only work with an editor who will enhance your voice without diluting or twisting it into something inauthentic (sometimes imposing their own values on your work). You won't always agree with every proposed change, but your line editor should be more experienced in the art of making sentences easy to read. At the end of this phase of editing, your writing should feel improved, enriched, and more fluid. It will seem less like a haphazard heap of words and more like a real book.

Copyediting

Copyediting is different from line editing in that it ignores substance and meaning. It might more commonly be thought of as proofreading. Its function is to hunt for errors related to grammar, punctuation, and spelling according to accepted style manuals, such as *The Chicago Manual of Style*. A professional copyeditor checks that things like hyphens, capitalization, and numerals are used correctly and consistently throughout a draft.

During copyediting is also a good time to fact-check declarative statements you've made about people, companies, historical events, or other easily verifiable claims in your draft. After all, you don't want readers scoffing at inaccurate claims or, even worse, attempting legal action against you. If you accidentally describe a place as located in Queens in one chapter and Manhattan in another, a thorough copyedit will catch and correct your continuity error. It will ensure all loose ends are tied up so as not to confuse your readers or cause you to appear incompetent.

If you do your own proofreading or copyediting, you may think you understand the rules of English because you know when to use an apostrophe with "its," that there should only be one space after a period, or why the Oxford comma is amazing. Yet, time and again, I've seen people with good grasps of English make simple and obvious mistakes they can't catch in their own work. Many even add their own rules that have no place in English grammar or think they can ignore some that are actually essential.

A copyeditor will:
- Fix punctuation issues such as poor comma placement, semicolon misuse, and missing hyphens from compound adjectives (e.g., so-called expert, 15th-century monastery, etc.).
- Check for spelling errors, including inconsistencies between British and American English variants.
- Capitalize all proper nouns, including trademarks (e.g., Kleenex, Rolodex, etc.), names of holidays, and names of days of the week.

- Change appropriate compound nouns from two words to one (e.g., caveman, pussycat, or goosebumps).
- Double-check the use of words that are similar in spelling and meaning (e.g., insure/ensure, immigrate/emigrate, or affect/effect).

Copyediting can often blend with line editing, as fixing these kinds of errors invariably affects how you word sentences and arrange paragraphs. You can choose to do them separately, but you may find it more efficient to tackle them together (or find an editor who can handle both).

Though this progression of different editing types is logical and efficient for many writing situations, you will likely have to switch between writing new content, performing one or more types of editing, and back again and again. You will catch ways to improve the wording of a sentence, followed by the epiphany that you've omitted a major philosophical pillar from earlier in your work. Then you'll realize you've been using commas incorrectly for 300 pages when a concerned reader points it out to you. On and on, the creation/destruction cycle will turn until your book is complete.

All this revision may seem unnecessarily tedious, but it's the best way to ensure the professional quality of your work before publication. The final 10% of the work on your book may result in changes that multiply the book's influence and accessibility 10 times over. That is the power of revising a draft from a functional state to one that exceeds the standards readers expect when they pay $10 to $30 for a published book.

Editing Your Own Draft

Author Jack Kerouac is said to have finished the first draft of his book *On the Road* in less than three weeks. However, he didn't finish editing it for another five years. How different do you think his first draft must have been from his final? How many precious pieces of prose do you think he painfully eliminated on the road to his own version of perfection?

Not everyone feels confident editing their own work, but it is vital to go over your writing several times by yourself before turning it over to other eyes. After all, no one is better qualified to confirm that a message is true to its intentions than the person who initially set those intentions. Most writers advise taking a break between writing something and revising it. All that matters is that your state of mind is clear and you are open enough to see your words as though you had no prior knowledge of what they were supposed to convey.

Revising your own work will drain the decision-making part of your brain more than everyday life ever does. English is a language that seems to always have either too many or too few options for clear expression. Writers frequently must choose to enhance the clarity of a statement at the expense of its beauty or vice versa. There is an array of ways to communicate in writing that will subtly alter, without destroying, the message you intend. The smaller the distinction made, the more deliberation you may incur over the options for how to distinguish it. Structure, grammar, punctuation, and semantic decisions all contribute to the meaning of your message.

When you edit your work, you will see that new ideas will have emerged during the creative process. New questions and potential points of confusion should be clear when rereading what you have written. You will see where you need to add more details or make some ideas precede others for your key points to make sense. During the refinement process, you may be able to measure your progress not by how many words you add, but by how many you eliminate.

Getting your latent ideas out of your head and onto the digital screen in front of you makes them tangible and malleable. You can manipulate clusters of thought. You can single out and modify specific parts of an idea to make its meaning have more worth. Perform these surgical maneuvers on the level of individual words or phrases when you see you're being repetitive or that another term would better capture your intentions. You can do it with paragraphs or long chunks of text when you realize they're in the wrong order and need to be moved to another section of the book to have the most influence in context.

Like every writer, you are a human being with finite amounts of time and energy. You exert your value preferences when you choose how much editing and rewriting to invest in your message before returns get too diminished to justify further effort. The point of non-equitability is different for each writer and each book. It will depend on your available time and energy resources, how cognitively demanding writing and editing are for you, and the expectations of your audience. You'll know you are done when you can't find any meaningful way to improve what's on the page in front of you.

Your goal from the outset of revision should be to optimize the use of your time and effort. Follow a logical pattern of evaluation for every portion of your text at whatever pace you feel your draft can handle.

Stage 1: Sculpting

"What is the purpose of this sentence? This paragraph? This section? This chapter? Should I remove this part entirely? Is it relevant to my message or not?"

First, ask yourself if there something of value present in whatever section, paragraph, or sentence you are evaluating. This question is the best place to start because the answer is binary and absolute. If there is nothing useful in a passage according to the purposes I have decided for the book I am revising, I delete it without hesitation. That's a scary thought for writers who grow attached to their work. Once they've sweated out the perfect prose, they can't bring themselves to destroy it.

The problem is that a reader doesn't care how hard you've worked on something or how much it means to you as the author. They only care if it entertains them and satiates the needs that drove them to read the book in the first place. So, if you've identified something in your draft that does neither of those things, all other justifications are moot. You can, perhaps, find some solace in the practice of saving well-written passages that have no relevance for your draft for some yet-undetermined future use.

I have done a lot of writing that was originally intended to be part of one book project, only to be temporarily set aside and later included in a book that was a better fit for it. Even some of the passages you've read in this book got their start in other drafts I worked on earlier or concurrently with this book. After cutting the passages out of their original contexts, I was able to retrofit them in a new context here. Sometimes I hardly have to change anything except a few pronouns to make the old text flow consistently in its new place.

As you refine your work, maintain the perspective that the reader only sees the end result of what you release to the public. It doesn't matter to them how many changes a book has undergone, unless you do a poor job unifying your vision before release and cracks in the seams still show. It is the same with every creative act.

When you order a meal at a restaurant, your enjoyment comes from what your server presents on the plate within the manicured atmosphere of the dining area. You don't see the hurried chefs and chaotic kitchen hiding behind the scenes (unless the restaurant does a poor job and lets their dirty dishes spill into its foreground).

When you pay to see a movie at the cinema, only the final cut of the movie should matter. You probably don't know how many rewrites, reshoots, cut scenes, and improvised decisions were made by the actors, directors, or various other crew members. If they are competent filmmakers, they will have made the whole thing seem seamless and intentional from opening to closing credits.

Reasons to possibly remove passages from your book include:
- The writing sounds nice, but it doesn't have any relevance in the context you've created.

- You're repeating information that has already been covered better in passages that come before or after it (and aren't doing so intentionally for the sake of emphasis).
- The passage made sense with your original vision for the book, but you have since evolved your ideas about what the book should cover.
- In researching your subject, you've seen that this type of information is already covered abundantly in other publications and your book won't be any more valuable for including it.

Stage 2: Surgery

"Is this passage in the right place to maximize its value? Could I repurpose it better somewhere else? What information should it come before and after to have the intended influence?"

A finished book is more than the ideas that go into it; it's the way those ideas are put together. Just as the function of a chemical compound is determined by the arrangement of its molecules and the function of a molecule is determined by the arrangement of its atoms, your draft has many layers of arrangement that affect it at every level of analysis. Through many rounds of expansion, rewriting, and elimination, you are going to realize the order in which you have presented your ideas may not be ideal.

You have it in your power to alter the meaning of your message many times over by simply rearranging what you've already written. You should not feel the need to force your message to conform to the structure you originally predicted in your outline. Revision is the time to make sure all sections lead into each other organically and you have not skipped over critical concepts in your writing.

Fortunately, it's easy to move large sections of text around in any modern word processor. Identify where a new set of concepts begins and ends, then cut and paste those paragraphs where they are better suited to go. You will figure out where to place them by finding a natural separation of ideas in another part of your draft, whether it's in the beginning, middle, or end of a chapter. Soon, whether you intended to delineate your draft as such or not, you will develop the vision to see subtle shifts in your monologue where you know you can attack with your scalpel.

You will then probably need to apply some polishing to the beginning or end of the passage you've moved and/or the passages that now come before and after it. The flow and context of the conversation will have changed. Some gentle stitching with new transitional phrasing and recontextualization will make the whole thing appear to be one uninterrupted passage of text to the unaware reader. Even the greatest surgeons tend to leave scars, but through further acts of polishing you can go on to make the evidence of your work invisible.

At this stage, you might also employ a tactic I refer to as "paragraphical mitosis," which is when you divide a single paragraph into two as its concepts are separated and expanded into new groupings. Maybe the first or final sentence in a paragraph isn't perfectly connected with all the others but is too important to delete. You can break the rogue sentence off from its paragraph and elaborate on it with another sentence or a few. You can also perform mitosis anytime a paragraph grows to absurd lengths because you keep thinking of new details to add. Just find the most appropriate point of separation and let line breaks do the rest.

Stage 3: Polishing

"Is this phrasing the best possible way to say this? Can I split this sentence into two? Should I join these two sentences into one? Have I used these words too often recently? Do these words add any meaning?"

When every passage is in its right place and there's a right place for every passage, you should evaluate if you have phrased them all to maximize their contributions. As I am an often verbose thinker, my biggest obstacle to writing as many books as I would like to has been my ongoing internal debate about the best way to articulate my thoughts without sacrificing the meaning of my ideas in their original states. If I try to make each sentence the ideal arrangement of descriptive words, I will never finish another book in my life. I will always be able to find something else worth changing.

Improving a passage doesn't stop at the level of removing unnecessary words. Look for any opportunities to use a more specific, descriptive, or engaging word or phrase in place of a vague or common one. Placeholders like "it," "this," "that," "stuff," or "thing" can often be replaced with something more specific that reminds readers of context and elaborates on your meaning without taking much extra space. Minimize the readers' cognitive load with your flow and style. A broad vocabulary is not a necessity to write an influential book, but you can easily rely too often on words like "really" and "very" to emphasize a quality or conclusion.

Guard yourself against using the same word many times in close proximity. English has many ways to say nearly the same thing. You can write with a thesaurus open on your desk or in your web browser to remind you of alternative words you already know when you get stuck in a creative rut. Just don't resort to forcing strange words into your text that you would never say out loud. It takes great skill and stylistic awareness to incorporate a variety of words and subtle meanings without sounding foreign or robotic. Do not betray your own voice.

If I may harken back to George Orwell and Occam's Razor for a moment, any time you can shorten a sentence without reducing its meaning, your draft may be better off for it (but not necessarily). Aim for a consistent meaning-to-word-count ratio as much as possible throughout your text. You decide if it is more consistent, authentic and appropriate to use three words for "in order to" instead of the single word "to." Ditto other examples like "in what manner" instead of "how." Choosing one or the other will modify the syllable count and cadence of your sentence.

The best way to simultaneously strengthen your voice and make your draft more concise is to eliminate qualifying phrases that weaken your assertions. When you preface every important conclusion with a caveat like "in my opinion…" or "the way I see it…," you lessen your readers' confidence in your message. A meaningful book only has the influence its creator intends when they aren't constantly having to apologize for or mediate their views. The book ought to be written on the premise that the author's point of view is valid, its conclusions earned, and its audience earnestly interested. Everyone already knows it's your opinion. You wrote it.

The inverse problem of making statements feel weak with modifiers is strengthening them to the point of absurdity. When your words are read by thousands of people, any reaction that can happen eventually will happen. Absolutisms can be easily misinterpreted to mean something other than what you intended. You can save yourself a lot of grief by tastefully including words like "most," "usually," some," and "often" and carefully working around the need for "all," "none," "always," and "never" (unless your meaning is dependent upon conveying an invariable absolute). Remove or reword anything that could conceivably be construed as pompous or offensive by your target audience, even if the chance seems small. Unless it's vital to your meaning, it's better to play it safe.

Check if your sentences flow when you read them out loud. Many factors affect this that you probably haven't considered. The number of syllables in a phrase affects its reception. Too many tightly packed phonetic similarities can leave a strange taste in the reader's mouth or mind. Because English is such a broad language with so many options for similar expression, you will almost always be able to swap out a problematic word or phrase for one that doesn't have the same stylistic issues in a particular context. You can employ contractions or different verb conjugations to change the syllabic breakdown of a sentence toward a stylistic advantage. Reading your work aloud at this stage can help you make sure everything is flowing the way you want it to through ideal syllabic groupings, sentence length, and alliteration.

Whenever you include something in your draft that is strange, unknown, unfamiliar, or unnecessary, there is a small uptick in the effort required by the reader to understand you. There is a delicate balance to maintain here. If your work is consistently too simple and easy, the conscious mind can, in a sense, go to sleep while reading it. If your draft is packed with intentionally opaque and impenetrable nomenclature, your readers will not retain it. The inclusion of interesting words and phrases in just the right amount puts a small demand on reader consciousness to stay involved and process what it is seeing.

During polishing is also the time to evaluate the negative space in your text. When you decide to break your long paragraphs into shorter ones with lines of white space between them, you affect how readers scan the page and evaluate the text. It will change how they cognize the separation of concepts within your exposition, how well they retain the information, and how easily they can return to a specific passage later. The ability to navigate your work is as important as the meaning of the work itself.

When you choose to break a long sentence into two or three short ones, you alter the flow and reading experience of your work. Making a sentence better often, but not always, means making it shorter and simpler for the reader to understand without sacrificing explicit meaning or implied connotation. The longer a sentence goes on, the more possibility of error in style or substance it holds. You may find there are times you can make entire sentences obsolete just by adding an adjective or slightly more description in preceding or upcoming sentences.

As you grow more confident and practiced in your articulations, you will be drawn into taking bigger risks with longer, more complex structures for your sentences and paragraphs. But so long as you remain unsure of your powers of articulation, polish with Occam's Razor in mind: the simplest solution is probably the best solution.

Recruiting and Working with Beta Readers

When you've been over every sentence of your draft multiple times, you may fall into the trap many shortsighted authors do of believing the work is done. The truth is you cannot finish refining your draft on your own, because your perspective is limited by your familiarity with the content you've written. The book revision process cannot remain self-contained forever. Eventually, you must open the door to outside opinions if you are to move past the boundaries of self-bias.

A book optimized for a purpose cannot be written in isolation. It requires interaction, friction, response, and correction. When you've got at least a portion of your manuscript to a point that approximates the message you intend for it, the smartest thing you can do is bring in a curated sampling of external minds to offer their interpretations of writing. The alpha stage of writing was the rough draft you've already surpassed by editing what you originally wrote. Your work was not yet ready for other eyes to see because it was not close enough to its ideal state.

When you craft a message from scratch, you see it only from your own point of view. To your mind, whatever you've written makes perfect sense. It exists in its ideal form within you because you see all unexpressed sides of it, easily overlooking the truth that your understanding hasn't necessarily translated to the page. You have complex mental models attached to every sentence. There is an elaborate backstory to how you arrived at what you wrote and where it is going. The words mean more to you than just the words themselves.

You can test your self-bias by taking a break from your book for several weeks. When you come back and pick up where you left off or edit something old, you will probably not be able to continue in the same way. Many of the concepts and the logical flow of the book that were clear to you when you were actively drafting are not present anymore. Now you have to try to piece it together like an outsider.

The job of beta readers is to let an author know whether their book succeeds in communicating its intended message, whether it is enjoyable to read, and whether it creates a unique influence. Beta readers imitate the role of strangers who have purchased a book while blind to anything beyond what is presented within the text itself. Perhaps you've been struggling to make it past a certain point in your draft. You know where you are trying to go, but have lost your vision for how to get there. You recognize there are errors to address, but you don't know what they are or what to do about them.

Beta testing is not unique to books. All wise creators perform controlled tests of their creations before full release. There is too much at stake once their work is out in the open, subject to criticism from the unmerciful public. Physical gadgets undergo rounds of experimentation with real-world use cases before they are manufactured en masse. Video game designers release early beta versions as they test new features, so players can spot glitches or tell them what isn't fun. Major movie studios recruit test audiences to screen rough cuts of their films, sometimes incurring millions of dollars of reshoots to fix issues they hadn't considered in the plot, effects, or character development during the manuscript stage. Don't be so brash as to believe that what is necessary for them is superfluous for you.

Your team of beta readers, no matter how large it is or of whom it is composed, can also serve a function as your book's "early adopters." Because they will have read your work before any member of the general public, they will be the first minds to contribute to the regurgitation and spread of your message. If they love your book enough to make it to the end of it, you should be able to count on them to preorder it before launch (thereby boosting the book's Amazon Best Seller Rank number and moving it up the subcategory rankings for greater exposure). They should be willing to leave positive reviews on the book's Amazon listing, tell their friends to buy the book, share it on their social media feeds at launch, or even promote it on their own websites if it is appropriate to do so. All these actions are important for a successful book launch.

There are many ways to find your beta readers. Beyond your existing friends and social media connections, you can join online groups, forums, and pages related to your book's topic (or related to writing in general). Put out an announcement that you are looking for early readers to give you critical feedback on your upcoming book. You'll be happy to include your beta readers in the book's acknowledgments and (if you're willing to foot the bill) a free paperback or hardcover (possibly autographed) copy of the book upon publication.

Being a beta reader is one of the best ways for aspiring authors to look behind the scenes of what goes into the production, revision, and marketing of a successful self-published book. Mention this fact while you are recruiting. You can even work out an arrangement with other writers wherein you will beta read their work in exchange for them beta reading yours. If your budget permits it, hire an editor or professional beta reader who can provide page-by-page or even paragraph-by-paragraph feedback.

Author Familiarity

You may be tempted to recruit your beta readers solely on the basis that they like your personality and writing style, and will, therefore, give you praise for your unfinished work. Don't fall into this trap. Do not only give copies of your draft to your best friends or an adoring aunt. The beta readers you recruit should be a mix of many types of people, including friends, strangers, experts in your field, and newcomers to your subject. Those closest to you may feel obligated to respond in a complimentary way. Set your ego aside and seek out a range of opinions, from the most negative to the most positive. From the different flavors of feedback they provide, you will learn to recognize what is useful for the purposes of your refinement.

With that caveat established, there is still value in the opinions of people who know you. The people closest to you have seen sides of you the rest of the world has not. They know more about your paradigm, personality, history, and intentions. They may have insight about what to include that

189

you've so far omitted from your draft. They can advise you when to write more personal anecdotes or go deeper into a subject they have heard you talk about. You don't have to accept every suggestion they give you, but feedback from those who know you, however biased, can be uniquely valuable for your book.

People who don't know you make good beta readers for the inverse reason that your friends do. They are not biased by any pre-existing relationship with you. Their interest will be more about providing helpful comments and learning something interesting from your draft. Their participation may even be motivated by a desire to learn about the book writing and revising process if they have their own aspirations of authorship.

Subject Familiarity

Beta readers who are novices on the subject of your book can be useful because of their freshness. This is particularly true if you are writing a book meant to provide an introductory overview rather than a lot of narrow, in-depth expertise. When you work with beta readers who have no relevant background in your field, ask them to summarize what they have learned from reading each chapter of your draft. You will soon identify where holes in your message still lie.

You should also recruit at least a few of your peers, experts to review your knowledge. Even if you are an established thought leader in your field, you may have overlooked important concepts. Your work might benefit from additional insights that have escaped your notice. Your expert peers may even challenge you to advance your knowledge further than what is contained in your draft. Working with knowledgeable people is a great form of quality control. Readers with no prior knowledge can give you helpful feedback, but only an expert can tell you if you have managed to communicate complicated theories or philosophies well.

Publishing Familiarity

You should recruit some beta readers who are experienced writers or editors. They can provide suggestions that non-writers won't. They understand book conventions better and have struggled through some of the same issues with their own drafts that you are now stressing about. Because they are probably used to receiving both useful and useless feedback during their revisions, they may be better equipped to formulate their advice in ways you can act on.

One possible problem with getting advice from fellow writers though is that many of them are so caught up in their own work that they have become vain about writing. They inflate their own experience or expertise, or they project their own standards and preferences onto your writing. They assume their job is to critique your work as though it were theirs. They critique with the implication that the best possible way to write anything is the way they would have written it. Other writers don't necessarily know what makes your book good by the standards you have set for it. Such people will have little respect for personal style or your independent goals. If you see a beta reader start to hijack your work, kindly ask them to back off a bit or kick them off the project.

Beta Draft Practicalities

If the text of your nonfiction book runs too long (perhaps more than 50,000 words), it might be more feasible to give different chapters or sections to different beta readers, rather than expecting each of them to make it all the way through the book in a timely manner. Remember that reading and giving quality feedback take a fair amount of time and effort. Different chapters might be more suitable for people with different expertise, experience, or interest. The last thing you want is a ton of great feedback for the first half of your book and then almost nothing from the handful of endurance readers who make it to the end.

Do your best to accommodate the format your beta readers prefer to read your draft in. I've found it most useful to break my draft into separate documents of 10,000 to 20,000 words each and upload them to the cloud as shared Google Docs. In that format, all beta readers can view them simultaneously.

Not every beta reader works well with the shared cloud document format though. Some may want your draft in a complete, free-of-markup Word document that they can digest without the interference of other readers or the necessity of constant online access. Some people refuse to read anything that isn't printed on paper in front of them.

During the beta reading stage of *The Influential Author*, I maintained seven shared Google Docs (one for each section of the book). In that format, my readers could leave their comments and corrections in a way that enabled me to easily incorporate, disregard, or probe each one for clarification. They could also comment on each other's comments, agreeing or disagreeing with each other with their own points of view.

Because I had conducted rounds of beta reading for several books before this one, I felt comfortable releasing each section of *The Influential Author* in sequence as I completed my own revisions of them. This allowed me to finish the book much faster than if I had waited until all seven sections were complete before opening them to external judgment. The patterns of feedback I got for the early sections of the book affected how I approached the later sections I was still drafting. It's slightly more complicated to write and revise a book in stages like this, but it's more efficient for the way I work.

Many authors make the mistake of bringing in beta readers only after they've spent months or years polishing their book to what they consider to be a state of perfection. They are shy about showing off what they have created while it is still premature. This shy approach defeats most of the purpose of using beta readers. You need input from them throughout each stage of revision. I encourage you to let go of your vanity and ask for help from a small, trusted circle as soon as you have something representative of your intended message. The size of the circle can expand as you make further revisions.

Beta Reader Instructions

As soon as you being beta reading, inform your beta readers that what they are reading is an intentionally unfinished draft. The purpose of their participation is to make sure it is moving in the direction you want. If they catch glaring structural errors or tonal incongruence early enough, you can course correct before wasting many hours working toward the wrong goal. If you wait until you have poured your heart and soul into your draft, you will be too deeply invested to be able to remove what isn't working or alter your assumptions.

The value of the feedback you receive from your beta readers at any stage of editing will depend on how well they understand their role in your work. We all know people who are too eager to give their unwarranted opinions on other people's work in non-constructive fashions. Picture your least favorite movie critic. Some people ignore all writer and director intent or the artistic talent that went into a film. They just rant about how the movie failed to meet their arbitrary and specific preferences about the number of explosions or sex scenes it should have contained.

I have used a disclaimer at the start of all the books I have submitted for critical review from beta readers, whether they have been books I authored or those of another author I had been working with. I always make sure it is the first thing they see before the actual content of the book. It goes something like this:

> *You are viewing an unfinished draft of this book. The goal with beta reading is to make it into an optimized communication. I need to know as much as possible when things are confusing, too short, too long, ordered wrongly, or just plain bad in your opinion. I also want to know*

what stands out to you as exceptionally good, so I can assess how to infuse more of those things into the book.

Everything is open to change at this point, so don't be shy about sharing your thoughts. Be brutal. I want your honest reactions as you go through the book one section at a time.

Try not to let your relationship with me as the author bias your opinion. Look at it as though you had picked it up off a bookstore shelf out of curiosity or had it recommended to you from a friend.

You can add comments/notes or suggest changes as you go. You can also collect your feedback in a separate document and give it to me when you've finished reading. Calling out typos or grammatical errors is highly appreciated, as are larger developmental suggestions.

Whenever possible, please try to state your feedback in a useful manner. Simply telling me you don't like part of it or would prefer to be reading a different kind of book doesn't provide much actionable advice to work with. Phrase your critiques in a way that allows me to arrive at specific changes I can make to improve the work. It helps if you understand my intentions for the book, so let me know if those aren't coming across clearly. This will make your contributions worth 100 times more.

The intended audiences for this book are…

Lastly, while I welcome additional beta readers, please ask me before sharing this document or any of its contents with anyone.

I will then provide my name and email address in case the beta readers need to contact me about anything while reading.

These caveats and premises are important for the beta reading process. Your readers need to understand your intentions if their feedback is going to be relevant. You also want to give them permission to share every opinion, positive or negative, about your work so that they won't feel rude voicing these things. That's the whole point of their participation at this stage. If some of your concepts don't make sense in the opening chapter, it might cause book buyers to give up reading at that point. Your beta readers need to be comfortable telling you this kind of raw truth so you can fix it.

If you are only looking for a certain kind of feedback, you can prompt your readers with specific questions up front. Ask them to take note of how confusing certain passages are or if the tone comes across as too serious or whimsical. See if the reasoning behind your boldest statements is clear or you are asking the reader to accept too much on faith. Ask where in the manuscript they start to lose interest and where they regain it. Ask them if all your book's central arguments make sense and have ample evidence to support them. See if your readers feel that their expectations were met from the time they started reading and that the promises that were made up front were fulfilled.

Your questions will let your beta readers know you're concerned about these things and they will direct their attention accordingly. You can even alert your beta readers to things that don't require their feedback because you are unwilling to change them or already have plans to do so. You are trying to get an accurate representation of how the world will respond once your book is published and available for purchase on the open market. Once you put it out there, you won't be able to monitor your readers' reactions directly. They might love it or hate it, and you won't know why.

Feedback Gradient

Some people will love your book to a fault. In their eyes, you will be able to do no wrong. Others will tell you that is just isn't to their taste, but that they assume someone else would like it. Others still will hate it to a shocking degree of severity. They will make it their mission to let you know how useless they think you are as a writer. When you encounter these people, it will be clear that their prerogative is only to posture themselves and express disapproval, not to help you improve your work.

Your goal is to improve your draft for your target audience and obviate it for everyone else. You cannot possibly please everyone, so don't try to. Assess all the feedback you receive according to your standards for refinement. Separate the helpful remarks from the unhelpful ones, and then make changes accordingly.

A helpful comment is clear, specific, actionable, and relevant to your goals:

"I found the language throughout the book to be clear, but the section in Chapter 3 on marketing tactics could use a case study or some specific examples to make it relatable to your readers."

An unhelpful comment is vague and irrelevant. It's more like a sneeze or a knee-jerk reaction than a thoughtful analysis:

"This is dumb. Your chapters are really long and you didn't even talk about my favorite city in the section about travel."

During the beta reading stage of every book I have written or produced (including this one), I have dealt with at least one critic who made it a point to write several paragraphs about how terrible they thought the book was. Their scorn went beyond telling me about a few fatal flaws that ruined the experience for them. Some demanded that the book wasn't just suboptimal but that it was wasn't fit for publication at all. Others insisted that I "go back to writing school" and work on my craft for at least a decade before I try to write a book.

I even had one beta reader glance over a document of more than 15,000 words, then confidently assert that it was worthless because there were no diagrams or pictures included. He only liked nonfiction books with diagrams. He hadn't read a single sentence of what I sent him, and he displayed no knowledge of my intentions for it. He only knew that his personal reading habits included books with visual aids, and therefore anything else was of no worth.

Do you think I completely overhauled the purpose and presentation of my book to appease this single reader's unilateral preference? Obviously, I did not. The value of his feedback was that it alerted me to the presence of people who might apply similar, inappropriate standards of evaluation. Even if 99% of people loved my book, there would always be some people who would be unwilling to see anything good about it. Such people just so happen to have the loudest voices sometimes.

No matter how negative or positive the feedback you receive during beta reading, you must distance yourself from your work enough to not let it personally affect you. Of course, it feels great when you receive heaps of genuine praise for something you have worked hard on. Conversely, it can be devastating when it seems no one appreciates your vision or efforts. But when you open your book to beta readers, you are no longer solely an artist. You are now a marketer. A marketer only has the goal of optimizing a product's presentation for its buyers. A marketer simply looks at the data and adjusts his product according to what it suggests. They know that no matter what they offer, some people are going to love it and others are going to hate it.

Even the most negative, least relevant feedback can still teach you useful things about the possible range of reactions to your work. However bad the reaction, it is representative of what might happen if the wrong person makes the mistake of purchasing your book. They will be upset they wasted their time and money on something that clearly wasn't a good fit for them. If you've ever bought a book with a captivating description or gone to see a movie based on a fantastic trailer only to find the experience was quite different, you understand the feeling of betrayal. Such a person will feel obligated to voice their opinions about your book to warn others like themselves from making the same mistake.

When you receive unhelpful comments, try to clarify what the beta reader actually meant. There could be a helpful morsel buried somewhere inside. If a beta reader describes your book as "a bit boring," they are giving you some blunt, non-specific feedback. It isn't a useful starting point for how to improve the draft. You can ask them, politely, to explain what they mean when they use words such as "boring," "bad," or "confusing." Ask them to point to specific examples within the text, without making it seem like you are just being argumentative. Ask what changes they would make to improve it. If they can't do these things and their negative response is not part of a larger consensus from other beta readers, you might be better off ignoring this outlier.

Be aware that not everyone will be able to articulate their issues with (or praise for) your writing in a viable manner. Vague comments can still be more useful than no feedback at all if enough readers voice the same reaction, even if they can't explain it. You may have sufficient evidence then to accept that something ought to be fixed about a particular passage. At the very least, you can get a sense of where a stumbling block may be or narrow down the right kind of reader for your work.

Watch for the patterns that emerge across the rounds of feedback you receive. If you get many of the same remarks, it is a reliable indicator that you should act on them. If two-thirds of your beta readers have told you that your book contains too many run-on sentences, trim some of them down and see how the reactions improve. Unless you believe it will ruin the meaning or artistic integrity of your work, there's no reason not to make your writing easier for your readers to stay engaged with.

While feedback often encourages discussion, you're not helping yourself if you take an argumentative stance against anything your beta readers tell you. You won't agree with everything, but it's still worthwhile for them to elaborate on their opinions. Information by itself can't hurt you. It just gives you more options to consider. If you flat out negate what beta readers tell you, they'll be discouraged from voicing their opinions peacefully or may stop reading altogether. Asking for more detail or correcting an inaccurate assumption is great. Telling them they are wrong or a bad judge of quality is not. If a beta reader is just causing problems with destructive and hurtful feedback, you can kindly tell them you don't think they are a good fit for the project anymore.

Remember that your objective at this stage of refinement is to discover how your target audience responds to the way you present your message. You must assess all feedback through that lens. Do not be too proud to alter the writing choices you have made just because you already worked hard to get the book where it is. This is another effect of the sunk cost fallacy. The amount of time or effort you have invested so far in producing your book has no bearing on its quality or effectiveness. Keep your eyes on the prize and do not get in your own way. When your beta readers have run out of suggestions for improvement, you might be ready to move on.

Summary of Chapter 7

Developmental editing, line editing, and copyediting all accomplish different functions in a book draft to bring it closer to its ideal publishing state. They can be performed many times and in any order by you or a team of professional editors you hire. The best way to apply them will depend on how well-organized your book is, how you've phrased each sentence, and how many typographical mistakes you've made.

— — — —

Every author should perform several rounds of editing on their own work, even if they decide to bring professionals on board to assist. You will need to go over every section of your words many times to determine if they are contributing something worthwhile to the message, if they are appearing in the ideal order for comprehension, and if they are phrased in the optimal manner for the reading experience. A large amount of your first draft may need to be eliminated, reordered, or rewritten to make your book as good as it can be.

— — — —

When you feel your book draft is in a state that approximates what you intend to communicate, you can recruit a team of beta readers from your target audience to critique your work. Their feedback will help you determine what you are doing right and wrong so far, giving you invaluable ideas about how to move forward. It will be your responsibility to determine what feedback is worth incorporating or ignoring depending on how relevant it is to your goals for your book.

CHAPTER 8:

Proofreading, Pedantry, and Punctuation

Why do perfect grammar, spelling, and punctuation matter so goddamn much?

Learning the rules of written English is not an idle or arbitrary endeavor. It is an important part of being a good communicator because using the language correctly is the best way to ensure that your message gets interpreted the way you intend. Good grammar and careful attention to comma placement and the like don't have to detract from your expressive abilities. You shouldn't feel forced to speak out of character because you have proofread your work. Casual writers tend to treat having to write in accordance with the pedantic rules of English like they treat having to dress up for a formal party full of people they don't care about. They resent society's highbrow expectations.

The way you use spelling, grammar, and punctuation is part of how you display your personality to readers. Messing up the structure or readability of your sentences is the written equivalent of slurring your speech in a conversation with people you are trying to create a positive impression for. Abundant errors will betray the high standards of traditional publishers that you have been hoping to emulate. Poor proofreading habits will also convey that you do not take your own message seriously. It makes it seem like you are not willing to put effort into perfecting it. Thus, neither should your readers.

All elements of presentation affect how readers interpret your message. It's more obvious how this comes into play with something like a cover design or author headshot, but it applies just as much to the presentation of the text itself. You might think that none of your readers will be fussy or academically inclined enough to notice (let alone care about) the fine details of your scripting so long as they understand what you are trying to say. The problem with this type of thinking is that there will always be at least some readers who *do* consciously care about pedantry. Your crappy writing habits will prevent them from getting the benefits of what you've written by failing to appeal to their temperaments.

Even readers who claim not to care about perfectionism are not immune to unconscious awareness of the effects of negligent proofreading. Though you may have never formally studied English grammar and vocabulary, native speakers have lived their whole lives with unconscious and mostly accurate understandings of the language's many complicated practices. You don't need to know what a subordinate clause is or what the limits of the passive voice are to sense when something is off in a book.

Writing, no matter the purpose or context, is almost always considered more formal and sophisticated than speaking. Writing leaves in its wake a static object. Speaking, unless recorded, is ephemeral by nature. This dichotomy contributes to the timeless power books and other forms of writing hold across history. The sound of spoken words disperses into the ether of existence as soon as those words are projected. Little mistakes in construction or presentation don't long stick around to reflect poorly on the speaker or grate the nerves of listeners. That is why we say that your written self is your spoken self on your best day, absent the minor mistakes that slide by, unnoticed by either party.

Because you have likely spent much of your life writing in casual and informal contexts, you have picked up bad habits few people bother to correct. When you send a text message on your phone or participate in an online chat, you will be forgiven for omitting unnecessary letters, parts of speech, or punctuation. Convenience and expediency are the goals in these contexts, not structure, accessibility, beauty, or consistent meaning. Now it's time to correct your bad writing habits in your book draft.

You don't have to train to become a master linguist to have a successful book. The level of cognitive investment you are willing to make for your book is up to you, but your writing only stands to improve by learning the finer details of English. Beauty is not lost by understanding the rules of its creation. It will help you think more clearly and then articulate your thoughts with fewer hesitations. When you understand the material that messages are made from, your messages will come to you more easily for as long as you remain a writer.

Grammar Myths and Legends

Traditional advice about English grammar is full of rules and suggestions, including many that accomplish little more than inhibit the communication abilities of writers who feel bullied to conform. Novices in a new domain might make it their goal to follow every rule for fear of making mistakes they won't even have the faculties to recognize. This is generally a cautious and advisable strategy to follow, but only to a point. A wise and experienced writer can, in any situation, determine which rules are worth following and which will only muddle their intentions.

I will begin with an overview of the basic parts of speech, the bricks that make up all English language communication. You've been using each of these in a mostly correct manner your whole life, but you may not have known the function each performs in your communication. Equipped with a deeper understanding of the building blocks of your language, you will be able to revise and optimize every element of your message.

Nouns are the words we use for various forms of static objects, whether they be concrete and tangible (like an apple, microbe, or galaxy) or abstract and intangible (like consciousness, pain, or epiphany). Pronouns are a form of collective shorthand for nouns within given contexts, depending on plurality and gender (such as she, us, mine, or themselves). Proper nouns are the names given to specific things (not the whole category of things they belong to) and are always capitalized in a sentence (as is the case with my cat named Fluffy or the New York Times newspaper).

Verbs are words that represent a state of being as applied to a noun, conjugated into specific forms based on plurality and a reference frame of the time that they occur. A verb either happens, is happening, has happened, has been happening, happened, was happening, had happened, had been happening, will happen, will be happening, will have happened, or will have been happening. Every complete sentence in English contains at the minimum a noun and a verb, a thing undergoing a change that ties its categorical abstractness to reality.

Adjectives add modifying qualities to nouns. They are single words or compound combinations that describe static things more acutely, altering their severity (light, extreme, simple, difficult), personality (friendly, strange, creative), or utility (Philips-head, 32-gigabyte, easy-open). Adjectives provide a means by which to reduce the whole category of a thing down to a smaller subset that holds a certain quality.

Adverbs add qualities to verbs or adjectives, describing the manner in which actions are performed or qualities embodied (quickly, easily, plentifully). Some adverbs are written the same as when they are used as adjectives (bright, slow, hard). With each new layer of meaning, the image becomes more precise in the mind of the reader, but the sentence more convoluted.

Prepositions denote a relationship between nouns, either spatially (above, throughout, beside), temporally (after, before, during), or epistemologically (of, from, through).

Conjunctions link concepts together, defining the meaning of their relationship to each other. They denote whether concepts exist within the same conceptual category (and), in opposing categories (but, yet, however), in causally connected categories (so, because, for, thus, therefore, nevertheless, until), or in alternative categories (either, or, neither, nor).

Articles indicate the specificity of a noun within its context. "The" is specific. "A/an" is generic. Other determiners like some/many, this/that, or numbers further contextualize the relevance the meaning of a sentence has to the abstract totality of its noun. A lack of determiner often implies universality.

Each component of writing is subject to principles that dictate how it must be used in a sentence, including how it can be modified or conjugated to add new meaning and fit its context. It's vital that you learn how to use and where to place the parts of speech, but most components also carry outdated or erroneous guidelines that may stifle your expression if followed too stringently. With experience, you will learn to trust your judgment about what English can and cannot do, as well as what the best choice is for all parts of your message.

Conjunct Beginnings

Conjunctions are supposed to connect or create a relationship between two nouns, implying nouns must come both before and after each conjunction. This is why many traditional grammarians believe it to be improper to begin a sentence with a conjunction. But in reality, there are plenty of times it makes sense to start a sentence in the middle of a relationship (such as this sentence beginning with the word "but"). You just need to remain mindful of starting too many sentences this way, as it may grow difficult to follow the flow of your message.

Prepositioned Endings

The same reasoning can be applied to the outdated advice not to end sentences with prepositions, which are used to show relationships between nouns. Often, ending a sentence with a word like "of," "from," or "to" is the best way to reduce the reader's cognitive load or feelings of dissonance about your voice. Some verbs are phrasal, requiring the specific placement of a preposition to alter their meaning. That's why *looking* in an upwards direction is not the same thing as *looking up* the lyrics to a song.

Dissected Infinitives

Every English verb exists as two words in its unconjugated state (i.e., "to _____"; to run, to walk, to eat, to drink, to sleep, to be merry, and so on). We call these infinitives. Uniquely, it is possible to modify infinitives with adverbs before, in the middle of, or after (e.g., "boldly to go," "to boldly go," or "to go boldly where no man has gone before"). While each of these phrasings should be considered to have the same meaning, they have different effects on a reader's interpretation of tone and personality. It's these weird little stylistic choices that make English such a frustrating and fascinating medium for expression.

Because in Latin the infinitive forms of verbs are expressed as single words, putting anything in the middle of their Latin roots is not possible. Traditional grammarians, therefore, declared it to be improper to "split" English infinitives by putting an adverb in between "to" and the verb. This is an example of where adhering to the habits of the past serves no function except to limit the options for expression. There is no reason English should have to suffer the same limits as Latin. You should modify your verbs in whatever manner best encapsulates your voice and meaning. If you prefer to come across to your audience as more traditional, then by all means remove split infinitives from your draft.

Passive Voice Resistance

One nearly universal piece of writing advice you'll hear is to avoid the passive voice whenever possible, deferring to the active voice in almost all cases instead. The passive voice states that a thing happened, while the active voice states that someone or something did the thing. The active voice is considered clearer and more engaging. It changes the emphasis of the information presented. The active voice places the importance of a sentence on the actor. A sentence is considered (or, if you prefer, readers consider a sentence) more concise and to flow better, incurring less cognitive load, when it is active.

Traditionalist grammarians will never admit, however, that there are situations where the passive voice is superior to the active voice. Passive voice constructions have a more detached, objective focus, which may be preferable for authors writing in a scientific, spiritual, or philosophical tone. This is why I have favored the passive voice throughout some sections of this book. The passive voice omits information about the actor, implying the action itself is what matters and not any person or entity behind it. There are times when a writer doesn't even know who or what did something, only that something was done. The identity of the actor may also be obvious through context, making their inclusion in a new sentence redundant (and therefore less concise).

Sometimes the impersonalization of the passive voice is more appropriate for how an author intends their message to be received. The passive voice aligns with how I think and perceive the concepts I write about. It's a more accurate representation of my cognition. That's enough reason for me to use it without reservation or apology.

Fragmented Sentences

You've probably been taught your entire life never to write in sentence fragments. Every valid sentence needs to contain its own subject and action for that subject to do. This is generally good advice to follow, but where it falls short is in the fact that people frequently speak in ways they are not supposed to write. They become accustomed to expressing themselves in ways that are technically incomplete or incorrect. These habits carry over to writing, and trying to change them might be more trouble than it's worth.

While it's usually easy to expand an incomplete sentence into a complete one, you don't necessarily have to. Sometimes the subject is implied by a preceding sentence. Sometimes you want to be punchy. Impromptu. Punctuated to make a point stand out within a paragraph. The danger of overuse is clear, but a tastefully executed sentence fragment can add the personality your book is needing.

Creative Terminology

Even the words you use in your draft aren't limited to what a dictionary prescribes. You can use any word you want, so long as it does not shatter understandable English grammar. It doesn't matter if your word processor and its squiggly red underline insist that your inventive word does not exist. All language is a human construction, shaped by spontaneous real-world use and filtered through a set of general practices. One measure of how well you understand the rules of English is your ability to modify and combine them into unprecedented results. Through consistent prefixes and suffixes, it is possible to expand the meaning of words without readers ever missing a beat or misinterpreting your meaning.

When I attach the suffix -fication to the end of a noun, you can logically surmise that I am describing the process of making or turning into that noun. My favorite example of this manipulation of the English language through its own rules is whatever astrophysicist coined the word "spaghettification" to describe objects stretching and compressing into long, noodle-like shapes under strong forces of gravity.

Likewise, to "-ize" or "-ify" something is to transfer qualities to it. Countries that receive a lot of American tourists, movies, and retail franchises might become Americanized over time.

Remember that writing is art. As long as your intended audience can understand you the way you want and their opinion of you won't degrade because of your creative constructions, you're good to go. You can nounify a verb or verbify a noun. English gerunds (using active -ing verbs as nouns) are a shortcut for accomplishing this and are made complicated by the fact that they can also be adjectives to other nouns (such as the case with the "writing" book I am actively "writing" through the act of "writing").

Problematic Placeholders

The overuse of vague placeholder terms, such as pronouns that substitute for specific nouns, can muddle your meaning. Your text becomes unclear when readers cannot tell what pronouns are supposed to be referring to, like if the same one is applied many times in sequence without restating its noun. If you use two nouns in a sentence followed by a pronoun, context might not make it clear which noun the pronoun is replacing. Pronouns, while quite useful for style and brevity, lead to clouded meaning when thrown around a draft without discretion.

Unlike some other languages, English breaks its pronouns into categories by their use as subject, object, possessive, and reflexive terms. This practice adds clarity to communication but also creates confusion if writers are not precise with them. "I" becomes "me," "mine," and "myself." "He" becomes "him," "his," and "himself" and so on. These pronoun possibilities must also agree in plurality and personhood with their subjects. The options for pronoun error are enormous.

The framing of your message will depend on the perspective provided by the pronouns you use, which can confuse readers if changed too often. If your book is primarily a memoir, it might make sense to tell it from your point of view, which English calls the first-person perspective (I). In an instructional book like this one, I slip into the first-person perspective when providing my personal experience or opinion to demonstrate the principle I am explaining (such as right now). I move into the second-person perspective (you) when offering specific advice and trying to get you, the reader, to take action with your own situation. The third-person perspective (he/she/it) often lays things out in hypothetical or universal terms not contingent on a specific actor.

Pronoun genderfication—a quite useful made-up word—is a sensitive issue. In English, there is no singular third-person perspective gender-neutral pronoun. We have no undifferentiated term for "he or she" in the way that "sibling" is an undifferentiated term for "brother or sister." For plural subjects where no gender is specified, they/them/their/themselves suffices. But what is an author supposed to do when the subject is just one person? "It?"

For centuries, it has been customary to use masculine terms and hope context would make it clear when women were meant to be included in the generic label. Many people, however, find the default masculine style to be unfair and imbalanced. Various pronoun alternatives have been offered, but none are without drawback. There is the clunky "he and she" and "his and her" option, the awkward and impotent use of "they" as singular, or even "she/her" in a neutral manner skewed to the feminine side (creating a now inverted imbalance).

The apparent misuse of gendered language is enough to deeply offend some readers. The safest (but not necessarily the most beautiful) choice is to shoehorn "they" and "them" as gender-neutral third-person singular pronouns. It will probably be a long time before the English language evolves to a point where some alternative pronoun has become accepted into common use. All authors should be aware of the responses of their target audiences when they use any form of gendered language, from "he" to "businessman" to "mankind."

In my upcoming personal development book, *The Exceptional Individual*, I chose the antiquated practice of using "he" and its derivatives as third-person singular pronouns in a gender-neutral manner—even though I've stuck with variants of "they" as the safer choice in the book you are currently reading. To me, each book requires a different style and tone to accomplish its function. *The Influential Author* exists to provide inspiration and advice for prospective authors. *The Exceptional Individual*, on the other hand, is meant to cause readers to question what they think they know about the structure and trajectory of their lives.

To strike an emotional chord with readers of *The Exceptional Individual,* the exact wording of each sentence was crucial. Using "they" or "he or she" in place of "he" would have altered much of the poeticness and elegance I worked so hard to craft. The book also makes many allusions to classic and modern mythology and timeless character archetypes. The antiquated way of writing with masculine labels as a catchall was more thematically appropriate and emotionally effective for that particular book. I couldn't be politically correct without feeling like I was sacrificing some artistic integrity.

Even the word "you," modernly employed for both singular and plural subjects (i.e., whether addressing a single person or a group of people), was exclusively plural until a few hundred years ago. That's why you don't see words like "thee," "thou," "thine," and "thy" used anymore. They were forms of the accepted second-person singular pronoun for a time, and it was considered improper to use "you" in the same way we now use "they" for singular third-person perspective subjects.

Prevalent Errors in Punctuation and Spelling

Impeccable spelling is not a worthy goal for most English writers. Much of the way we put letters together to make words relies on the rote memorization of uncommon letter arrangements. Compared to other languages, we are inconsistent with how we create sounds with our symbols. Our vowels can be pronounced so ambiguously that it's impossible to determine whether a word should have an a, e, i, o, u, sometimes y, or some unholy combination of two or three of these options. The times we choose to double a consonant in a word are generally arbitrary and have no bearing on pronunciation. English steals so many words from other languages that we now have many possible ways to spell the same phonetic outcomes.

While digital spelling, punctuation, and grammar checkers have made it easy to fix most common errors during editing, they have their shortcomings. Computers have a hard time determining from context exactly where commas ought to go or the ideal way to conjugate a complex sentence. When you use any type of automated revision tool, you must still rely on your knowledge to judge whether the program is correct in its analysis of errors and the best way to resolve them. This isn't a problem with words you use every day and can identify the solution to, but it can lead to errors anytime you try to branch out a little with your vocabulary or sentence structure.

The most overlooked problem with machine correction comes from distinct words that are spelled almost the same. Your spell checker won't always know which option is the best one to correct a misspelled word to because it's not good at understanding context. It also probably won't even register an error if by misspelling the word you meant to use you inadvertently spell another word correctly. Eventually, you need a keen pair of human eyes to come in and catch what the machines don't know to look for.

Though hiring professional help is often a good idea, your own eyes will be the first line of defense against mistakes in English. You should learn your language well enough to know "affect" is a verb and "effect" is a noun (usually). The same is true with "advise" and "advice," respectively. "Accept" and "except" are pronounced almost the same but are spelled differently and mean unrelated things. "Lose" is not the same as "loose." The problems associated with "their," "there," and "they're" shouldn't need repeating here.

Crown vs. Colony English

English spelling habits are further complicated by the fact that valid but distinct variants exist for Americans and Britons. Writers often don't realize the extent of these differences and inadvertently slip a British variant into an American text or vice versa. Whichever version of English you decide is appropriate for your subject and audience, you should stay consistent with it. British spellings are more traditional in the sense that they are closer to the original spellings of words rooted in Greek or Latin or borrowed from other modern languages (such as German or French).

American variants have been modified over time to be spelled more like how they are pronounced.

The British include a silent "u" in many cases where Americans omit it, such as behavio(u)r, colo(u)r, and favo(u)rite.

You may need to reverse the order of -er and -re at the end of words like center/centre and theatre/theatre (but not in words like river or mediocre).

The British read their catalogues and the Americans their catalogs.

British sports teams play offence and defence while American teams play offense and defense.

Brits take their sick children to paediatricians, while Americans keep things slightly more modern with their pediatricians.

The British like to add unnecessary l's before the suffixes of certain words. In England, they will write that the traveller cancelled their trip to the beach, not that the traveler canceled.

You could ask that same traveler where they would have leapt or dived into the water if they come from the U.K., and where they would have leaped or dove if they are from the U.S., as they might not agree on irregular past conjugations.

Americans move toward or backward, while Britons move towards or backwards.

Americans are more inclined to end verbs with -ize or -yze, while the British are more likely to use -ise or -yse. So, while you can recognize or realize this fact in the United States, you would recognise or realise the same in the United Kingdom. Because not all verbs spelled this way share the same Greek origin from which this practice derives, some exceptions remain the same in both spellings. Whether you are in the U.S. or U.K., you can still despise to circumcise your baby without changing a letter (although, surgical statistics would suggest the British despise it somewhat more than Americans).

Punctuation Faux Pas

On top of minor spelling anomalies, we must also worry about the little non-letter marks we place within and between our words to give them structure.

Punctuation plays a large part in dictating the speed and voice of a passage of text even when we read silently in our heads we apply speech patterns to words beginnings middles and endings of sentences and phrases feel different to us reading a passage of text without punctuation is like reading a music score without rests or measures it is a futile attempt to organize the meaning of words and phrases without the appropriate containers to hold them.

Whew. Still with me?

You must learn the roles of each manner of punctuating a sentence if you wish to amplify the meaning and enhance the organization of your message.

Commas

Commas play a vital role in showing the reader when parts of a sentence are connected or independent. Although it takes a great amount of effort to ensure you are using commas consistently through the full text of your draft, their functions are worth learning. There are times where commas are required for clear communication, times where they are optional (but often preferable), and times where they cannot be used at all.

- Commas, which act like parentheses to isolate secondary parts of a sentence from the rest, help the reader identify the main point and most important parts of a sentence.

- Commas that act like parentheses to isolate secondary parts of a sentence from the rest help the reader identify the main point and most important parts of a sentence.

In the first example, the information that commas act like parentheses is displayed as an afterthought or optional piece of information not integral to the point of the sentence. In the second example, acting like parentheses can become a vital qualifier to the conclusion of identifying the most important parts of a sentence. The meanings are similar, but distinct because of the comma placement.

- A writer can determine which elements of a message appear first in a sentence through the use of commas.

- Through the use of commas, a writer can determine which elements of a message appear first in a sentence.

Which version of this sentence is superior? There is a value declaration made by an author whenever they choose which aspects of their sentence should appear first. In the first sentence, the author is implying that a writer being able to determine the order of elements in a message is more important than the use of commas. In the second sentence, the author is implying that the use of commas is more important than a writer being able to determine which elements appear first in a sentence. These and many other authorial choices subtly shape the meaning of a message and display the creator's personality.

There is still debate about the necessity of the inclusion of a comma before the final item in a list, known as either the serial comma or Oxford comma. Following the principle of Occam's Razor, the simplest practice is the best practice. To my knowledge, a convincing argument has never been made to change the rule and exempt the final item from comma separation. Doing so can obscure the meaning of a sentence, such as making the final two items appear as one item joined by a conjunction or even as a description of the item that preceded them. The future belongs to authors who appreciate the Oxford comma.

Writers who are too eager about their comma use may inadvertently use them where a period or semicolon would rightfully belong. To separate two complete sentences with a comma (instead of making each its own sentence) is known as comma splicing. All it succeeds in doing is creating a run-on sentence that will stand out as flawed to keen eyes. To fix comma splicing, you can split the sentence in two or add a conjunction such as "and" immediately after the comma. The inverse error, omitting a comma when two complete sentences are joined into one by a conjunction, is just as common.

Semicolons

A semicolon is a temptuous thing. Placed correctly, it's extremely satisfying for both author and reader. Placed incorrectly, it's an awkward reminder of the author's ignorance and a distraction from their prose. If you aren't super clear on how and why to use semicolons, it's probably best to ignore them.

A simple way to think of semicolons is somewhere in between a comma and a period. They indicate a breaking apart of mostly separate ideas, independent enough to stand on their own but related enough to stay connected. If you have two complete sentences in sequence and the second is a continuation of the first, it *might* be appropriate to connect them with a semicolon instead of keeping them separate with a period. Of course, you could also use a comma and conjunction of some kind to make them work as just a single sentence of multiple clauses.

You can also use semicolons with commas in a manner analogous to how brackets are used with parentheses. You can list a series of items with semicolons and then a comma within an item in the series so that you can elaborate on or modify it. If that sounds too complicated, do yourself a favor and steer clear of semicolons in your first book.

Hyphens and Dashes

Hyphens are versatile little tools for writers, but (as with commas) their versatility is precisely what makes them so difficult to remember how to use correctly. I'll save you the trouble of trying to remember all the rules endorsed by style manuals and grammarians. If inserting a hyphen will improve the clarity of your writing, do it. This guideline will most often come into play with compound adjectives (combining an adjective with another word to create a sort of super adjective) placed before the nouns they describe.

Why is "backyard" one word and "front yard" two words? Who knows? Perhaps backyards come up in speech and writing often enough to have made the jump to a single label and front yards have yet to receive the same upgrade in stature. To complicate the matter, it's sometimes considered acceptable to write "back yard" as two words when used as either a noun or adjective. You can even hyphenate the term when using it as an adjective, as in "back-yard garden."

You've probably also heard of the differences between en dashes and em dashes, both of which are often mistaken for hyphens and vice versa. The en dash (so named because it runs the length of a lowercase letter n) can be used to denote a range of things between two defined limits (e.g., "January–June 2016" or "Monday–Friday"). The em dash—so named because it runs the length of a lowercase letter m—can be used like commas, parentheses, or colons to offset clauses you want to stand out in a sentence. With both styles of dash, there should be no spaces between the dash and the words on either side of it.

Apostrophes

Apostrophes denote possession and contractions, either the ownership of a thing or the combining of two words into one.

When you make a singular noun ending in the letter "s" possessive, you can either add an apostrophe or an apostrophe plus another "s." Whichever approach you choose, you should remain consistent with it throughout your book.

"Its" is possessive. "It's" is a contraction of "it is" or "it has." No one knows why. Embrace the anarchy and move on with your life.

Sometimes an apostrophe is optional. A word that might work as possessive could also be a plural adjective. A farmers' market is a market possessed by farmers. A farmers market is a market containing the quality of farmers. Both meanings could be considered valid for the same intended purpose, though you should never use an apostrophe to make a noun plural (as the designers of many storefronts and restaurant menus seem to believe they should).

Quotation Marks

Place periods and commas inside quotation marks instead of outside ("Like this," instead of "like this".). For other punctuation like dashes, colons, and semicolons, place them outside the quotation marks. For question and exclamation marks, context determines where they go.

Capitalize a quotation if it's a complete sentence.

Use single quotation marks to denote quotations within quotations.

Use quotations around a term to indicate you are talking about the term itself, not what the term means (as I have done many times throughout this chapter). You can also use scare quotes to indicate that you are using a term ironically or that you disagree with its conventional meaning.

Question and Exclamation Marks

Question marks and exclamation marks are generally straightforward in their use, but creative writers still find ways to mess them up.

Are you the type of author who has fallen into the habit of putting two question marks in a row for emphasis?? Such a practice does nothing more than make you look silly to your readers, as though you were unaware you had left your finger pressed down a moment too long on your keyboard. In approximately 99% of cases where expressive terminal punctuation is called for, a single question mark or exclamation mark will suffice. If the extra emphasis is vital to your communication, three of the same mark in sequence (??? or !!!), no more and no less, will convey the intended importance (though superior wording or bold formatting might accomplish the same function in a less jarring way)!!!

Occasionally, the need may arise to combine a question mark with an exclamation mark, either when exclaiming a question (?!) or questioning an exclamation (!?). If you're feeling particularly innovative, you can try to slip the rare combination-question-and-exclamation mark known as the interrobang (‽). You may just confuse readers more than anything else with this approach, however.

Handing Your Draft over to Professional Pedants

There's no getting around the brutal truth of proofreading: for many writers, it's the most tedious and mind-numbing part of creating a book. Hunting down every single errant punctuation mark or incorrect spelling convention in a long draft will take many hours of your time. You will strain yourself staring at the details, even with the aid of spelling- and grammar-checking software to point out the obvious mistakes for your fallible human eyes. One small concession is that modern word processors have "find and replace" features that will allow you to correct every instance of a specific mistake in a document with a few inputs, but only as long as you can identify every mistake you've made.

Fortunately, you don't have to subject yourself to the full hardship of proofreading on your own. There are many reasons you might feel more comfortable hiring a professional editor or proofreader to manage the tedium of revision in your stead. You may simply be too busy with the demands of your life or profession and you deem it not an equitable use of your time. You may lack confidence in your opinion on what warrants revising. You want an expert's eye to ensure your book fits the standards of quality readers expect from traditionally published books (at least for your first publication).

Hiring a professional isn't a statement on how adept you are as a writer or how worthy your message is. Even the most accomplished writers turn to professional editors (often ones provided by their publishing houses) to ensure their books are in their finest forms before they reach readers. The authors who forego professionals, choosing to rely on themselves or the input of friends, will still need to rethink, restructure, and rewrite much more than they presume. When they are too close to the work, they fall into the habit of seeing only what something is supposed to say and not what it actually says.

Finding the right editor(s) and proofreader(s) to work with can be complicated, however. The job requires more than a firm grasp of the English language and a passing familiarity with the prose of Bill Shakespeare. A professional editor should intimately know the standards expected of traditionally published books as they apply to structure, style, grammar, and punctuation. It's not always easy for a new author to evaluate these qualities in someone else, especially if you are not well-versed in them yourself. Some editors get certified through organizations by demonstrating their knowledge.

Beyond knowledge of the conventions of the medium, your editor should be one who has shown a clear understanding of your voice and the intention behind your message. Otherwise, their revisions will just move you further from your goal instead of closer toward it. A bad editor will superimpose their values onto yours instead of trying to help bring yours to life through your work. Often, what appears to be a mistake or bad writing depends on the context of the author's intention. Your editor cannot help you get where you are going if they don't know where that is.

The type and quantity of professional experience the professionals that you hire have will matter. For good developmental editing, they need to be familiar enough with your subject matter to understand the progression of your concepts and whether you are covering everything necessary for comprehension. For good line editing, they need to know how your intended audience will respond to the many possible ways of phrasing the same things. For good copyediting or proofreading, they will need a perfectionist's eye and to be intimately familiar with the guidelines of *The Chicago Manual of Style* (or whatever style guide they follow).

Sometimes what an editor or proofreader catches in your work will be what you expected. You probably have many little doubts about your work before you hand it off but aren't confident enough to act on them. Hearing someone else who is "qualified" call out the same things you suspected will validate your feelings. You won't argue when you hear these issues brought up, so revision will be swift and easy. Your hired gun will probably also call out things you would never have considered necessary to improve in your draft. Some of these corrections will seem reasonable to you. Some will hurt your ego. You might sometimes agree with an editor's assessment that something is wrong, but you might disagree about the best way to fix it.

As when working with beta readers to refine your draft, it is best not to react impulsively to professional revisions you were not expecting. After mulling upon them, you may come to agree with many and still reject some others. No matter how skilled or experienced your editor or proofreader, you still hold veto power over your work. You mustn't be afraid to disagree with the expert you hire to fix your errors, yet you must still remain open enough to consider their wisdom. A good editor should be able to explain the reasoning behind their critiques, so don't be afraid to ask.

While some things like grammar are supposed to be absolute and inviolable, most stylistic changes are a matter of subjective preference and momentary interpretation. Even an editor with more experience in book production than you can hold invalid interpretations because they don't understand your message the way you do. The subject matter might be far beyond them or they may simply be biased against the values you support in your work. Learn to accept and reject criticism with poise and perspective.

It's always easier to leave things as they are than to consider how altering your structure or style might improve your message, while also necessitating other changes throughout the draft. If you accept the suggestion to delete or reorder large passages, it will affect other references you may have made before or after the deleted passage. Areas that were densely populated with content before might now be too short to justify their inclusion. After editing, you will either have to expand them with better content, integrate what remains of them into other sections, or remove them completely. The cascading effects of one change can be numerous, but necessary. Resist the inertia of laziness.

Whenever I've edited or proofread other authors' drafts, I've had to take it upon myself to learn their mindsets. If I don't understand where they were coming from when they wrote, including elements of their professional brand identity, personal biases, intended audiences, and communication preferences, I run the risk of overruling important parts of their messages. Good editing is as much about developing a fluid working relationship with an author as it is about understanding good writing and traditional book conventions. I advise authors to edit and proofread their own work as much as they can before turning to any form of professional assistance.

Even when you've poured everything you've got into your work, you should still reach out for help in whatever forms you are comfortable with. You need someone to spot your errors, whether they be developmental or grammatical in nature, because it is difficult to see your own words as they actually appear when you have grown accustomed to the ideal version of the text you hold in your mind. You easily skim over passages of your writing and tell yourself you see things that are not necessarily there, or else you selectively ignore things that are really there. Someone else will be better equipped to perform this vital function because they will lack the expectation of what your words ought to be. Even if you end up rejecting most professional suggestions, the perspective they provide should open your eyes to other ways you could present your message. The input might also give you greater confidence in your writing.

When you've finally refined your message to the point where it embodies the standards required by modern book readers and sellers, you can shift your focus to the many ways it will be represented on the open market. You can think about the overall impression you will create well before anyone actually gets to the point of digesting every paragraph, sentence, word, or comma.

Summary of Chapter 8

While grammar, punctuation, and spelling matter for the quality and experience of reading your book, there are many antiquated rules you do not need to worry about following if they inhibit your ability to express yourself the way you want. You can split infinitives, begin sentences with conjunctions or end them with prepositions, or even invent new words if doing so adds to your style and meaning. You can get away with a lot so long as you understand the immutable patterns of English composition.

— — — —

There is a long list of common spelling and punctuation errors committed by amateur authors who skimp on editing and proofreading. The societal prevalence of mistakes like misplaced apostrophes or combining different English spelling variants among common writing in society makes it easy to overlook them in your own work before proceeding with publication, but they will still affect your book's reception.

— — — —

If you decide to turn your editing and proofreading over to professionals, you'll need to hire ones with the correct type of experience for your needs. You'll need to find ones who understand the subject and intent of your book and won't try to overwrite your personality with their own. Just as it is with dealing with beta reader feedback, you will need to determine which corrections and pieces of advice are relevant for your work and which to ignore.

PART 5:

PRESENTATION

CHAPTER 9:

Book Appearance and First Impressions

Congratulations. You're entering the home stretch of bringing your message to the world in the form of a book that is as clear as it as attractive. Everything that follows from here relates to packaging and promoting your book in its optimal format for reach and transmission. On the surface, tailoring your book's appearance seems simple compared to the cognition-wracking war of writing and editing you've already endured. Don't get cocky just yet. There are countless mistakes you can make here that may sabotage your book's reception, so you must take these tasks seriously.

The title, cover, and description are the first things readers will see about your book. These elements are so concentrated and important that the consequences of errors within them are magnified. A poor wording choice in the title, ugly color combination on the cover, or typo in the description can prevent thousands of sales from happening. It may not seem fair that such small details can determine the life and death of your book, but there's no getting around the need for good presentation. The acts of buying, reading, and recommending your book all depend on how readers respond to their first impressions.

In the domain of marketing, the process of prospects becoming paying customers is called conversion. Without the ability to convert non-readers into readers, nothing else about your book gets a chance to matter. If people don't want to pick up your book and look inside, none of the words you've drafted will be read. Your meaning will have no chance to influence.

Good presentation makes the crucial conversion possible. Imagery is the catalyst for influence, as a buyer's decision to spend money can be made in moments of intrigue, not hours of careful study.

Because online shopping is so convenient, buyers often assess the merits of many similar books simultaneously. They buy the ones that, at the moment of analysis, seem to suit their interests and address their concerns the most. If your book is presented the same as or worse than every other book, readers will have no reason to pick yours. Shoppers will also turn to other indicators of quality, like the number of positive reviews or a high category ranking, to make their choices for them—but you cannot control these other factors as precisely as you can control your book's title, cover, and description.

In these chapters, you will come to see that creating and refining a meaningful message was only the middle of your journey as an influential author. Your role will now shift from writer and editor to designer and marketer. This is where the publishing part of self-publishing really begins. The image of your message will impress an urgent desire upon the right readers to buy, read, retain, and spread your book. Optimizing your book's presentation is an investment that will pay off with greater sales, readership, and influence for the lifetime of your book.

Choosing the Most Effective Title and Subtitle

It seems unfair that an author can spend more time and incur greater stress while crafting the perfect title and subtitle than they do while writing entire chapters. Because titles are limited to so few words, the influence of every syllable must be carefully considered. Adding or removing a single word can affect how attractive and saleable the book appears. If you phrase something in a less-than-optimal way, you might ruin the title's memorability. If you try to stuff in too many keywords to appeal to search algorithms, you will make your title ugly for human shoppers.

It's not an exaggeration to say that a book's title and subtitle are two of the most important factors for its commercial success. The title is the primary means by which readers will share the existence of your book with others. It must contain enough accurate, specific, and attractive information to be effective. Think carefully about the purpose of your book and how it could be conveyed in just a few short phrases. Under most online or in-person browsing conditions, you may have fewer than 10 seconds to catch and hold interest. The perfect title and subtitle combination just might be the hook that keeps a browser around and convinces them to move forward with a purchase.

A great nonfiction title doesn't just say what's in the book. It invokes selective curiosity from a certain type of person by informing them about the book's practical benefits and the ways it will accomplish them. Newbie authors often want their work to carry an important-sounding, hyper-creative, often cutesy label. That's how they want the world to know them and their work. But too much elegance in what should be a simple and straightforward title obscures the meaning of a book. The fancy phrase you think captures your message might be lost on other people who don't hold the same insider perspective and associations as you.

Fiction titling requires different strategies than nonfiction titling because its readers are typically in a different buying mentality. They read to open their imaginations, excite their emotions, and get lost in wonder. Readers of nonfiction typically want to think deeply, refine their knowledge, improve their abilities, learn useful skills, and resolve problems. The more prescriptive your message, the clearer its presentation should be. Clarity creates sales (though a nonfiction book that encroaches into narrative or philosophical territory might adopt some of the same qualities as fiction).

An effective nonfiction title and subtitle combination should:

- Contain the most commonly searched keywords related to the book's message.
- Sound pleasant and easy to say out loud.

- Stick in the memory.
- Paint a clear picture of the book's tone and subject.
- Be free of obscure or esoteric jargon (unless the book is targeting obscure or esoteric readers).
- State or imply what kind of readers the book is written for.
- Not be easily confused for the name of another creative work.
- Incite curiosity and intrigue from the book's target audience.

While there are plenty of fallback titling gimmicks made popular by famous authors, they are not always appropriate for the first-time self-publisher. Many authors name their books after popular sayings or quotes, or they riff on other book titles to get attention. While often attractive and memorable, these types of titles don't always reveal anything important about the content or tone of the book. They rely on external context to be meaningful or recognizable to buyers. They don't stand out well enough in isolation to create conversions.

Single-Word Titles

Authors hoping for their books to become synonymous with popular concepts might opt for one-word, impactful titles:

- *Color: A Natural History of the Palette* by Victoria Finlay
- *Contagious: Why Things Catch On* by Jonah Berger
- *Flow: The Psychology of Optimal Experience* by Mihaly Csikszentmihalyi
- *Krakatoa: The Day the World Exploded: August 27, 1883* by Simon Winchester
- *Outliers: The Story of Success* by Malcolm Gladwell
- *Positioning: The Battle for Your Mind* by Al Ries and Jack Trout
- *Salt: A World History* by Mark Kurlansky
- *Vagabonding: An Uncommon Guide to the Art of Long-Term World Travel* by Rolf Potts

One-word titles like these can be powerful and authoritative approaches under the right circumstances. However, it's not a tactic I recommend for most new authors who lack the budget or ability to acquire mass exposure. Ultra-short titles run the risk of having their meaning lost in the obscurity of brevity. They work well for tightly defined and easily categorized subjects where the chance for misinterpretation is low, especially if there isn't much competition from other books on the same subject. It also helps if publishers know they can get the book in front of enough eyes to make the mental association they are seeking.

Books with one-word titles often rely on their subtitles or author reputation to provide details about their contents. After all, if an author is already successful and maintains a large following around a given niche, it might hardly matter what they choose to call their next book. The author's fans will read it anyway, and some of that association will naturally spill over to new fans just through word-of-mouth and repeated exposure. For your first book, where you cannot safely assume these external factors will apply, it's safer to err on the side of detail and exposition in your title. This is true even if it seems a single word is enough to denote the subject of your book, such as the case might be with certain places, people, or historical events.

Cookie-Cutter Guides

Another overdone titling approach is to call a book some variety of a guide and let readers determine what that entails. For my money, the world has enough "ultimate guides," "beginner's guides," "quick guides," "complete guides," and so forth about almost every subject you can imagine. You'd think that by now authors would be coming up with more original ways to describe their guides. There's nothing necessarily wrong with a "how to" titling approach or calling something a "10-step plan" to whatever. These types of titles are shown to be very effective under the right conditions. They just paint books in a certain light that might cause them to be viewed poorly by readers wanting greater depth or originality. Decide how user-friendly you want your title to be, as that will set readers' expectations for the scope and tone of its content.

Your book's title is a manifestation of the position you desire your book to hold in the market as a whole and within Amazon's ecosystem. It defines the first impression of your message for unfamiliar readers. Your title should, therefore, manage to tastefully summarize what your book does, how it does it, who it does it for, and (if there is enough space left) why it all matters. You just need to be careful not to do this in a vague or clichéd way that could apply to any other book on any subject. Bold and unique claims will draw attention and increase memorability, so long as they are worded in a way that can be believed.

When professor Jordan B. Peterson published his wildly successful self-help book, *12 Rules for Life: An Antidote to Chaos*, he (or his publisher) eschewed conventional wording. He could have fallen back on a more conventional and exciting title like *How to a Live a Great Life in 12 Easy Steps: The Ultimate Guide to Getting Rid of Chaos So You Can Live the Life of Your Dreams!*, but he wisely chose not to. How do you think a title like this would have affected the book's reception? Would readers have expected it to be more or less original? Deeper or shallower in content? Fluffier or more grounded in tone? Unique or rehashed advice?

Title Pools

Begin collecting words and phrases related to your subject that seem catchy and meaningful while you draft and revise your content. These could be adjectives you think fit your tone and outcome in a unique way. They could be an action your reader should associate with your book. They could be a description of the type of person who should read it. List every conceivable benefit readers stand to gain from your book. The more unique and powerful, the better. You've probably seen dozens of book titles that promise to help you "take back your freedom," "be happy," "live the life of your dreams," or "get the results you want." These fail to convey compelling value because they don't offer discerning buyers anything meaningful. They don't make it past a skeptical mind's defenses.

While brainstorming title and subtitle ideas for *The Influential Author*, I had a list of words and phrases that looked something like this:

- write a book that matters
- meaningful authorship
- write, publish, and sell your message
- important book
- spreading your philosophy
- write to make an impact
- share your message
- impact through authorship
- write a book and change the world
- your message deserves to be known
- publish something meaningful
- change the world with a book
- publish your ideas / philosophy / message / legacy
- a deeper / more philosophical approach
- nonfiction that makes a difference

The difficult part was figuring out which of these and other concepts would be most relevant to what my buyers were searching for, clearly communicate the purpose of the book, and create a yearning to know more. Then I had to decide which terms to include in the main title, which to relegate to the subtitle, and even in what order they should appear for optimal flow and memorability. The possible ways to arrange even a limited number of terms is large, and the effects on sales and influence are larger.

Aside from the intuitive appeal to readers, there is the matter of appealing to Amazon, Google, and other online databases. Getting your book's title to rank for search terms on Amazon is similar to common Google SEO, but also distinct. Amazon has its own search engine, exclusive to the products it sells. This engine can be segregated into categories of items its store carries, like Computers, Luxury Beauty, and Musical Instruments. With Amazon keywords, you can assume that searchers are there to make a purchase within the category they have selected (such as Books or Kindle Store). The products that appear when you search for a term on Amazon are those that have been shown to sell well when other buyers have searched for the same thing.

Use this market data to learn what terms to incorporate into your book's title and description. It is easy to see if terms are competitive or uncompetitive by the number of books that appear when you search them (as well as how many reviews the books tend to have and how they are performing in Amazon's Best Seller Ranking system). If you can identify terms that don't have much viable competition, you can surmise that you may be able to get your book to appear on the first page of their results (maybe even in the top spot).

Amazon's search bar will automatically suggest similar, commonly searched phrases. You can reverse engineer this feature to conduct market research and brainstorm more terms within Amazon's Book category. For the guide-type books I have produced, I have aimed to make the titles and subtitles clear, informative, and keyword-laden without appearing forced. I wanted the names alone to be enough to drive sales.

For Olivier Wagner's tax book, *U.S. Taxes for Worldly Americans: The Traveling Expat's Guide to Living, Working, and Staying Tax Compliant Abroad*, market testing showed that this specific combination of adjectives, verbs, and nouns was the most informative and attractive for our target audiences. Olivier and I believe the title and subtitle combination is one of the primary reasons the book continues to sell well years after publication compared to other tax books with short, dull, and vague titles.

The tax title may seem a little boring, but there is no doubt about what you will learn if you read it. The way it's worded displays the specific value of the content and qualifies who should be reading it to receive that value. No one should be interested in reading *U.S. Taxes for Worldly Americans* unless they identify as a "worldly American" or "traveling expat" who "lives or works abroad" and needs to "stay tax compliant." If you are not this type of person, you will not receive the full intended value of the book. When the right person reads the title, they will know the book is meant for them.

Unconvincing Repetition

Countless successful books have been published with extremely short and vague titles, but that doesn't mean following this trend with your title will produce the same results. They are also often followed by simplistic subtitles like "A Memoir" that provide little insight about the tone or content within. Without additional presentation elements like cover design, author notoriety, media exposure, descriptions, or reader reviews, there are few means by which to differentiate these books. There is no compelling reason to buy one over another:

- *Boy Erased: A Memoir* by Garrard Conley
- *Drunk Mom: A Memoir* by Jowita Bydlowska
- *Elena Vanishing: A Memoir* by Elena Dunkle and Clare B. Dunkle
- *Garbage Bag Suitcase: A Memoir* by Shenandoah Chefalo
- *The Glass Castle: A Memoir* by Jeannette Walls
- *The Invisible Girls: A Memoir* by Sarah Thebarge
- *Real American: A Memoir* by Julie Lythcott-Haims
- *Three Little Words: A Memoir* by Ashley Rhodes-Courter
- *Welcome Home: A Memoir* by Jude Ezeilo

Some authors, perhaps recognizing the weaknesses of this titling approach (but not wanting to deviate too far from convention), add minor differentiating details to let readers know what type of memoir to expect. These work slightly better because they prompt inquiry from book browsers, possibly leading to more purchases:

- *Between Breaths: A Memoir of Panic and Addiction* by Elizabeth Vargas
- *The Bright Hour: A Memoir of Living and Dying* by Nina Riggs
- *The Electric Woman: A Memoir in Death-Defying Acts* by Tessa Fontaine
- *Hillbilly Elegy: A Memoir of a Family and Culture in Crisis* by J.D. Vance
- *I'm Just Happy to Be Here: A Memoir of Renegade Mothering* by Janelle Hanchett
- *A Long Way Gone: Memoirs of a Boy Soldier* by Ishmael Beah
- *My Fair Junkie: A Memoir of Getting Dirty and Staying Clean* by Amy Dresner
- *On Writing: A Memoir of the Craft* by Stephen King
- *Shoe Dog: A Memoir by the Creator of Nike* by Phil Knight

Notice how much easier it is to tell what the experience of reading these books will be like due to the additional details provided in their subtitles. Though, while an improvement, they still don't offer as much about the content and tone of the book as nonfiction titles could. First-time authors who aren't Stephen King or the creator of Nike will not be able to get away as easily with such basic labels. A longer title offers the opportunity to increase clarity and incite curiosity. The most influential and informative titles are those that do not waste the precious Real Estate each word offers. They avoid vague phrasings that don't add anything useful:

- *Bad Choices Make Good Stories: Going to New York: How The Great American Opioid Closet Epidemic of The 21st Century Began* by Oliver Markus Malloy
- *Breaking Night: A Memoir of Forgiveness, Survival, and My Journey from Homeless to Harvard* by Liz Murray
- *Fear and Loathing in Las Vegas: A Savage Journey to the Heart of the American Dream* by Hunter S. Thompson
- *Memoirs of an Addicted Brain: A Neuroscientist Examines his Former Life on Drugs* by Marc Lewis
- *Memoirs of a Surgeon's Wife: I'm Throwing Your Damn Pager into the Ocean* by Megan Sharma

These titles demonstrate more convincing arguments for purchase than alternatives published with brevity or poetry as their priority. They have been written with marketing (not solely artistry) in mind. When these details are complemented by strategic search terms, the title and subtitle of a book work as powerful sales assets. They ensure that a book will always receive some readership, even if the rest of its presentation and promotion are lacking.

Concise Main Titles

No matter the subject of a book, its main title should be short enough to display in large print on a book's cover. It will need to be easy to read in many contexts and sizes, as the cover will be displayed across Amazon and the rest of the internet. A short main title will also be easier to say and remember, contributing to word-of-mouth virality. A longer subtitle offers the opportunity to expound upon the value promise of the main title. In the subtitle, you can list the categories of information the book contains, instantly answering many questions a reader might have about what they will learn inside.

To construct my main titles, I look for 3-5 words from my brainstormed list of meaningful phrases and search terms that summarize the process, outcome, or meaning of a book. I try to accomplish this using rhyming, alliteration, or a play on a popular phrase whenever I can without it feeling forced for my audience. The broader your book's purpose, the harder it will be to summarize within its short main title.

Short and effective main titles include:

- *The 7 Day Startup*
- *Chicken Soup for the Soul*
- *Eat, Pray, Love*
- *The Elements of Style*
- *The End of Jobs*
- *Everything Men Know about Women*
- *The Feminine Mystique*

- *Guns, Germs, and Steel*
- *How to Change Your Mind*
- *Man's Search for Meaning*
- *Maps of Meaning*
- *Never Split the Difference*
- *The Plant Paradox*

Employing these principles, I narrowed my main title possibilities for the book you are reading to three similar but distinct choices:

1. *The Impactful Author*
2. *The Effective Author*
3. *The Influential Author*

I had plenty of my own ideas about what the best choice would be according to which adjective fit the content and tone of the book, sounded the best when spoken aloud, and was most memorable. I wisely realized I couldn't finalize such an important facet of my book's presentation on my own, so I resorted to several rounds of market testing that revealed some unexpected truths.

First, I learned that the public reception of the word "impactful" was all over the map. There exists a vocal community of language snobs who consider "impactful" to be a redundant derivative of "influential" and "effective" that some marketing guru likely dreamed up in the 60s to make his company sound important. I had no idea this perception existed. In my mind, impact, effect, and influence are three distinct things. I considered ignoring what seemed to me like a faulty language bias but knew it wasn't worth risking sales or positive reception of my title just to stick with a word out of principle. I knew that if I titled my book *The Impactful Author* that I would offend enough people to make the launch into the market measurably more difficult.

From there, determining this book's title was simply a matter of figuring out which option, *The Effective Author* or *The Influential Author*, generated the most interest and would induce more clicks and sales from my audience.

Repeated testing showed about an 80% preference for "influential," so the choice was clear.

Elaborate Subtitles

For my subtitles, I want approximately 7-15 words that expand the promises, themes, methodologies, audiences, and/or outcomes of the book. Depending on the tone of a book, its subtitle can have a hands-off "how to" approach, a direct command or promise for the reader, an introductory statement about the book's perspective, or foreshadowing for something important to come. The extended length of the subtitle also offers the opportunity to include more searchable keywords without sounding stuffed or unnatural.

For most nonfiction books, the subtitle is a manifestation of what marketers call a positioning statement. Any product on the market can be framed as that it "does X to accomplish Y" (sometimes with the addition of "in a Z way" to add more uniqueness to its image). In other words, a positioning statement reveals the compelling features of a product and the benefit they create. What does your book do and what outcome will it create for your readers?

Detailed and effective subtitles include:

- *Artificial Intelligence and the End of the Human Era*
- *The Hidden Dangers in "Healthy" Foods That Cause Disease and Weight Gain*
- *How to Use Advanced Learning Strategies to Learn Faster, Remember More and be More Productive*
- *One Woman's Search for Everything Across Italy, India and Indonesia*
- *Ten Reasons We're Wrong About the World--and Why Things Are Better Than You Think*
- *The Surprising Science Behind Why Everything You Know About Success Is (Mostly) Wrong*

- *What the New Science of Psychedelics Teaches Us About Consciousness, Dying, Addiction, Depression, and Transcendence*
- *What The Rich Teach Their Kids About Money - That The Poor And Middle Class Do Not!*

For unknown authors who cannot rely on mass exposure or prior associations, titles and subtitles should drive sales independently of external factors they cannot control. If the only perceptible difference between two books is how clear their titles are, the less ambiguous one will win the purchase. You are wise to avoid some of the more obscure titling approaches of traditionally published books, even if those books happen to be successful in the market. All this, of course, depends on your readers being the type of people who appreciate detail and specificity, instead of instant promises of some large and vague concept of value.

For the subtitle of *The Influential Author*, it was clear to me that I would need to include certain specifics about what the book covered (such as its relevance for the separate acts of writing, publishing, and selling books). I also knew I would need to add some modifiers that targeted readers only interested in being a certain type of author, which meant excluding fiction writers and anyone looking for just another guide to quick and easy self-publishing. I had to find that crucial balance between making it clear what kind of book I had written but also standing apart from the many, many other options on this topic.

The word "nonfiction" obviously had to be included somewhere. I struggled with the right way to phrase my conception of the type of book prospective authors should be interested in writing in order to get the full value of my words here. My ideas included "meaningful books," "important books," "remarkable nonfiction," and "books that make a difference." Lastly, I needed to somehow point out what was unique about my approach to covering the subject of nonfiction authorship.

I considered using lengthy and intimidating modifiers like "a deeper approach to" and "the philosophy of," but these sounded too off-putting to be one of the first things shoppers see on my book. I knew I had to be more inviting and guide them into the deep content within, but still not sound like every other generic self-publishing book.

Then one morning while I was showering, the simple solution came to me. If nearly everyone else was using some variation of a "how to" titling approach, why not just tweak things slightly and add a hint of more depth by making mine a "how and why to" title? After more rounds of market testing and confirmation, I ended up with the combination title and subtitle I am using now, *The Influential Author: How and Why to Write, Publish, and Sell Nonfiction Books that Matter.* This subtitle includes the unique elements of what the book does, how it does it, and whom it does it for—all without taking up too much space or appearing too confusing for casual browsers.

Title Testing

Like every other area of your book's presentation, you shouldn't trust solely your own opinion about the title and subtitle. You are too familiar with the implied meaning of your tentative title to be objective about its reception. You cannot isolate its wording from your background knowledge. The most basic title test you can perform is to ask people, without further prompt or context, what they think your book is about when they hear or read its prospective title. Their responses might be different than you expect. They might have a different interpretation of the tone or intended audience. Repeat simple title tests like this with your beta readers and other people who fit your target readership. Eventually, you will find unity between intention and interpretation.

When you've narrowed down some viable options for titles and subtitles, search them on Google and Amazon to see what other entities might be using a similar combination of words. Although there are no American copyright restrictions for titles, it's a bad idea to publish your book with one already in use for another book, blog, podcast, etc. Doing so creates potential brand confusion. Furthermore, the other entity will have a head start for placement on Google and recognition among consumers. They probably own the .com domain name, which might prove useful for promoting your book. It's also perceived as rude to encroach upon someone else's intellectual property, even if doing so is legal. If the title you want is similar to a name already being used by someone else online, you're probably better off modifying it until the potential for confusion is gone.

For your next rounds of title testing, you can use social media groups and dedicated online forums to create polls among the people who represent your target audiences. Test your favorite title and subtitle combinations among at least one group representing each type of reader you've identified as needing your book. How many distinct target audiences can you anticipate? Where will you find them gathered online?

In the case of Sean Plotkin's book, *Get Bail, Leave Jail: What Every American Needs to Know about Hiring a Bondsman and Getting Released before Trial*, our title testing groups included family members of ex-convicts, criminal defense lawyers, law students, recovering drug addicts, and members of criminal reform movements. Though the author initially had strong opinions about what the title of his book should be, I convinced him its success depended on letting the market speak its mind. Our testing showed all target markets preferred a clear and detailed title over the short, exciting one the author initially suggested. We later relied on these same groups to test a variety of cover designs.

Be aware that this type of testing can be subject to sampling errors that may give you misleading results. Your tests should be repeated as often as possible among the largest, most appropriate groups you can find. If the poll results come back ambiguous or contradictory (perhaps with only a slight preference for one title over another, such as a 60-to-40% split, or each group strongly preferring a different option), you should modify your testing options and try again until a clear preference emerges among all groups.

Choosing Your Ideal Cover Design

Along with a book's title, its cover is often its first point of contact with potential readers. Unavoidably, people judge books by their covers the same way they judge other people by their hair and clothing. Being aware of this, you can think about what kind of visual first impression you want your book to make. Your cover carries the burden of representing the value of your book in an accurate and attractive form. Do not neglect this opportunity to show off your book's meaning and convince readers to look inside.

In self-publishing, book covers (much like book titles) are often sabotaged by overzealous authors who hold deep attachments to their work. These authors have detailed preferences about what their books should look like because certain colors or imagery hold meaningful associations for them. You have to be cautious, especially if you are a creative person, about falling in love with your book cover concept. Accept that you are not creating it for yourself. You already know the value of your book. An unfamiliar reader does not. Your cover is the fastest way to draw their attention and initiate sales and the desire to begin reading.

Notice how quickly and mindlessly you often scroll through Amazon or other online retailers when you shop for books, or even as you walk past the shelves of a bookstore. You unconsciously do the same thing with the "Customers who bought this item also bought" and "Sponsored products related to this item" sections that appear on each book's Amazon listing. Almost instantly, you decide whether you are curious enough about a book cover flashing before you to click on it and investigate it further. Many people will notice a book's cover image before even the title, number of reviews, or average rating.

Title Legibility

To ensure your book's cover design and text send a cohesive message, the title, subtitle, and author name should be displayed in an easy-to-read way. Their meaning should be simple to discern without blending into the graphical elements behind or around them. It is not hard to find books with titles that are practically illegible on their covers. Either the typeface is too fancy, or the words are overlaid on images of similar color, making the letters blend with the background. Covers with this type of problem do not merely fail to convey information; they actively kill any desire to learn more. Your meaningful title may be overlooked because elements of your cover fail to attract the right attention—or, worse, offend your target audience by showing what they consider to be indicators of poor quality.

Consider the somewhat humorous example of fiction author Lisa Jackson, who wrote seven detective novels in her popular *To Die* series, each with a name like *Left to Die, Chosen to Die*, or *Born to Die*. Her book covers all use a similar layout of placing her name in large font at the top, followed by the book title slightly smaller and lower down with a fair amount of space between the two. For most of the books in the *To Die* series, this layout is quite clear and legible. There is obvious differentiation between author name and book title because of sizing, spacing, typeface, color, and grammar.

The title for book six in the *To Die* series, however, is *Deserves to Die*, which wouldn't have been a problem if not for the fact that it is written in the same color and font as the author's name just above it, with little space between the two. The unfortunate combination of design elements and grammatical structure create the illusion that the title of the book is *Lisa Jackson Deserves to Die*, not *Deserves to Die* by author Lisa Jackson.

For fans of the series, this probably isn't an issue that can't be overcome by their familiarity with her work, but it serves to highlight a potential mishap that can occur if you do not pay attention to how your title shows up on your cover. There's a possibility of arranging the words on your cover in such a way that viable readers might not understand what they are seeing at first glance and move on to something else, costing you many sales. Remember that once you go public, the negative effects of every seemingly minor mistake will be amplified many times over.

There is no universal formula for good book cover design, just conventions that are popular in every category. Good art and marketing are matters of personal appeal. Your cover will have different mental associations and emotional connotations for every reader who looks at it, depending on their background and desires. What you can control is whether the primary and commonly shared connotations of your cover are true to the book's content and tone. Like your book's title, its cover should clearly represent the type of content within, the voice you write with, and the type of reader your message is intended for.

Besides the initial impression, think about your cover's long-term influence on your readers. If someone reads and loves your book, it's possible they will feel like sharing a link to it on their social media profile or carrying a copy with them in a public place. These actions will expose your book's cover to their friends and anyone else in their immediate vicinity. Will your cover look like something they will want to keep on their desk or coffee table, displaying it proudly to guests and colleagues? Or will they be embarrassed to be seen reading it on a city bus?

Color Theory

Almost always, the first thing readers notice about a book cover is its dominant colors. Human brains are hardwired to pay attention to color and respond differently to each shade. On most covers, background colors occupy more space than text or graphical elements, so color selection clearly deserves your attention. There are important reasons the colors red and yellow show up often in the branding elements of fast food companies. It's also no accident that products companies intend to be perceived as "natural" are frequently portrayed in a green-toned color scheme. Some color connotations are the products of our evolutionary history. They are universal and unchanging. Others are cultural imprints that vary across nations and generations.

When I published my first book, *Brand Identity Breakthrough: How to Craft Your Company's Unique Story to Make Your Products Irresistible*, I was new to the world of publishing. I didn't understand what would constitute an effective design for its cover. I was, however, well versed in online sales and split testing. Because Amazon allows authors to update the covers on book listings at any time (with changes usually taking less than a day to appear online), I saw an opportunity to test how changing my book cover's color scheme would influence sales.

I initially launched *Brand Identity Breakthrough* with a simple, white cover with large title text at the top and subtitle below it. The author name and a simple business-oriented graphic rested at the bottom. The book received a decent amount of sales at first, already making me a couple thousand dollars per month in royalties from sales of all its formats combined. I was happy with the results but wanted to know if I could improve them. Once the book had been on sale for a few months and sales had stabilized, I tested six new cover designs, each a differently colored variation of the same basic layout. I had my own ideas about which color was best, but I also knew that it was not my opinion that mattered here. What mattered was how the market would respond.

To control for other variables, I didn't change anything else about *Brand Identity Breakthrough*'s promotion during the time I cycled through the new designs. I tested covers done in red, green, orange, yellow, white, and blue for one week each (to account for natural buying variations across different days of the week). The red design showed the clearest indicators of increased interaction from online browsers. In fact, I sold more than twice as many copies across all formats with the red cover than I had been selling with the original white design.

I can't say for sure why red worked better than the other colors, but it's easy to surmise that a bright red rectangle stood out as confident and bold among business books. My shoppers were mostly business people seeking important information from a reliable source. Red works well for branding books because branding is the practice of promoting one's unique existence and standing out from the crowd. The color red, associated with importance and strength, serves this purpose perfectly.

It would be misleading to assume that any book could see an increase in sales simply by adding red to its cover. It doesn't work that way. It depends on context and expectations. Red can be the color of aggression, intimidation, emergency, and conquest. It doesn't function the same for every genre or target audience. It should be used with contextual awareness if you don't want to send the wrong message to your audience about the topic and tone of your book. How red is used in conjunction with other colors will also affect how readers interpret it.

The Same but Different

When you look over the covers of popular books on your subject, there should be some obvious trends in the types of layout and design elements used. The challenge, as always, is figuring out how to match what readers expect your type of book to look like, while also standing out as superior and unique in some important way. Too far in either direction (more of the same or wildly different) will cause you to lose attention and sales.

The more complex the ideas contained in your book, the more difficult it will be to convey them in the limited dimensions of its cover. Adding layers of nuance adds to the amount of care you must put into each subtle new element. Amateur cover designers often try to take up as much space as they can on a cover, sacrificing the clarity of the message with confused and clashing imagery. Err on the side of simplicity for your first book cover. Concentrate on one or two ideas and make them clear. Additional visual details beyond a legible title and one or two complementing elements, more often than not, will hurt your book sales.

There are subtle, yet effective ways to convey deep meaning in a simplistic cover design. My second book intentionally pushed the boundaries of its categorical conventions, and its cover needed to show that. *Travel as Transformation: Conquer the Limits of Culture to Discover Your Own Identity* was a thought-provoking travel memoir that blended travel, philosophy, personal development, and social commentary. I found myself in a conundrum about how to display its exceptional nature to the public without obscuring the point or turning viable readers away.

In *Travel as Transformation*, you won't find a list of the world's best beaches or tips to save on flights and hotels, even though this is what travel readers have come to expect. The book is an account of deep personal discovery through a decade of uninhibited world travel, starting at age 18. For the next 10 years, I wandered nearly 50 countries trying to make sense of the world and my place within it. The book walks a delicate line between personal memoir, practical advice, and spiritual mentorship that I think not many books can pull off.

To showcase *Travel as Transformation's* purpose-driven divergence from conventional travel books on its cover, I went against design trends and avoided clichéd travel imagery (such as luggage, plane tickets, picturesque beaches, and passport stamps). While the book has some elements of adventure and recreation, the real meaning of the book lies in exploring uncomfortable truths and establishing an authentic identity.

After various rounds of cover testing, I chose to use the profile of an introspective, bearded young man as the centerpiece of the design. This image was important to the message of the book, as it represented the personal nature of the journey. Taking the symbolism a step further, my designer repeated the image three times in different shades, blurred into a single transitional image. The result was an eye-catching effect of transformation, conveying the changing nature of the human figure.

To contrast the human-centric foreground of the cover, the designer thought it was best to place a faded map landscape behind the model's profile. The map had an authentic old-world aesthetic, even featuring names of prominent places in their local languages to remove any Anglo or western bias (and to keep with the theme of expanding beyond initial perceptions of the world). The map imagery made it unmistakable that travel was the context in which the human story of transformation would be occurring.

If you're brave enough to produce an unconventional book, explore the subtle ways you can signal to readers that there is something unique going on inside. Don't limit yourself to ordinary, overdone design elements, or your book might seem typical and unappealing. Whenever possible, test your assumptions against real shopper feedback and draw your design conclusions from that data.

Graphic Taste

In arriving at a cover design for Olga Petrenko's unorthodox cookbook, *Intimacy On The Plate: 200+ Aphrodisiac Recipes to Spice Up Your Love Life at Home Tonight*, there were many types of images we could have used to blend its themes of lust and cuisine. Appetite-inducing shots of ingredients, an attractive couple enjoying a romantic meal, or even just a scantily clad woman in a kitchen could all have served the purpose. Yet, however thematically appropriate it was, such imagery would have been unremarkable among other cookbook covers.

Sex has always been an effective tool for grabbing attention in advertising, but it is usually shoehorned into niches where it's neither tasteful nor relevant. In the case of *Intimacy On The Plate*, the author wanted to take a simple, appropriate idea and execute it in an elegant manner. The cover we published featured an image of the world's most famous aphrodisiac, the oyster, arranged to resemble the vulva of a woman's genitalia. This eye-catching design worked well to draw attention to the book's listing on Amazon, yet it didn't contradict the contents of the book.

Choosing a sexual image for the cover was a bold move. There was no guarantee that the market would respond favorably, perhaps being offended or confused by what they saw. Although the cover was certain to get attention, we didn't want empty clicks from non-buyers with no real interest in the content. The goal was increased sales and satisfied readers. With some of the advertising channels we were using to promote the book, the author was paying money for every click made on the ads we ran. We only wanted shoppers to click if there was a good chance they were going to complete a purchase. We had to be sure we could recover the cost-per-click investment of advertising.

We also didn't want the cover of *Intimacy on the Plate* to appear vulgar, which can be a difficult balance to strike with sexual imagery. The professional photo of the oyster with a pearl created a luscious, expensive, and desirable aesthetic that appealed to our target audience. We tested the idea and received positive feedback from our beta readers and social media groups containing samples of our target audiences. We had proof that the cover delivered the message that we had created a tasteful, erotic cookbook with recipes of aphrodisiac foods. It stood out from other cookbooks, but its imprint remained clear and unmistakable.

Whatever the subject of your book, what will it take for the cover to capture its content in a way your target audience will understand at a glance? You will likely need to test several designs against the opinions of qualified readers. Will your cover blend in and disappear among its competition? Will it be so unconventional that it pushes your target audience away? Or will it stand out in an influential way without divorcing itself from its meaning?

You also must consider how your cover will look in a variety of sizes and contexts. Amazon displays book covers at thumbnail size in its search results, category listings, related books, "customers also bought" lists, and sponsored ads. Will your cover still carry the same influence and be legible when it's smaller than a driver's license photo? When a customer visits your listing, they see the cover at about the same dimensions as a credit card turned vertically. Only if they then click on the cover will it be enlarged to full size. Your cover must be intriguing and legible enough, even while tiny, to incite clicks from qualified buyers.

Hiring Design Help

Graphic design is not something the average writer is equipped to do. Unless you are a competent designer with experience marketing to book buyers, you should entrust your cover to professionals. Finding the right designers is a crucial part of producing your book, and managing them well is a skill unto itself. If you are willing to put the increased labor and capital into experimenting with many designers and design concepts, you'll be happier with the final product. If you do your market testing well, you'll also make your cover investment back through increased book sales.

When you hire a graphic designer, you are hiring a creative human being with their own ideas about artistry, professionalism, and subjective interpretations of beauty. These differences can create either synergy or conflict between you two. You will have to communicate with your designer throughout the design process, offering your opinions, testing components, changing color palettes, and more. All these adjustments are best entrusted to somebody in whom you have the confidence to bring your message to life.

The burden is yours to make sure your designer understands the content and purpose of your book. You can do this by sending them a summary or the full text of the book, images of covers you like from similar books, or just briefing them on your personal vision. Experienced designers will have their own design briefs for you to complete, so they will have all the information they need. The final decision about what design to publish is yours, but bear in mind that, while taste is subjective, tried and tested design tactics work for a reason. Your cover designer might know some things worth listening to.

Your designer should know the file submission requirements of the printers and distributors that will produce and sell your book (including Amazon's Kindle Direct Publishing (KDP) for e-books, KDP Print for paperbacks, Audio Creation Exchange (ACX) for audiobooks, IngramSpark for e-book, paperback, and hardcover, and possibly several others). They will need to prepare different versions of your cover for each format of your book, conforming to the standards set by the parties who print or distribute them. Submission requirements can be found on each company's website and are subject to change, but your designer should be prepared for them.

Other decisions like the trim size of the book and number of pages will affect the final forms your cover takes, such as the width of its spine. Your designer will need to come up with a back cover design and spine design that complement the front cover image. They should also know the best way to arrange your back cover description, author bio, author headshot, and any other text elements like endorsements.

Every aspect of the book market is subject to change, including trends in cover design. Every year sees new developments in typography, colors, layouts, and shapes. A modern graphic designer should be familiar with programs like what's included in Adobe's Creative Cloud Suite, such as Photoshop and Illustrator, but this standard could change in the future. It doesn't hurt for you to keep up with these developments, even if you never plan to do any graphical designing yourself. They will also be relevant to much of the presentation of the promotional tactics you employ for your book.

If you aren't in a position to recruit a freelance designer or get referred to one, there are services that enable you to host design contests where many designers will compete to fulfill your requirements. Options like this generally cost more than hiring a single designer but will give you many more options to choose from.

Knowing how heavily the market response to your book cover can affect ongoing sales and royalties, the best strategy may be to hire a designer or several to produce many different designs up front. Then you can test them in controlled online settings for market response, or even months after your book has launched on Amazon by cycling through a different design each week and monitoring the change in response. The hardest part of cover design is simply moving your own preferences out of the way long enough to let the market speak its mind.

I have been fortunate to be able to curate a group of trusted designers who understand the necessary marketing principles behind how their work will be displayed. The designers I work with know that the goal of a good book cover goes far beyond making something that looks pretty or evokes a certain emotion. The woman who designed the cover for *The Influential Author* was savvy enough to test several different ideas to narrow down which would be most appropriate for the book's readership.

Together, she and I discovered that some of the designs she prepared worked better to attract instant attention, while some others did a better job at conveying deep meaning and originality. Each of these qualities was important for different reasons. With such detailed feedback, we eventually arrived at a cover design that combined both kinds of appeal and proceeded to publish the book with it.

Writing Your Book Description

At the start of every online book listing is a brief description that lets readers know what to expect when they buy and read the content inside. The same text will also appear on a book's back cover or the inside flap of its dust jacket. The description functions both as a synopsis and sales pitch for a book and is usually not longer than just a few hundred words. Its role is vital in convincing readers to exchange their money for the chance to read what's inside.

Your book's description will also serve as a sample of your writing that shoppers will use to begin shaping opinions of your style and perspective. Everything that applies regarding editing and proofreading to your book's content applies just the same to its description. Mistakes in spelling, grammar, or punctuation signal to buyers that your book is not a professional publication. The description is seen as indicative of what readers should expect to find on every page within. A single error here can be the cause of hundreds of lost book sales.

Keyword Stuffing

Like your book's title and subtitle, its description should be populated with the search terms you've identified as relevant and uncompetitive, so long as it can be done in a naturally pleasing manner. For Becca Tzigany's spiritual and sexual memoir, *Venus and Her Lover: Transforming Myth, Sexuality, and Ourselves*, the search terms we wanted to target included:

- archetypal psychology
- consciousness science
- feminism
- goddess
- history of sexuality
- integral philosophy
- polyamory
- sacred sex
- soul awakening
- spiritual energy
- spiritual sex
- tantric sex
- transpersonal psychology

For Veronica Kirin's study on the lifestyles of generations of Americans past, *Stories of Elders: What the Greatest Generation Knows about Technology that You Don't*, our keywords included:

- American technology
- American history
- centenarians
- cultural anthropology
- Dust Bowl
- evolution of technology
- Great Depression
- Greatest Generation
- history of technology
- technology and culture
- technology and society
- technology change
- technology growth
- society and technological change
- U.S. history
- United States history

Some terms are easier to incorporate than others into their books' descriptions. A crafty copywriter can always find ways to make the words go where they need them to go without seeming forced. However good of a writer you are, it may be in your best interest to outsource your book description to someone familiar with online marketing and the elements of good sales copy. To ensure their voice doesn't overtake yours, you can provide a rough draft and the list of keywords you want to include. Then you can make touch-ups to the version they craft for you.

Copywriting Best Practices

When amateur authors write their own book descriptions, they often inflate their own importance by making hyperbolic promises, hoping to excite or trick people into clicking Amazon's "Add to Cart" or "Buy now with 1-click" buttons. Overpromising will sabotage a book's public reception at or shortly after release. Projections of grandeur tend to turn off discerning readers and disappoint the small percentage who fall victim to the gambit, causing them to expect one thing and get another. Disappointment leads to canceled purchases, negative press, and long-term marketplace failure.

Once more, there are category conventions to consider for your book description. Look at the descriptions of the most popular books on your subject. Pay attention to commonality in phrasings, style, tone, or other elements. These conventions are how readers have come to expect a book like yours to describe itself. You risk confusing readers if you stray too far from them. People need easy ways to conceptualize the new information they are exposed to, or they quickly abandon trying to evaluate them. When readers are confused by what they read, they click away before investing more time to decipher what a book offers.

Resist the temptation to be too drawn out or innovative in your book's description. Within this short length of words, you can cover the most compelling features and promises of your message. Your description should be laid out in such a way that readers can scan it to get the overall impression or find a specific detail. This is accomplished with short, standalone paragraphs, bullet points, and clear language. Clarity and directness can create more book sales than any other factor.

Opening Hook

Copywriters know that opening lines are often the most important part of a message. If a customer's attention is not captured from the start, the customer is likely to move on to something else. When the first sentences make them want to know what comes next, they will continue reading until their curiosity is satiated. You might start your book description with an important question that will be answered in the course of reading what's inside. You might call attention to a major problem the reader is dealing with. If your book offers strategies or solutions for solving that problem, hint at them to entice the reader.

Examples of opening lines introducing the reasons for a book to exist:

1. Does your business have a story to tell? It should! From the moment you first opened your doors, you began crafting it. With every new product you release, you carve out an even more unique niche in your industry. This all builds up to one thing—brand identity. Does yours stand out from the crowd?

2. Are you a citizen of the United States who lives abroad? You probably know America is one of only two countries that taxes its citizens on their worldwide income, regardless of where they live or work. If you're thinking about becoming a digital nomad or expatriating to another country, do you know how to avoid paying unfair taxes on your income while abroad?

3. When you travel to a foreign land, do you experience this new place as your old self? Or do you become a new version of you?

4. What started the War between the Sexes? When two artists, Becca Tzigany and James Bertrand, began a worldwide investigation into the forbidden history of humanity, they could not have predicted the clues they would uncover across cultures to what holds us back from deep intimacy and spiritual sex. *Venus and Her Lover* is their long-awaited opus.

5. America's Greatest Generation (born before 1945) witnessed incredible changes in technology and social progress. From simple improvements in entertainment to life-changing medical advances, technology changed the way they live, work, and identify. Sadly, with each passing year, fewer members of the Greatest Generation remain alive to share their wisdom as the last Americans to grow up before the digital revolution.

Unique Approach

Once you've introduced why your book and its solutions are needed, you can outline the unique approach it takes to provide those solutions. Include why your book is superior to others (at least for a certain type of reader) so people will know they need to read it, even if they've read others on the same subject. The reader should begin to believe they will be entertained, learn something valuable, and be prompted to take meaningful action… but only if they read your book.

Examples of detailing the unique way a book solves its reader's problems or fulfills its purpose:

1. By combining the right strategies for citizenship, residency, banking, incorporation, and physical presence in other countries, most Americans abroad can legally lower their U.S. tax owing to $0. In *U.S. Taxes for Worldly Americans*, Certified Public Accountant, U.S. immigrant, expat, and perpetual traveler Olivier Wagner shows you how to use 100% legal strategies (beyond traditionally maligned "tax havens") to keep your income and assets safe from the IRS.

2. In 2015, Millennial author and cultural anthropologist Veronica Kirin drove 12,000 miles across more than 40 states to interview the last living members of the Greatest Generation. *Stories of Elders* is the result of her years of work to capture and share their perspective for generations to come.

3. *Stories of Elders* preserves the wisdom, thoughts, humor, knowledge, and advice of the people who make up one of America's finest generations, including the Silent Generation. Their stories include the devastation that came from major events in U.S. history like World War I, the Dust Bowl, the Great Depression, and World War II.

4. By recounting the existential lessons from his journey, Diehl challenges the reader to question how their identity has been shaped by the culture and lifestyle they know. He argues, compellingly, that travel can transform your perception of yourself along with the world. By losing your comfortable sense of self, you learn to examine your life through the structure of everything it can become.

5. Accompany Becca and James behind veils, deep into shadow realms, and through the pleasures of liberation beyond our dominator society. Their two-volume memoir is the result of decades of Tantric sex, meditation journeys, and intellectual scrutiny, which weaves tales of personal struggle, encounters with mythological archetypes, and the ecstasies of sexual union into a powerful new view of our planet in transition.

6. Olga Petrenko is a housewife who dedicated years of her life to crafting original dishes that combine tradition with innovation, creating new tastes that everyone can enjoy. In the process, she discovered something new: by applying scientific research to her recipes and by using the correct ingredients, all meals had the potential to be the perfect aphrodisiac. After a decade of hard work and experimentation, she finally had an extensive collection of recipes designed to make every bite erotic.

With this perspective, it's easy to see that the primary function of your book's description is to advertise, not merely summarize. It does not need to document every little detail about the book. Its purpose is to convert browsers into buyers by generating interest. Because readers have access to a wider range of books now than at any other time in history, you need to give them reasons to read yours. If you've philosophized and strategized amply, you should already be clear on this angle. Your book's uniqueness will be the essence of its hook and something you reference throughout the description.

Poignant Bullet Points

For the benefit of shoppers who skim (i.e., most of them), it is wise to summarize the promises and benefits of your book in a short list of bullet points near the end of its description. If a reader is looking for a specific type of information, this is likely where their eyes will go. Finding a bullet that mentions what they seek may be all that is needed to persuade them to click the buy button. Bullet points also happen to be an excellent place to include additional keywords you were unable to fit naturally into the paragraphs of description that came before.

Examples of bullet points containing a book's benefits:

1. In *Brand Identity Breakthrough*, you will learn...
    *   How to incorporate a unique selling proposition into your branding.
    *   The best methods for selling products to customers as a small business.
    *   How to use business storytelling to sell products in both physical and online marketplaces.

2. Olivier covers a wealth of international tax information, including:
    *   Step-by-step instructions for the Forms and Schedules you will use to file your offshore tax, no matter where you are.
    *   How to qualify for special deductions, credits, and exemptions on international taxation.
    *   Why opening bank accounts and corporations in foreign countries is easier than you think.
    *   How residency or citizenship in another country can legally lower your taxes.
    *   How your spouse and children (whether American or of another nationality) affect your tax situation.
    *   Practical advice for moving, living, and working with tax-free income in other parts of the world.

- What to consider before renouncing your American citizenship and saying goodbye to the IRS for good.

3. Follow the artists' adventures across Peru, Mexico, Puerto Rico, New York, California, New Mexico, Italy, Greece, Hawaii, Thailand, India, and Nepal to discover:
    - The influence of mythological archetypes and archetypal psychology.
    - Where we are in the Spiral of Evolution, according to Integral Philosophy.
    - The primal sources of sexual passion channeled through Tantric practices that lead to soul awakening.
    - How the "Return of the Goddess" goes beyond Feminism to calling up the Divine Feminine and Mature Masculine.
    - How to heal trauma and break disempowering patterns through consciousness science.
    - How surrendering to one's destiny path leads to magic, synchronicities, and miracles.

Summaries and Action Calls

Finally, it's good to round the end of your book's description off with a few sentences summarizing its purpose and unique appeal. Give readers a concentrated zing that will make them certain they will be happy with what they get if they choose to buy and read your book right now. You should also include some form of a "call to action" that encourages them to act on what you have just revealed. The call to action doesn't have to be a direct command to make the purchase, which often comes across as tacky.

Examples of final value summaries with or without calls to action:

1. By chronicling more than 8,000 years of life lived during the most transitional time in American history, *Stories of Elders* offers old-fashioned wisdom and insight for America's future generations.

2. As a non-resident American, there is no single easy answer to lower your taxes. If you don't understand every possibility, you could end up paying too much. Embrace a worldly lifestyle with confidence as you master the U.S. tax system for Americans living overseas.

3. *Travel as Transformation* will give you the wisdom, the inspiration, and the resources to conquer the limitations placed by your arbitrary past. Whether traveler or non-traveler, its lessons about approaching the uncomfortable and unfamiliar apply to everyone.

4. Whether you lead a growing company or are just starting out, *Brand Identity Breakthrough* will give you a smarter way to think about product development flow, branding, brand mapping strategy, and business model generation. With proven, and well-organized logic, it will set you on the path to selling more—and at higher prices—giving the customers exactly what they want and sending your profits through the roof.

5. A revolutionary spiritual memoir 20 years in the making, *Venus and Her Lover* will reveal to you how ancient spiritual principles and the secret history of sexuality offer the path to personal wholeness and fulfilling relationships.

With the title, cover, and description optimized, your book will be primed to sell to qualified buyers once traffic begins flowing to its various online listings. To complement the effect of this tailored first impression, you'll want to make sure your book is available in every popular format. The more chances you give shoppers to buy your book and the more attractive you make it seem, the more success you will know as an author.

Summary of Chapter 9

Your book's title and subtitle are usually a reader's first exposure to it, often presented in isolation from the cover or any other descriptive information. Therefore, they must be accurate, specific, and enticing enough to prompt further investigation from anyone who might find value in your book. It is safer for new nonfiction authors to pick a long descriptive title than a short generic one.

— — — —

Your book's cover will appear in many sizes and contexts, including being quickly scanned over by hurried online shoppers who don't know anything about its message. It should be able to attract attention and instantly convey what the book is about and who it is for. Ideally, one or many graphic designers you hire should be able to produce a variety of designs that you can test for effectiveness both before and after publication.

— — — —

A book's description is an essential selling tool that needs to accurately summarize the most compelling promises of your book's message without dragging on too long or getting lost in its own grandeur. As well, it should contain important search terms and specific benefits readers will receive so they can quickly determine if buying your book is a wise investment of their time and money.

CHAPTER 10:

Preparing Each Format of Your Book

You've done almost everything you need to prepare the imagery through which you will make readers aware of your book and convince them to take a chance on it. Now, to optimize the effectiveness of your imagery, you will need to prepare your book for every major format that appears in the modern world. More than that, you will need each version of your book to follow the rules that have come to define how each format is consumed— whether it be in the form of an electronic book, printed book, or audiobook.

It may seem superfluous to go through all this formatting work for a book that isn't even for sale yet. You may not understand why you should prepare each format up front since doing so will incur additional expenses and you have no proof you will see a return on the market. Most self-published authors prepare only the bare minimum for launch, usually just their hurriedly formatted e-book for immediate release on Amazon. What these cautious authors don't realize is that by taking this approach, they lose most of their visibility and conversions.

If you don't make your book available in every format, you will put a cap on your readership. Many readers who might love your book will decline to purchase and read it if their preferred format is not available. People don't buy e-books if they prefer the feel of turning a page and don't own e-readers. Some readers are too mobile and don't want printed books piling up, so only digital media will do. If a reader wants a hardcover edition, they may be reluctant to settle for a less-enduring paperback instead. Most audio listeners stick to narration only, out of convenience or necessity, declining other formats that would occupy their eyes or hands.

Publishers rely on many esoteric formatting practices you've probably never given much thought to, even though you have been exposed to them since you started reading books. Most people lack the discerning eye needed to notice these interior design conventions. Once you know what to look for, though, you may begin noticing consistencies throughout every traditionally published book you own. You may also notice when those conventions are absent from self-published books because the author did not understand the minutia of proper formatting. Breaking tradition here lowers readers' opinions of a book's quality. It can even prevent a book from being accepted by printers and distributors.

Learn the standards that are expected of each format of publication so that you will be ready to offer yours in as many ways and to as many readers as possible. Dressing your message up in the expected attire will help it overcome the negative stigma of self-publishing, convincing readers to take you more seriously as a communicator of important ideas. If you master these formatting conventions, it may be that the question of your book's origin never even enters most readers' minds. Your message will be unconsciously accepted as existing on the same level of prestige as those brought forth from the most impressive publishing houses on the planet.

Formatting for Paperback and Hardcover

You know why the exterior elements of your book matter for your success, but you may not have considered the importance of how the inside appears to readers. Text formatting plays an important organizational role in written communication, and this role is often overlooked by writers who focus exclusively on the meaning of their words. Good formatting makes it easier to digest your message in an orderly, comfortable manner, reducing fatigue during long reading sessions.

If you open your wardrobe and see your clothing neatly stacked and folded, you will have a clear idea of what you own and can wear for any occasion. If your closet is stuffed with crumpled and disordered garments, featuring no means by which to separate them by color, fabric, or function, you will not even be able to assess your options. The organization of your wardrobe affects how you dress yourself and the way you feel about the process. The same will apply to the visual organization of your book's text, helping readers find the passages they need when they need them.

Many self-publishers who choose to format their own text will use common word processors like Microsoft Word or Apple Pages because they are the same programs they drafted in. However, these programs are not made with publishing in mind. They make it difficult to keep text precisely aligned, especially if there are graphic elements involved. Authors just like them because they are simple to learn. You can apply page and section breaks as needed to make your text appear where it should. Margins, page numbering, footnotes, indexes, and other formatting conventions are present, though limited.

Professional book formatters work with programs like Adobe InDesign that are made with book interiors in mind. With InDesign, you can easily work with text in columns or move chunks of it around a page. The downside is that InDesign is more difficult to learn to use than common word processors. If you hire a formatter, this is likely the program they will use to work on your book. It helps for you to at least know what the program capable of. If you don't want to hire someone to format your book, your next-best choice may be to use a design template that will enable you to plug sections of your text into the appropriate places as you go.

Content Structure

Review the structure your nonfiction book should be taking, with the caveat that not every section is necessary for every book and the order they appear in can be subject to change:

Front Matter

Title Page

Copyright Information

Dedication

Quote

Table of Contents

List of Illustrations (if needed)

List of Tables (if needed)

Foreword

Preface

Body Matter

Introduction

Main Chapters

Conclusion

Back Matter

Afterword

Appendices

Glossary (if needed)

Bibliography/References (if needed)

Index (if needed)

Acknowledgments (can also appear in front matter)

Author Bio

Trim Size

The first decision you will need to make is what size you want the print version of your book to be, which is called its trim size. The trim size will not only affect how many words you can fit on each page but also other practical matters like how easy it will be for readers to hold or transport your book. The most common trim sizes for nonfiction books are 6" x 9" and 5.5" x 8.5". Other types of books, like mass-market paperback fiction, are designed with a mere 4.25" x 7" trim size for portability and cheap production. Big workbook-type books that benefit from a two-column layout on each page or lots of images might use a 7" x 10" trim size or larger.

Page Margins

Next, think about the size your book's page margins should be. The empty space of margins acts as a buffer between your printed words and the end of the paper. In print, the outside margin (the one furthest from the spine) is generally between .5" and 1" thick and gives the reader a place to hold the book without obscuring the text. The inside or gutter margin (the one closest to the spine) gives pages the extra space they need not to have words get lost in the crease of the spine. For this reason, inside margins are usually slightly wider than outside margins. Publishers refer to these as mirror margins.

Because the production cost of a print-on-demand book is determined by its page count, some authors attempt to save money by reducing the number of pages during formatting. Unfortunately, the ways they do this can ruin the appearance of their books. They set their margins too narrow so that the text runs almost all the way to the edge of the page. They reduce the spacing between lines of text (known as the book's leading) or make the font too small for comfortable reading. Do not be tempted to ruin your book's visual appeal just to save a few cents per copy.

Headers and Footers

The top margin or header is a useful place to put some combination of the book's title, subtitle, author name, or chapter name. Typically, the title will go on the left-page header and the chapter name on the right-page header to aid with navigation. With short books, however, it may be more appropriate to have the author name on the left header and the title and subtitle on the right header. There won't be enough pages or chapters to necessitate navigational assistance. Find a combination that both looks good and serves readers' needs.

The bottom margin or footer is usually where the page number goes. It may be in the center of each page or at the outside corner. Traditionally, the first numbered page begins on a right-side page. Thereafter, all odd-numbered pages will be on the right (known by formatters as the recto side of the page) and all even-numbered pages will fall on the left (known by formatters as the verso side of the page). This will remain important for the consistency of the book's formatting. New chapters should begin on the right side, sometimes necessitating a blank left-side page if there is not enough text to populate it from the end of the preceding chapter. Headers are always omitted from the first page of each chapter.

Pages belonging to a book's front matter (such as the foreword and preface) are numbered with Roman numerals, starting with i, ii, iii… on the first page of the foreword and continuing until the book's introduction. This numbering convention is useful because it allows you to make changes to the front matter without changing the running page numbers of the main chapters that follow. Pagination changes to Arabic numerals (1, 2, 3…) on the first page of the introduction and continues until the end of the last chapter.

A book's back matter (i.e., everything that comes after the conclusion) can either continue with Arabic numbering from where the body matter ended or begin again with Roman numerals from where the front matter left off. The latter tactic might be particularly useful if your book is part of a series, and you want to keep the body content numbering consecutive between books. No header or footer content (including page numbers) should appear on a blank left-side page before the beginning of a chapter on the right side.

Body Text Style

Books are traditionally published with fully justified text, meaning each line of text is spaced to extend evenly from the left margin to the right margin. This is a departure from the way most people use word processors or write things out by hand. Our writing is, by default, justified to the left of the page, so that each line of text only lines up on that side. The right side of the page therefore has a ragged, uneven look as each line ends at a different place depending on how close its final word is to the right-side margin.

Print books are almost always formatted with their body text in serif typefaces, which have stylistic embellishments at the ends of letters. This practice creates an elegant and classic feel compared to more modern sans serif typefaces that lack embellishment. However, when shrunk down to a small size, fonts without serifs will retain their readability better, which makes them preferable for low-resolution e-reader devices.

Your printed book will almost certainly be best served by a common serif typeface like Garamond, Baskerville, or Caslon for its main text and a sans serif font like Futura, Helvetica, or Myriad for its headings and subheadings. The goal here is not to stick out and make the reader wonder why your fonts look so strange compared to the ones used in the traditionally published books they are used to. If your text is hard to read or evokes an inappropriate feeling, it may dissuade shoppers from buying the book when they flip through its pages or preview it online. It will negatively affect their cognition of the content as they read it.

Although the body text of most books is printed with font sizes between 11 points and 13 points, each typeface takes up a different amount of space on the page (even at the same point size). Your best option to minimize the number of required pages in your printed book without sacrificing readability is to choose a typeface that doesn't take up unnecessary width in or between its letters.

On the level of paragraphs, traditional publishers either indent the first line of each one to provide a visual marker for where it begins (excluding the first paragraph of a new section), or they omit the indent and separate each one with a line of space (creating block paragraphs). Often, fiction publishers prefer indentation and nonfiction publishers favor block paragraphs. Fiction tells a story that is meant to be seamlessly carried between paragraphs as the narrative proceeds. Nonfiction paragraphs contain structures of ideas that should be able to stand in isolation and for consumption at whatever pace the reader prefers. For creative or narrative nonfiction (such as memoirs), however, indented paragraphs may be the ideal choice.

Orphans and Widows

One of the consequences of breaking up book text across many pages is the possibility of the first or last line of a paragraph getting separated from the rest of it between pages. A broken line of text at the start of a page is called an orphan; one at the end of a page is called a widow. Orphans and widows hurt aesthetics and comprehension because they make the eye jump from the bottom of one page to the top of the next in the middle of a thought. They may even require the turning of the page.

Professional book formatters painstakingly remove orphans and widows before publication so as to make the reading experience as pleasant as possible. For the same reason, a subheading should never be the last thing a reader sees on a book page. Some formatting programs are equipped to eliminate orphans and widows as they occur automatically. Other times, a formatter may have to manually increase the spacing between characters (known as the text's tracking) or add extra line breaks to correct the issue.

Quotes and Transcripts

Many print formatting choices depend on a book's specific purpose and function. Because it was derived from a series of interviews, Veronica Kirin's book, *Stories of Elders: What the Greatest Generation Knows about Technology that You Don't*, contained many quoted passages of varying lengths throughout the text. The author and I needed some way to visually distinguish when an interviewee was speaking directly rather than the author. Big chunks of text contained in opening and closing quotation marks interspersed throughout the primary text would have been difficult to distinguish and ugly to look at.

For short quotations, we left them within the same paragraphs of the main text and used quotation marks to denote them. For longer transcribed passages, we separated them into their own block paragraphs and indented their entire length on the page. This visual distinction negated the need for quotation marks. The result was attractive, space efficient, and made it easy to discern when the words belonged to the author or interviewee. If you're not sure about how to format certain parts of your book like this, you can brainstorm strategies from your favorite classics.

Image Arrangement

If you want your book to contain images, you'll need to consider some additional formatting factors. Firstly, realize that unless you are willing to pay about twice as much in printing fees per copy, all your images will be printed in grayscale. Depending on the nature of the images and your reasons for including them, this may negate their effectiveness. Secondly, you'll need to secure high-resolution versions of your images so that they won't appear pixelated or blurry on the page. Print-on-demand facilities like IngramSpark and KDP Print recommend a minimum image resolution of 300 dpi ("dots per inch") to ensure everything will look the way it is supposed to, though 200 dpi may be sufficient for simple images.

The images you include can take many forms and serve many functions, no matter the subject or tone of your book. If your book mentions real-world locations, a map in the front matter or within the body matter will help show readers where you are talking about. For *Stories of Elders*, author Veronica Kirin felt adamant about including a map of the contiguous United States with a line denoting the route she took driving across 40 states to conduct her interviews. If it serves the transmission of your message, you can also insert charts and graphs where appropriate in the text or relegate them all to a designated section of the back matter.

Images in books are often accompanied by captions that include snippets of vital information about them. Across both volumes of *Venus and Her Lover:*

Transforming Myth Sexuality and Ourselves, author Becca Tzigany curated roughly 50 images depicting ancient and sacred works of art from around the world that were central to her message. In addition to each picture needing to appear at a specific place on a specific page so that it would line up with the body text discussing it, almost all of the images required captions ranging in length from a few words to a few sentences directly beneath them. This kind of precise image and caption arrangement just isn't feasible with common word processors like Microsoft Word. Finishing her book required the expert hand of someone well-versed in the much more robust program, Adobe InDesign.

Formatting Sabotage

Unfortunately, when much skill and attention are required, the possibility of error or sabotage grows larger. I'll now share with you my most painful experience as a publisher, which occurred when I made a major error in judgment and hired someone woefully underqualified for a difficult formatting job due to my personal bias and relationship with her. The experience not only cost me an enormous amount of time and money but also permanently ruined one of my most valued friendships.

Venus and Her Lover Volume 1 became something of a painful learning experience about the complexities of detailed formatting, human resources, and workflow management. At the time that Identity Publications began working with Becca Tzigany, someone I had a longstanding personal and professional relationship with was hired to be in charge of the book's visual elements related to cover design and interior formatting. Although the friend I brought on board had done a good job on a few previous Identity Publications projects, this was the first time she had taken on a book with layout requirements so precise.

Still, my associate seemed confident in her ability to adapt to the needs of the project. Initially, the timeline she provided for formatting the first volume was only a few weeks.

Flashforward three months. Despite endless corrections to inaccuracies about where certain images, subheadings, italics, and footnotes were supposed to go, it still seemed we were still no closer to getting the formatting for volume one of *Venus and Her Lover* completed. It became our production bottleneck, as everything required for its printing, launch, and promotion had been ready to go for several weeks, but we could not do anything with the rest of our work until the print formatting was done. My associate in charge of formatting kept feeding me lines insisting that work was proceeding as quickly as it could and that the delays were vaguely the author's fault for requesting new changes throughout the process.

Just as I thought we were finally ready to put the final touches on the book's interior and send a printed proof to the author, I received an email from my associate stating that she would immediately be ceasing all work on *Venus and Her Lover* and the few other books I had in production at the time. I quickly realized that the stress of getting the job done as required had become too much and she refused to continue, despite the fact that she had already been paid thousands of dollars for the book projects she was working on many months prior.

Shockingly, the friend I had hired to handle the formatting then attempted to exploit me for further company funding before she would hand over the incomplete Adobe InDesign source files for the interior of *Venus and Her Lover*. In a matter of moments, I went from dealing with normal publishing tasks into emergency mode, having to defend my company and months of labor from internal sabotage by someone I thought I knew and could trust completely to be a character of reliable work ethic and great integrity. If I didn't give in to her demands, we would have to start from scratch on a formatting job that had already taken far too long.

Up until this time, my formatting friend had been consistently baiting me with promises about the book nearly being done and only requiring a few more basic corrections. However, the source files she eventually delivered were riddled with amateurish errors, jerry-rigged fixes, and inconsistencies with the master Word document I had provided for conversion to InDesign. Images and captions weren't anchored where they should have been in the text, so any attempt to add or remove elements invariably caused them all to shift around to the wrong locations. Text that was supposed to flow from one page to another within the same thread was arbitrarily cut off halfway through, again requiring an enormous amount of manual reformatting.

It became clear that the friend I had trusted to do a good job, perhaps in an attempt to get it done quickly and keep the large amount of money she had been paid up front for minimal effort, had employed the simplest possible solutions to create the *appearance* of conforming to the formatting instructions. Instead of addressing the document holistically from the start, she had outsourced the task to inexpensive formatters in Ukraine with little knowledge of the complete functionality of Adobe InDesign or how to adhere to Western book formatting practices. Because she was unwilling to oversee and check their work personally, her repeated promises that the work was being done to the standards we expected were based on nothing.

When I brought the problems to her attention and asked for help in explaining the work that had been done so far to a new formatter who could take over where she left off, my friend attempted to extort me once more for thousands of dollars. I knew then beyond doubt that I had made a series of very large mistakes in letting my personal relationships influence my business decisions by trusting her with such a big project. I accepted that I would be on my own to salvage the project and my working relationship with the author. When all was said and done, the author and I had found nearly 400 inaccuracies between the master Word file of the book's text and the partially formatted InDesign file my friend had delivered.

After spending more than $1,000 with a new formatter and waiting another three months to be able to check that everything was how it was supposed to be (including having the book's author volunteer many hours of her own time to help check and correct the mistakes), we finally had *Venus and Her Lover Volume 1* ready to go and could begin formatting the second volume with our difficult lessons firmly learned. It's a shame that it took us so long to realize it actually would have been more time- and cost-effective to begin formatting the book again from scratch than to try to manually repair the many hidden errors we had just become aware of.

I am telling you this story because I value transparency and disclosure. I want to give you a glimpse of everything that can go wrong with preparing a book for launch if you are not aware of the character and capabilities of the people you work with. Even with my experience and the success I found early on with producing and launching books, one bad call such as hiring someone based on my pre-existing relationship with them and not their genuine experience or work ethic royally screwed things up for everyone involved with *Venus and Her Lover*.

I urge you not to just hire the online freelancer who offers to handle a complex task for the lowest price, unless you are certain they have the abilities and experience to complete the job to your specific expectations. Pay attention to the early impressions you get about someone's ability to perform and their attitude about the job, as initial warning signs can turn into catastrophes at crucial moments of a tight production process. Even if you find someone with the right skills, the burden is then on you to oversee their work and ensure it is getting done to spec and on schedule while you are organizing the other elements of your book's production and preparation for launch. I am fortunate now to have professional formatters that I know I can rely on for all styles of book formatting, no matter their complexity.

Although most self-published books will not have layout demands as intensive as those for *Venus and Her Lover*'s two volumes, there are still many things that can go wrong if you are not familiar with good formatting practices or how to manage the talent that you hire. My fatal flaw in this instance was projecting too high a level of professionalism and ability onto someone who was still an amateur at heart. I didn't see the danger in time because I projected my hopes of what she could become with the right opportunity to prove herself professionally. Because I had vouched publicly for my underqualified partner, I was left bearing the blame and having to work harder to make amends for her indiscretions. It's the only thing I could do if I wanted to maintain my own integrity.

Paper Color

Once your interior formatting is ready, you can begin thinking about the finer details of printing your book. You will first choose whether you want the pages of your book to be white or cream colored. Publishers tend to prefer to print longer nonfiction, technical subjects on white paper, while shorter books with philosophical or narrative elements (especially fiction) look better on cream paper. Another thing to consider is that if you have any images in your book, their appearance will be affected by cream-colored paper. Take a look at books with cream and white pages to determine which will look better with your book's length and subject matter.

Cover Finish

You'll also choose if you want your cover is to have a glossy or matte finish, each of which offers some subtle pros and cons. Glossy finishes look more modern and vibrant, which can be good for attracting a certain kind of attention. Matte finishes have a slightly more muted coloration, which comes across as more natural and elegant. Each also carries its own textural qualities for the hands of the readers who hold them. Once all these creative decisions have been made, you just need to choose one or more printers for your book.

Print-on-Demand Providers

The most popular print-on-demand company in the world was once CreateSpace (a wholly owned subsidiary of Amazon) but it has since merged with Kindle Direct Publishing (KDP) to become KDP Print. Amazon does not add any fees to books printed through KDP Print (beyond their normal distribution percentage). You will be able to update the interior content, cover, or information for your books on KDP Print at any time with no revision costs. Their association with Amazon makes KDP Print the preferred print-on-demand company for authors who sell primarily through the Amazon.com platform (i.e., almost all of them).

IngramSpark (the print-on-demand branch of The Ingram Book Company) offers a similar service, but with some other advantages and disadvantages. IngramSpark makes their books available to a wider variety of retailers, including Apple, Barnes & Noble, libraries, and many others. IngramSpark has printing facilities in the United States, Europe, and Australia, making it convenient to ship to customers there. Through their Global Connect Program, they are even able to partner with third-party printing facilities in Brazil, China, Germany, India, Italy, Poland, Russia, South Korea, and Spain. With these unique features, many self-published authors prefer KDP Print as their primary printer to fulfill sales on Amazon and IngramSpark as a supplemental option for greater global reach.

The biggest advantage of IngramSpark is their ability to produce hardcover books, something KDP Print has yet to provide. IngramSpark's hardcovers can be produced with either case laminate binding or cloth binding (with or without a dust jacket), each at a slightly different cost of production (though typically about twice as much as a paperback). There's little reason why you shouldn't proceed with producing a hardcover format of your book, even if you don't foresee it selling well. The additional formatting and setup costs are minimal, so even a few extra sales will compensate for it.

The mere existence of your book in a hardcover format may help improve the perception of other formats. Buyers will see your book available in many forms and surmise that a lot of work has been put into their production. Most self-published authors don't bother to take the extra steps of hardcover and audiobook production, so these formats are still associated with top-quality traditional publishers. Even people who don't prefer these formats will be subconsciously affected in a positive way by their presentation.

Formatting a book's text for print is more complicated than most authors assume. That realization is probably why many self-publishers omit both paperback and hardcover editions of their book from publication, sticking only to e-books (at least for the first several months of publication). This is a mistake because it eliminates the possibility of readership and revenue that those versions of the book would have generated, which could be vital for a book's early growth and long-term success. New authors shouldn't be choosy about how they allow the world to consume their work.

Formatting for E-Readers

Preparing an e-book is much simpler than preparing a print book (whether you do it yourself or outsource it to an expert) because e-books are read on e-reader devices that make many formatting elements superfluous. There will be no fixed pagination for e-books, so readers can change the font size however they like. This, combined with the size of a device's screen, alters how much text shows up at a time and the number of total screens (or "pages") a book contains. You won't even need to select a trim size for your book, as that will depend solely on the device each reader uses.

Regardless, as with print books, it's still good practice to start each chapter after a page break on a new screen instead of running continuously from the end of the preceding chapter. This makes for easier navigation.
E-books, unlike their printed counterparts don't require denoted page numbers, fixed margins, or even headers and footers on each page to contain the title, chapter, or author information. Your readers' devices will automatically adjust these factors as needed. You can still choose the typeface you want, but your readers might have their own preferences that will overwrite whatever you set.

Of the hundreds of typefaces, many were designed before the advent of digital reading and writing. Therefore, they aren't optimized for presentation on screens, under sometimes backlit conditions, taking into account factors like pixel resolution and modified text sizes. Popular printed typefaces have a lot of variability in the sizes, shapes, and stroke widths of their letters. They look great presented in a static, physical format, but lose many of their attractive qualities when forced through the limitations of a screen.

Reading long texts under suboptimal conditions, such as those created by inadequate typefaces, can strain readers' eyes and ruin the reading experience of your e-book. You have an obligation to make things as comfortable as possible for your readers. Complex graphics you want to incorporate into your e-book may also appear ugly and obtrusive, so you will need to verify how they look on actual devices.

There's even the possibility of e-reader devices not carrying the font you desire. Anything outside of the old standbys like Baskerville, Georgia, Helvetica, Palatino, or Verdana might not be able to render properly, causing devices to default back to something else.

Because digitally displayed typefaces sacrifice their finer details at lower sizes and resolutions, most publishers opt for sans serif typefaces as body text (with the possibility of serif or themed display typefaces for larger titles and headings). The typeface Georgia, created way back in the early internet days of 1993, was the first serif typeface designed with digital display in mind. It accomplishes this through the use of "ball serifs" (little balls instead of flat lines coming off the ends of some letters) that don't lose their finer detail, as well as a mostly consistent stroke width between the thickest and thinnest parts of each letter.

In 2015, Amazon went so far as to design a proprietary typeface called Bookerly as the default for their Kindle e-reader devices. Amazon describes their Bookerly typeface with these words: *"Warm and contemporary, Bookerly is inspired by the artistry of the best fonts in modern print books but is hand-crafted for great readability at any size. It introduces a lighter, more graceful look and outperforms other digital reading fonts to help you read faster with less eyestrain."*

With printed books, the arrangement of the text is determined by the publisher before the book is printed and purchased. Because electronic books give that control to the reader, you should experiment with how your book looks under a variety of reading conditions. Look at your book on different-sized tablets, e-reader devices, or Amazon's online Kindle Previewer feature. Check that the spacing between paragraphs and sections ends up the way you planned it and images are where they are supposed to be. Play with different size and typeface settings until you are confident in every angle of the appearance of your work.

E-books offer some additional functionality that print books cannot. Their digital nature allows for hyperlinking to sections within the book or to websites outside it. You can direct readers to your personal website, to your social media profiles, or to compose an email to your inbox with a click. If you talk about other books you have written in your author bio, you can link to their Amazon listings. Your e-book's table of contents too should be hyperlinked to each chapter (and possibly subsection) so that readers can just click to whatever part of the book they desire.

To prepare e-books in their appropriate .epub file format for publication, special software like Vellum, Calibre, or Sigil is required to go beyond what normal word processors can do. These will allow you to arrange your text and set any images in navigable sections. Set properly, your .epub file will be accepted by every major e-book distributor, including Amazon's affiliated companies and IngramSpark's e-book branch. Amazon also maintains their own proprietary .mobi format for Kindle books, but they will be happy to convert .epub files as required.

As mentioned, Amazon's e-book publishing division is Kindle Direct Publishing (KDP), which is designed for authors to create an Amazon book listing for presale or immediate release in just hours or days. Other e-book publishing platforms like Apple's iBooks, Kobo, and Google Play (and even aggregators that publish your book to many platforms) can expand your digital reach, but most e-book sales still happen for Amazon Kindle. KDP even offers a 90-day exclusivity deal for authors called KDP Select, which makes their e-books available only on Amazon in exchange for additional promotional benefits that can be of great value to an author's launch strategy.

Enrolling in KDP Select makes your e-book available for free to Amazon shoppers who subscribe to Kindle Unlimited. For about $10 a month, Kindle Unlimited members can read as many e-books enrolled in the program as they want without paying anything additional. Book royalties are structured quite differently under this program. Amazon divides the total royalty fund of all members' monthly fees based on how many pages of your book are read each month. Amazon calls these Kindle Edition Normalized Pages (KENP), which are Amazon's way of standardizing content quantity by variations in font size and image placement across e-readers.

Narrating Your Audiobook

Audio narration did not begin to gain industry popularity until the 1980s. Today, it seems it has still reached only a fraction of its potential. The audiobook format is considered unconventional (or even a form of cheating) by some readers, but that hasn't stopped it from continuing to grow. In some genres, such as business books, it's estimated that audiobooks now sell more than three times as much as e-books and at higher prices. More than 50,000 audiobooks were produced in 2017 (out of the hundreds of thousands of books published), and it's estimated the numbers will continue to grow 20% each year.

Founded in 1995, Audible (now the world's largest audiobook vendor) is Amazon's sister company for audio sales. They offer a backend for audiobook production and publication called the Audiobook Creation Exchange (ACX). Like KDP for e-books and KDP Print for paperback books, ACX is designed to make uploading audio files and linking to an existing Amazon book listing easy. Once you have set up a profile on ACX and produced your narration, you simply need to provide a newly formatted version of your book's cover set to square audiobook proportions. This is the image Audible and other audiobook retailers will use to display your audiobook beside its other formats.

Many readers/listeners who prefer audiobooks will eschew other formats, so not having your narration available for purchase on your book's Amazon listing means losing all sales that would have come from them. By having your audiobook ready for purchase at the time you launch the electronic and physical formats, you create the possibility of increased sales from a whole new type of audience. Omitting audio simply because it's not your preferred format may cost you many thousands of dollars in book royalties. Yet, most self-published authors never bother to narrate their own books or hire narrators to do it for them.

Especially for people with long commutes or busy schedules, audiobooks offer many advantages that e-books and print books do not. They have opened all types of writing to new audiences who may not have the time or preferred learning style necessary to sit and read a book in the traditional manner. The speed at which audiobooks are played can be adjusted up or down on most media players, including Amazon's native Audible app. If a listener is busy or just prefers to go fast, they may prefer to play the recorded material at 1.25x to 2x speed and still retain most of the information. The mind adjusts to the pace of data it is given.

By occupying the ears (and not the hands or eyes), audio narration enables listeners to multitask in ways that traditional reading does not. Whether it's driving to work, taking a walk, going to the gym, or washing the dishes, audiobooks cater to people whose time is occupied by tasks that do not require their full cognitive focus. Rather than daydream and accomplish nothing while they fulfill repetitive tasks, they can be engaged in any of the dozens of books they have downloaded to their tablet or smartphone. By not providing your work in audio format, you are cutting your message off from this demographic. Your sales will be lower, and your message will not have the same influence.

Hiring a Narrator

If you don't feel confident narrating your own book, it's easy to find freelance narrators who will work for a fixed cost. ACX has even integrated a service to match authors with a selection of narrators on their platform. When you want to release your audiobook, ACX will give you the option of providing your own .mp3 audio files, paying a fixed price to one of their narrators, or offering a 50-50 royalty split in the hopes that a narrator will see the opportunity for long-term royalties from your book.

With the royalty split option, you must convince narrators your book will sell enough to justify the hard work they will put into recording, editing, and mastering your audio files. This is more likely to happen if you are already a popular author or your book's subject matter is extremely topical.

I don't generally recommend sacrificing ownership of a portion of the revenue from a book. To do so negates much of the benefit of self-publishing. You will no longer be eligible for as much financial return on the investment of crafting and promoting your message, and it can affect how you prioritize its promotion. If you have enough confidence in the commercial success of your message to write the book in the first place, it makes more sense to pay a flat fee or figure out how to record and master the audio yourself. If your book is as meaningful and in-demand as you have strategized it to be, you will see the investment returned to you in due time, possibly within the first month of its availability on Amazon through a windfall of immediate audiobook sales.

Self-Narrating

Before you record anything or search for a narrator, think carefully about who will listen to your book. Remember that there are differences between readers and listeners. A reader is a relatively captive audience. An audiobook listener may have other stimuli competing for their attention. They may be engaging in other activities like driving, working, or doing housework. Think about what voice and reading style will be required to keep them focused on your words. What best serves the nature of your message? Should it be casual, formal, or theatrical? Would a male or female voice suit the subject matter? Should the narrator be young or old? What about a regional accent?

Narrating your own book is not complicated, but it is tiresome, time-consuming, and tedious. If you've never recorded spoken word before, you might think professional narration is as simple as reading aloud into a microphone. It's not. Aside from investing in the right kind of recording equipment (which is the easy part), you will need the endurance to maintain consistency in your pace, pronunciation, and tone for many days of recording.

It's hard to picture how draining narration is if you've never had to speak without interruption for more than a few minutes at a time. In regular conversation, two or more parties exchange less than 30 seconds of speech each and then patiently await their turn to speak again. The strain placed on their voices is nothing compared to an hour or more of constant and measured vocal output. You will be surprised to see just how quickly your mouth dries out and you lose a bit of your voice.

Because professional narration is about the consistency of sound, you can't just plow through the whole book with a deteriorating voice. Your listeners will notice that the first hour of your audiobook sounds bright and chipper, while the final hour sounds like you're in the throes of a bad cold. Unless your book is extremely short, you will probably need to break the recording sessions up across several days, so your voice has time to recover from the strain. If you can record 10,000 words a day or more (about one hour of finished audio after editing) you're making good time.

There's also the distinct possibility that you don't have a good reading voice. The fact that you have written an exceptional book has nothing to do with your ability to speak it out loud in a compelling manner. If you cringe every time you hear a recording of your own voice because it sounds different than what you expect, you're probably not ready to narrate an audiobook. For the recording to be any good, you need to be in control of your voice. You can't be in control if you don't even have an accurate conception of the sounds that come from your mouth.

Despite the labor and skill required, being your own narrator comes with some unexpected benefits. You'll be contributing to your personal brand by letting people hear your voice, with your intended emphasis on your own words. It simulates a relationship between you and your listener. Narrating your book also gives you the opportunity for one final, metered read-through of the full text of your book before publication. You may spot errors that spell-checking and silent proofreading missed. You may realize that some of the ways you've worded things sound awkward out loud. You may decide to cut out sentences or paragraphs that no longer serve the purpose you intend. After all, your vision for the book should have changed at least a little now that you have the perspective of its full context.

Audio Recording Dynamics

If you choose to proceed with narrating your own audiobook, you'll need to acquire some simple recording equipment. You will need a computer with basic recording software like Audacity, GarageBand, or ProTools. Do not be tempted to use the internal microphone on your laptop or tablet, or any other cheap microphone you may have lying around. Your voice will sound hollow and tinny, and you will capture excessive background noise that will make your narration worthless. Though you don't need top-of-the-line pro audio equipment, you should spend at least a couple hundred dollars on a dynamic USB microphone with a pop filter.

Find a quiet place where you can record at least an hour of narration without interruption by people or random background elements like traffic, construction, birds, rain, or the sound of water rushing through pipes. Turn your phone off and ensure that all sounds are disabled on your computer. If any unexpected noise arises during recording, you'll have to stop, wait until it dissipates, and then re-record whatever portion of your speech it interrupted. Afterward, you will need to edit out the mistake without ruining the flow of speech or making the cuts obvious.

You'll also need to eliminate as much potential for vocal echo as possible. Professional recording studios are padded, floor to ceiling, with a special type of foam that prevents sound from bouncing around the room. Echoes get picked up by sensitive microphones and ruin the recording. They are difficult to remove in post-production, even by a skilled audio master. You can purchase recording studio foam if you want, but an easier solution is to hang thick blankets on the walls of a small closet or hallway. So long as your recording space has floors of carpet (definitely not hardwood or tile), you shouldn't need to worry much about echo. If you lack small, enclosed spaces, you can even drape a blanket over your head and keep your computer and microphone underneath with you. It may not be comfortable, but it gets the job done (and you finally have a valid, professional excuse to build a blanket fort in your living room).

Keep the microphone a consistent distance (about six inches) from your mouth while narrating, and practice speaking slowly and clearly. Be careful about making any noises that might distract from your content and betray your amateur status. Loud breathing, lip-smacking, and whistling "s" sounds are off-putting for listeners. Professional narrators have learned to eliminate such distractions from their diction. When you make mistakes, such as reading a word wrong or tripping over your voice (and you will make many, many mistakes), you will need to re-record them and edit out the bad takes afterward. Minimizing mistakes while recording will save you hours of editing time.

Make yourself comfortable. Have a glass of water close by as your record, as you will need to take sips when your mouth and throat become dry from speaking. Aim to record at least one complete chapter per session if length permits it. Save each chapter as its own track on your recording software. If you need to vary your voice, to shout or scream (which you should not do without theatricality as your goal), move your face further from the microphone. For whispering, move it closer.

When you make a mistake (such as skipping or mispronouncing a word), don't stop recording. Use a signal word like "delete" or "whoops" and return to the beginning of the paragraph or sentence in which things went wrong. Snapping your fingers or making a popping sound with your mouth into the microphone after you make a mistake will create a visually distinct spike on your recording track and make it easy to edit it later. Edit each chapter soon after you have finished recording it, so that your memory from the session will be fresh. This will give you the chance to review your work and see if there are any passages that need to be re-recorded. Taking breaks to edit between chapters will also give your voice a chance to recover and be fresh for another round.

When you've edited your recordings down to flawless and consistent read-throughs, you'll need to prepare them for the technical format required by ACX (or whatever audiobook platform you seek to publish through). It's best to keep your audio in uncompressed .wav format throughout the editing process until you are ready to publish. Alternatively, .mp3 files are compressed into more convenient file sizes with some loss of audio quality. Once you've uploaded your audio files to ACX according to their .mp3 audio requirements with the right amount of room tone and the start and end of each track, the files will be reviewed and approved for distribution through Audible and Amazon.

With your e-book, paperback, hardcover, and audiobook formats ready for distribution, you can begin thinking about the upcoming launch and promotion of all the hard work you've done so far. Now you're ready to put your face and message (and perhaps your literal voice too) out in front of the world for evaluation. The only task that remains is to keep the image of your book in front of the people best suited to consume and appreciate it. Promote your book well, and your life will never quite be the same.

Summary of Chapter 10

Modern print book formatting practices are the result of centuries of slow evolution. You will have to follow the established trends for headers, footers, pagination, paragraph style, font use, text justification, and more if you want your book to appear professional. These standards also aid in navigation and reading comfort, but they are easy to mess up if the formatter you hire is not familiar with them or is inexperienced with the formatting program they use (e.g., Microsoft Word or Adobe InDesign).

— — — —

E-book formatting is comparatively simple and obviates many of the complex practices of print book formatting. E-readers allow their users to tailor many aspects of the reading experience to their tastes. Regardless, you'll still need to make a few tactical choices about how you want your book to appear on the screen, especially if you plan to include images or tables in your text.

— — — —

Audio narration is rapidly gaining popularity and is a potentially significant source of additional royalties and readership for some types of books. You can narrate your own book if you have the skill, equipment, and time required. Otherwise, you can hire a professional narrator to deliver your audio files in the format that will be ready for upload and publication.

PART 6:

PROMOTION

CHAPTER 11:

Setting Your Book for Launch

Your manuscript has been refined to the point of something approximating completeness. You have monitored the results of testing titles, book descriptions, and cover designs with people who represent your audience. You are ready to set a date and begin telling the world about the release of your upcoming book. For many self-published authors, this is the critical flaw in their process and the part they dread most. They assume their success is secured by the strength of their book's content alone. They see only the blood and sweat they've poured into crafting it. With such a simplistic "write it and they will come" mental model of success, they fail to respect the entrepreneurial side of giving visibility to their artistic endeavors.

When you release your first book, you are offering a new type of message with an identity the world has never known behind it. You are pleading with strangers on the internet to take your work seriously and invest themselves into it with both their time and money. You must effectively convince them they will receive something of enormous value that justifies the sacrifices they will have to make to surrender to your promotions.

Everyone who sees your book's cover, hears its title, or reads it description will instantly begin to form their own interpretations of what your creation means. Targeting your promotions helps you focus on only the people who will form the right impressions, but it only works to a point. At the end of the day, each of us comes from a different background and has a set of values and expectations. You cannot control with total precision exactly how the market will respond to the many possible ways you could show them your message. You will have to become clever, resourceful, and adaptable to find success in the short run or the long one.

There are many ways to tell the world about your book. Some work better than others. Some are free and others expensive. Some take a lot of time to set up and others only a few clicks of a mouse. Some are available only for specific book categories or formats. Your first priority in marketing is to figure out what types of promotion are most appropriate for your book and audience. Otherwise, even if the quality of your writing is extraordinary and the value of your knowledge immeasurable, you may find that all your production efforts have been a waste.

You must also determine the amount of resources you are willing to dedicate to promoting your work in the hopes of eventually earning them back and then some. No promotional activities are without some cost to the promoter. If you aren't paying for advertisement, you are giving away your time (or the time of someone you employ). That's why it's crucial to concentrate on channels that bring the highest return for what you invest, especially if your time or money is limited. When the most obvious methods have been exhausted, you can expand your outreach by turning to more risky and creative ways to promote.

Book marketing should ideally begin months before publication, but you can also cover the most important bases with just a few weeks of preparation before launch. By the time your early manuscript is ready for beta reader feedback, you should have cultivated a small but passionate audience of people who represent your ideal readers. Though often overlooked, simple word-of-mouth publicity is one of the most effective ways to ensure the launch of a new product with a specialized audience. It's more personal and authentic than paid advertising. Word-of-mouth is difficult to fake, and this builds a deep level of trust with new readers.

Like most authors, you probably don't think of yourself as a salesperson or marketer. The reality is that you sell and promote things every day of your life. Marketing is just the act of making people aware of new things. Sales is just convincing people to take actions they otherwise wouldn't have taken. When you see it this way, much of the intimidation surrounding the idea of promotion begins to dissipate. Marketing and selling are as natural as talking to people about something you care about. Since you obviously care about whatever you took the time to write a whole book about, these necessary processes should come to you with ease.

Framing Your Author Brand and Bio

It is said that a work of art should stand alone and be evaluated solely on its own merits. Evaluation never works this way, however. Any work of art creates a conversation between its producer and consumer. A reader's experience of a book is shaped by their perception of its origins. They interpret it as a message directed at them from a person with definable qualities.

Your readers' opinions of your books will be affected by their perception of your identity as the author. Long after they've finished reading your work, the specific things you wrote about may fade from their memories. However, their impression of you as the author can linger far longer. When someone feels that they have identified with you, you never truly leave them. Readers may decide to reread your book someday. If you've published other works, they'll want to investigate them too. They may also just carry you around as a passive force in their cognition, reminding them of the tone and lessons of your book.

What you publish will be a reflection of your personality in the public domain for the rest of your life. The residual impressions readers retain of you after reading your book form your author brand. It is the image readers conjure in their minds when they think of you, no matter how accurate or inaccurate it may be. Since no one can ever know everything about another person, personal brands are always incomplete representations of complex, real-world human beings. They are relevant windows into a person's identity emphasized in the public eye for a calculated purpose.

Your author brand will play a large part in drawing certain readers to your writing and keeping certain others away. If your book represents your first attempt to enter the public eye, you should now decide which aspects of your identity you want your readers to acknowledge most. People like to listen to others with whom they identify or share respect in some manner. They need to see themselves in you (or see what they wish they were). Anyone who is turned off by your appearance, personality, or values is almost certainly not going to read your book. If they do read it, they almost certainly won't like it. If you don't fit the stereotype your audience expects, you may need to work harder to win them over.

For the ideas in your book to be taken seriously, readers must perceive you as qualified to dispense your wisdom. Without authority, you may be dismissed from the outset, regardless of the quality of your words. The funny thing about authority is that it rarely makes sense. In a sane universe, the only reason we would trust the opinions of other people would be because they had the knowledge and experience to hold their conclusions. In our world, people use many kinds of unconscious, often nonsensical indicators to determine whom they should listen to, such as age or physical attraction.

Your author bio is your chance to tell your readers who you are, focusing on the details about you that are relevant to their decision to consume your message. Here, you can illustrate the type of person you are and portray an image of yourself that will positively affect your readership. What you should put in your bio depends on what your book is about and the impression you are trying to create. Fiction writers often tell stories about their personal lives that show off what life experiences lend themselves to the kind of story they are telling.

Author Qualifications

For nonfiction writers, the details of your personal life that are worth including are those that make readers believe you are qualified to have written your book. There are many ways to accomplish this besides listing traditional credentials. Did you run a software company for years before writing your first personal development manifesto? Your readers might not care about software, but you probably had to be pretty driven, dedicated, and adaptable to make your company a success. Those types of underlying traits might be relevant to someone who wants to learn your philosophy about how to be a better human.

If your book's subject is building a successful export business in a competitive industry, mention your time as International Sales Director, Logistics Manager, or General Manager of an overseas subsidiary. If yours is a self-improvement book, say a little about where you came from, what you've achieved, the gap between the two, and why helping others in the same area is important to you. Are you an artist? You might want to mention where you studied, where your works are exhibited, and any prizes you've won.

Have you written any previous books? Mention the most prominent ones in your bio. Do you have a website or social media pages you maintain for business purposes (and not to share pictures of the latest stray cat you rescued, unless that's part of your deal)? Do you have an email list to which people can subscribe? Tell readers where they'll find the signup link. Have you won awards or commendations, or been mentioned in relevant publications?

Social Proof

Social proof is another trait that makes an author more likely to be taken seriously. When you command a small audience, it gets easier to command an even larger audience because the assumption will be that you must have something to say worth listening to. What influence do you have? How can it be construed to be relevant to the message of your book? How does it qualify you to write about the things you care about?

Author Personality

Readers also want to see personality from you. This works best if you can showcase it in an uncommon and memorable way. Talking about the fact that I've been living around the world since I was 18 in my bio makes me stand out from other authors, regardless of the subject I'm writing on. You'll get an even better sense of me if I mention my penchants for homesteading in off-the-beaten-path countries like Ecuador and Armenia and rehabilitating stray cats as I go. What kind of person do you imagine I must be for these unusual claims to be true? Plenty of authors can talk about their families and favorite hobbies. Not many mention something truly unique and interesting about themselves.

Many self-published authors fall prey to vanity when they write their own bios. You may be the best civil engineer ever to walk the earth. Other civil engineers may speak your name in hushed reverence—but be mindful of the line between modesty and grandiosity. No one likes a know-it-all, even when considering buying your book because it appears you actually *do* know it all about your subject. There is not a 1:1 correlation between the number of positive things you state about yourself and the degree to which people will want to buy your book. What have you said that you didn't need to say?

Author Photo

Everything that applies to demonstrating your personal brand through your author bio applies all the same to your author photo. The type of person you are trying to portray yourself as must come through in the headshot you put on your book's back cover and which will appear on your its online listing. It seems unfair that a person's physical appearance has such a big influence on how they are received, but if you neglect it your reception may suffer.

Think about how someone in your position of authority is expected to look. Stereotypically, an astronomer looks different than a world-traveling backpacker, even though appearance has no bearing on the ability to perform either of these tasks. Your clothing, jewelry, hairstyle, makeup, posture, and physique all matter. All can be altered, within reason, without betraying who you are or misleading readers. You can't make yourself physically older (which can be a problem if you are writing on a subject where youth is perceived as a sign of ignorance or inexperience, as I often do at my current budding age of 30), but you can make yourself appear more confident and mature through proper grooming, attire, and attitude.

Through Amazon Author Central, you will also be able to place videos, display recent blog posts, and upload several photos besides your primary author photo. All these additions have the capacity to help you increase the influence of your author brand for readers who want to get to know you (either before or after reading your book). You can even use a different photo for the back cover of every book if you want to. Maybe they are so different in subject and tone that there is no single best photo for all of them.

Personal Branding Gateway

The author branding you establish on Amazon and with each copy of your book should be a gateway into the rest of your personal online presence, whether that be a dedicated author website or something else. You can generate many new visitors to a business you run, a podcast you host, a blog you write, or any of various social media channels you control. If readers like what they see in your book, it's only natural they will want to see what else you are involved in.

In the years to come, you may to decide to write more and more on the same topic you find your initial success with. You may also choose to do the opposite by writing about many unrelated subjects. The more varied the topics you write on, the more your personal brand will expand.

Your author brand and bio are not set in stone. As the years pass, your goals may change. When you produce more books, you may think of other things to include and some to eliminate. You may start writing on other subjects or branch out into fiction. You may have more interesting life experiences or improve your credentials. While you can't change what's already gone into printed copies of your books, you can update your online bio in Amazon Author Central at any time, as well as the interior and exterior production files for future sales of the book.

When I started Identity Publications, it was a way to link the various categories of books I knew I'd be writing and audiences I'd be writing for under a common theme and mission. I never wanted to be limited to typecasting myself as the branding guy, the travel guy, the self-help guy, or anything narrow like that. I write what I do because I believe the things I have to say carry the potential to affect people's sense of identity, and therefore their actions, in a positive way. The authors I want to work with are those who carry a similar mission and can foresee the importance of what they want to put out into the world, hence the existence of the book you are reading.

Effective Pre-Launch Outreach

I often advise authors to make the e-book format of their book available as a pre-order on Amazon for at least a month before they launch. This will give them time to finish preparing the other formats and begin promotional outreach. Once they set the future date of their e-book's release through Kindle Direct Publishing (KDP), the Amazon listing goes live. They can then begin sending traffic to it, whether it be from their existing social connections or promoters and reviewers they are ready to begin reaching out to. The paperback, hardcover, and audio formats of the book will appear on the same Amazon listing once they have been submitted, approved, and processed by their respective platforms.

In some cases, choosing the right time to launch and promote your book can accelerate its sales. Releasing an aphrodisiac cookbook before Valentine's Day ensures increased demand during the romantic holiday. Releasing a tax book after the national tax deadline would undermine many of the book's promotional efforts, as there would not be as many people looking for tax help. If your book's theme depends on seasonal changes or particular dates, consider these factors when planning its launch.

If you choose to publish your print books through both KDP Print and IngramSpark, it makes sense to complete KDP Print's paperback version first. Setup and revision are free on KDP Print, and they are directly affiliated with Amazon. Publishing there and then making any necessary changes to the inside or outside of a proof version of the book will make publishing a hardcover version on IngramSpark much easier. IngramSpark charges small fees for initial setup and each subsequent revision, so it's wasteful to have to keep making changes to your book on their platform. Books published through IngramSpark also will not show up as quickly on your Amazon listing as those published through KDP Print.

With both KDP Print and IngramSpark, you can update your book's pricing, metadata, and other details for free. KDP Print makes these changes almost instantly. IngramSpark generally faces long delays between the time you update your book's details and when its listing reflects your changes. These rapid results make KDP Print better suited for testing different prices to sell your book at and monitoring the changes.

During your book's pre-order is a good time to set the ideal Amazon subcategories. The ones you choose will affect how much visibility the book gets during its fragile infancy. They will change what kind of shoppers see it and how well it appears to be performing compared to its subcategory competition. If you can get your book to the #1 spot in any subcategory, you will be the first choice shoppers see when they browse through it. You will have also earned the right to call your book an Amazon bestseller (for whatever that's worth).

Amazon enables you to move your book out of its present categories and into new ones any time you want simply by contacting its support team. Changing subcategories is a useful strategy when your book starts ranking highly in a non-competitive or loosely relevant category. You can then move it into something with more competition and that more appropriately matches its subject. Since your book will have had many sales when you make the switch, it has a good chance of continuing to rank highly in its new subcategory. If you place your unknown book in a competitive category without a strategy to boost its rankings, it will likely remain hidden from view forever.

Figuring out how hard it will be to rank in a certain place within a subcategory is easy because of the Amazon Best Seller Ranking (ABSR) system. If the book currently in the #5 spot of the subcategory you want to be in has an ABSR number of 30,000, your book will have to get to #29,999 to replace it. #30,000 is an impressive but not impossible ABSR to beat, so it's a realistic goal for new authors to shoot for.

However, in the same subcategory, the book currently in the #1 spot might have a substantially better ranking, like #1,000 of all books on Amazon. If you want to be an Amazon bestseller in that category, you'll need an ABSR of #999 or lower, which is exponentially more difficult. Through massive promotion, it's possible to shoot up in the rankings and cross that threshold temporarily, but don't expect to maintain it unless you've found a niche with high demand and low competition.

Getting to #1 in an Amazon subcategory confers some useful promotional advantages, but it does not guarantee long-term commercial or critical success. During the time your book occupies the top spot in a subcategory, a small orange label will appear beneath it in search results reading: "Bestseller in (name of subcategory)." This small visual indicator can have a strong effect on how many shoppers click on your book and purchase it.

Whenever we perceive something as desired by other people, especially people we identify with, it changes the way we evaluate it. The bestseller label attached to your book's title and image creates an instant impression of popularity. The label will even appear on your book's sponsored ads and when it shows up as a suggested pick on other books' Amazon listings.

On the one hand, it can sound impressive to readers to hear that your book is a bestseller. On the other hand, being an Amazon bestseller is not the same thing as being a New York Times bestseller, for example. Bragging that your book got to #1 in a non-competitive Amazon subcategory for a brief time will make you look like a boisterous amateur to people who know better. It will also imply that you have no other merits to brag about, such as the number of copies sold, royalties generated, coveted awards won, lives affected, or opportunities created. There are plenty of great books that earn many thousands of dollars in royalties every month but never get to #1 in any Amazon subcategory.

In general, you want to have your book ranking as close to the top of its most relevant subcategory as possible, as that is where the highest quantity of qualified buyers will be browsing. Online shoppers rarely look past the first page of results, so it's fairly useless to be ranking low (even in a popular subcategory).

Guest Blogs and Podcasts

While your book is on preorder, you will have the opportunity to begin reaching out to reviewers and promoters and prepare them for the upcoming release. Review, again at this time, who your ideal reader is, where you can reach this type of person, what their interests are, and why your book can benefit them. When you look at book promotion through this filter, it gets much easier to focus only on actions that will result in exposure and sales. Now you know where you or your virtual assistant can compile a list of contact information for blogs, podcasts, video channels, and other internet media outlets that represent your audience.

Whatever the subject of your book, somewhere on the internet are people interested in it. Some of these people have gathered in various groups across all social media platforms. Others are posting content regularly and cultivating a following of like-minded people. If you can identify institutions that have already earned the attention of your target readership, you can work out a mutually beneficial arrangement.

Targeting the right promotional platforms plays an essential role in how effective your promotion will be. If you've written a book about mending broken family relationships, you probably don't want to guest post on a blog about teenage girls' fashion. What you'd be looking for in that situation are blogs related to marriage, parenting, emotional issues, counseling, and more. No matter what you've written, there's potentially a big range of tangential niches to belong to. Finding them all and contacting their owners could keep you busy for a while.

Among the many millions of blogs on the internet, most are relatively small and uninfluential. There are a few well-established blogs in any industry that are followed by many thousands or millions of people. Naturally, everyone wants to borrow the influence of such valuable online Real Estate by guest posting on them. Unless you have a connection with the owners of these blogs, are already well-known, or have something unique and incredible to share, you may find it difficult to get past their gates. So, at least at first, look instead for blogs that are small enough to welcome an approach from an unknown entity like you. Any efforts you have already taken to secure your authorial brand identity will aid you here.

The most basic offers you can make to bloggers are:

1. A complimentary copy of your book for them to consider for review on their platform. If they agree, ask them if they'd mind also adding the review to Amazon and Goodreads. Remember, though, that Amazon prohibits requiring someone to leave a review in exchange for a free copy. This approach will probably only work on bloggers who have a history of posting book reviews or you know are avid

readers. Remember that reading a full-length book, even if it's a great one, is an investment of many hours of someone's time.

2. A prewritten article about your book that they can post on their blog and attribute to you as the author. You can pick out interesting passages from your book of approximately 500 to 1,000 words in length (or whatever specifications the blogger indicates) and re-contextualize them as guest posts. You can do this only if they work as standalone pieces and you don't submit the same passage to more than one blog. Google frowns on duplicate content and blogs usually have policies against it. With some minor editing though, you should find plenty to use within what's already going in your book.

   You can ask the author of the blog what subjects they are looking for in their guest content or offer them a predetermined selection of topics. In your guest author bio, you will have the chance to link back to your author site and/or your book's Amazon page.

3. An interview with you, the author, about the process of writing your book or one of its specific themes. The blogger may provide you with a list of questions, or they may invite you to a real-time interview on their podcast, videocast, or radio show.

When you reach out to blog owners, treat it like any other sales approach. Make it simple and make it direct, but also make it appeal to their emotions. Tell the blog owner right up front who you are and why you are making contact. Try to make it clear that you are familiar with their blog. When you've done that, describe what your proposed post will be about and say why you think it would be useful to the blog owner to accommodate it. They will probably want to see a pdf of your book or its Amazon listing. You can also send them to your website if you have one. If they like your style, they'll be more likely to agree to a guest post.

You should also briefly research each blog before contacting its owner. Do they have guest post guidelines? If so, take care to follow them. Look at the posts they write themselves. What sort of subjects? What sort of tone and angle? It should be fairly easy to deduce what kind of content their audience would like.

If you are trying to be a guest on someone's podcast, use an approach like this:

> *I'm the author of the (subject of the book) book, (title and subtitle of the book with a hyperlink to the Amazon page). The book is going to be released on Amazon on (date of release) and available as a free download for a limited time shortly after.*

> *I'd be honored to be a guest on (name of the podcast) to talk about my experiences and the lessons of the book. The book is designed to (details about the unique merits and approach of the book). Just let me know the topic or angle you think would be most appropriate to talk about for your audience, or I'll gladly come up with one myself.*

> *I'm also happy to send you a copy of the book in pdf, epub, paperback, or audiobook format if you'd like to read it. Just let me know where to send it.*

> *My past media appearances include… (share any links to previous podcasts or guest blogs you have posted—the more famous the platform, the better).*

> *I look forward to hearing back from you,*
> *(your name and contact information)*

While this approach works well before your book launches, it can also be even more effective a few months later while the book is still considered new enough to be noteworthy. At that time, you'll be able to fortify your outreach with statistics about how successful the book is, such as:

The book became an Amazon bestseller in two categories upon release and generated a lot of positive feedback. It currently has 153 reader reviews with a 4.8- out of 5-star average rating.

If you want to submit a guest post to someone's blog, change the details of the message to be relevant for that purpose. Include a paragraph like this:

I'd be honored to contribute a guest post or article to your site that would be appropriate for your audience and help promote the book at launch.

Short messages like this are vital for promotional outreach because these platforms tend to get many requests every single day. No one wants to sift through several paragraphs just to figure out why you are contacting them and whether it is in their best interest to respond.

You should strive to give some kind of personal and specific reason why your book is a good fit for their audience. Do your best not to make your message seem like a template you sent out to hundreds of other platforms, even though most will recognize the approach you are using. Think of things from your recipients' perspectives. If you were running a successful blog or podcast with thousands of regular visitors, you would only want guests who had something valuable to say that would fit the brand identity of your platform. That impression is what you must convey in the short space of your outreach if you expect to get any positive responses.

When you post as a guest on other people's websites, you are essentially borrowing the market appeal of influencers who have earned the attention of their audiences. If the bloggers' audiences overlap, they will receive repeated exposure to your name and book from multiple respected sources. This will only enhance your appeal in their minds. If your guest posts create backlinks to your website, your SEO receives a boost too. You will appear closer to the top of search engine results for terms related to you and your book, hopefully resulting in more popularity and book sales.

Every time you post an article to someone else's blog, there's a possibility that its followers will share your post on their social media profiles, re-blog it, or otherwise spread it around. There could be a viral network chain reaction, where more and more people keep showing it to more and more people. Don't hold your breath waiting for overnight internet celebrity status, however.

Your Own Audience

Not all your book launch outreach has to happen with blogs, podcasts, and other forms of internet media. If you have an email list or a large social media following yourself, you have people who have self-identified as your fans. They are people who have shown enough interest in your personality and subject matter to allow you some precious space in their email inbox or social media newsfeed. If your book is in line with your existing public message, it's reasonable to assume that many of your followers will take an interest in it.

With subscribers and followers who would be genuinely interested in the subject matter of your book, you can figure out the best way to send out a sequence of emails about your book launch in the weeks leading up to it, encouraging recipients to read and review your work (or download it during a free promotion). These messages don't have to be purely promotional. You will probably get a better response by sharing valuable or entertaining information about your personal experience with writing the book, the information it covers, or how you plan to promote it. You can also provide excerpts from its content.

If, however, your book covers something unrelated (or even antithetical) to your existing brand image, you may not be able to use your existing audience to promote it. The fact that some people like what you have to say about stock tips does not mean those same people will want to hear your input on special needs parenting or ancient Egyptian religious practices. At best, you may be able to get away with a small mention of your off-brand book contained within a larger message that is more in line with what your followers are used to seeing. It could be something in the vein of, "Oh, and just so you know, I am about to release my first book on (unrelated subject).

You can find out more by clicking here." Anything more than that may be alienating and cause you to lose subscribers or lower their opinions of you.

Traditional Media

While blogs and social media outreach are great ways to get your book in front of some readers, they cannot achieve the same exposure as traditional media. If you want to get your book into newspapers, magazines, or on the websites of reputable news authorities, you are going to have to play the media game by their well-established rules. The easiest way to do that is by writing and distributing a press release for your book.

Journalists have columns to write. More than that, they love easy stories. A press release allows you to present your book to conventional news outlets and journalists in a form that is easy for them to share as a noteworthy story. The best press release for your book will be one that makes it seem newsworthy.

Journalists skim the headlines of press releases, hoping to find one that will be a winner. They don't have time to waste on something that doesn't instantly interest them. The headline should fulfill at least one and ideally more of these objectives:

- Intrigues the journalist and make them want to read on to find out what the story is about.
- Arouses worry or excitement so they won't want to miss out on sharing its contents.
- Makes a big claim, meaning unusual, mysterious, or powerful.
- Promises to reveal something valuable that readers will want to know.

With that in mind, mundane press release headlines like "Local Woman Publishes her Late Mother's Journals" will do very little to contribute to the appearance of newsworthiness.

There are a few proven concepts that tend to draw attention to books. If your book is about something utterly unique that has never been covered in other books, it might be newsworthy. Maybe your book has hit some important sales milestone or won a well-known reward. If you have an interesting story behind the book's creation (even tying into your personal life as the author) that adds uniqueness and intrigue. If the headline refers to an idea or trend that is popular right now, so much the better.

Once you have a press release ready, you need to make sure it gets in front of the right journalists. There are syndicates that will send your press release all over the world. These distributors certainly save a lot of time, but writers get better results by targeting publications individually. Your press release is most likely to get accepted by the publications you target if they can use it with little modification. Newspapers and magazines won't want to rewrite every press release they use in a way that suits their readers and fits their bias. Minor modifications will be fine, but a press release that has to be substantially rewritten is unlikely to be used.

As well as choosing the outlet you write your release for, you should choose the person you send it to. If you simply address it to a magazine, it may never find its way to a journalist interested in the subject. Newspapers and magazines have individual editors who look after the various sections. Find out who the editor is that might want to use a story about your book. Most magazines and newspapers make this easy by providing information about editors on their websites.

Book Pricing and Royalty Strategies

The question of how best to price each format of your book is one that cannot be answered without understanding the nuances of how pricing affects marketplace perception. It's foolhardy to assume, as many new entrepreneurs do, that lower prices directly correlate to higher sales. While some book shoppers hunt for bargain buys, others perceive that higher prices indicate better quality. Many readers don't want to waste their time and money on something they assume isn't good enough to command a respectable price.

You can spend a lot of time studying the pricing strategies of books like yours, but there's no substitute for real market testing. Fortunately, Amazon and its publishing partners make retail prices extremely easy to adjust in near-real time. You can change the prices of all your book formats (except audio) at any time and monitor how your sales rise or fall. With enough testing, you will come to see what prices maximize total readership or royalties, depending on your priorities.

With some of the books I've produced, price testing showed that twice as many copies were sold when the retail price was twice as high. In those cases, the market demonstrated that it would rather pay $20 than $10 for a paperback. The author was making roughly eight times as much money from the sale of their paperbacks due to receiving four times the royalty per sale (for reasons detailed below) and twice the quantity of sales. However, just as with strategies for writing or design, no author can assume the same scenario will apply to their own work or even to more than one of their own titles.

E-Book Pricing

E-book pricing on Amazon is fairly limited. Amazon has structured their royalty percentages for e-books such that those priced between 99 cents and $2.98 earn 35% royalties for their authors. For a traditionally published book, this retail price range would be considered extremely cheap. Though cheap e-books will draw sales from people who don't want to risk a lot of money on unknown authors, they will also devalue a book's presentation.

E-books on Amazon priced between $2.99 and $9.99 earn 70% royalties for their authors. At twice the royalty and a higher retail price, the earning potential is clearly much higher within this range. Above $9.99, the author royalty drops back down to 35%. It rarely makes sense, therefore, for independent authors to price their e-books above $9.99. Clearly, Amazon encourages its authors to price their e-books in the 70% royalty range.

Print Book Pricing

Printed books, unlike electronic books, have a cost of production per copy that must be factored into every sale. For print-on-demand providers, the price per copy is determined predominantly by page count. If your non-fiction book is a typical length of 60,000 words and formatted to fit roughly 250 6" x 9" pages, it will cost less than $4 to print a single copy through KDP Print.

Taking into account the 40% that Amazon keeps from each sale, the minimum price an author would be able to sell such a book for on their platform for would be about $6.50 (excluding shipping costs), negating nearly all author royalties. The same 250-page book priced at $10 on Amazon would earn its author roughly $2 in royalties per sale. A $15 retail price would earn roughly $5 in royalties; for $20, $8 in royalties; for $25, $11 in royalties; for $30, $14 in royalties; and so on.

Print books command higher prices than e-books. They are physical possessions buyers touch and hold on to for potentially their entire lives or which they can otherwise resell or give away. Readers are not just paying for the information within, but the ownership of the object itself. For the same reason, hardcover books tend to sell at retail for about $10 more than their paperback counterparts. The physical quality of a hardcover is superior enough to warrant a higher retail price from readers who care about such qualities.

Through KDP Print's expanded distribution (which caters to platforms other than Amazon), you will have greater exposure but lower royalties per sale. KDP Print keeps 40% of sales made through Amazon and 60% of sales made through its expanded distribution. Through expanded distribution, however, institutions might purchase dozens of copies of a book at once for resale or internal use, depending on the type of book.

It can be a little disappointing to see royalties on a paperback priced at $19.99 drop to $4 or $5 compared to the usual $8 or $10 from sales originating on Amazon, but this will more than be made up for if you get a bulk order of 50 to 100 books from an unknown source. You probably won't be complaining that you just made a surprise few hundred extra dollars. Since customers who buy your book through expanded distribution probably wouldn't otherwise have purchased through Amazon's retail front, you won't be cannibalizing many retail sales and replacing them with those that earn a lower royalty rate.

Although printing and shipping costs with IngramSpark are slightly higher than with KDP Print, most authors report the quality of the printing is a little better. IngramSpark also makes up for its higher print costs with the ability to let you set your own wholesales discount rate between 35% and 55% (as opposed to the fixed 40% and 60% rates set by KDP Print). Opting to receive a lower royalty gives greater incentive for independent retailers to purchase copies of your book for resale. IngramSpark further incentivizes resellers by allowing authors to make their books returnable if they go unsold, which KDP Print does not.

Audiobook Pricing

For reasons not entirely known, you will not be able to set the retail price of your audiobook through the Audiobook Creation Exchange (ACX). They use their own pricing structure, based on the length of an audiobook and their experience with what sells well. ACX's pricing guidelines by length are:

Under 1 hour: under $7
1 to 3 hours: $7–$10
3 to 5 hours: $10–$20
5 to 10 hours: $15–$25
10 to 20 hours: $20–$30
Over 20 hours: $25–$35

Audible, the retail front of ACX, offers its premium members the opportunity to purchase audiobook credits at discounted prices that can be redeemed for any title, no matter the retail price. When they run out of credits, premium members can still purchase audiobooks at a 30% discount off the full retail price. These three purchasing options (full retail price, 30% member discount, and pre-purchased credits) affect the royalties you will receive from your audiobook.

ACX provides two author royalty tiers: 40% of the sale price if you agree not to distribute your audiobook through any other platforms and 25% for non-exclusive distribution. The amount of money you receive for each audiobook sale will depend on whether you chose the 40% or 25% rate. It will also depend on whether a buyer purchased your audiobook at full non-member retail price, member discounted retail price, or with one of their prepaid audible credits. Figuring out the breakdown of your audiobook royalties can be a little confusing, but the possibilities are large.

To further complicate audiobook pricing, ACX offers a $75 bounty as part of their referral program for every new Audible member you recruit by sharing a referral link to your audiobook. Taking advantage of this will require you to use specifically generated links to your audiobook, however. People who download your audiobook as part of their free Audible membership trial will need to maintain their paid membership for 61 days afterward. Even with these restrictions in place, it's possible to leverage ACX's bounties to earn thousands of extra dollars in revenue.

Monthly Royalty Breakdown

If acquiring passive income is one of your reasons for publishing, it's easy to break down how many sales you need to reach a certain income goal each month. Here's what a realistic pricing and royalty scenario for a 250-page book might look like:

E-book
Retail price: $9.99
70% royalty through Kindle Direct Publishing (KDP)= $7 per sale

Paperback
Retail price: $19.99
60% royalty through KDP Print after ~$4 print costs= ~$8 per sale

Hardcover

Retail price: $29.99

40% wholesale discount through IngramSpark= ~$9 royalty per sale

Audiobook

Retail price: $19.99

40% exclusive distribution royalty through ACX= ~$8 per sale

In such a pricing situation as this, the number of monthly sales necessary to reach $1,000 profit would be 110 to 140—or about four or five per day across all formats. Even a totally unknown author with a desirable message and only a basic understanding of book promotion can come to achieve these numbers consistently. These numbers can also go much higher if your message is particularly hot or you take the time to master its promotion.

Keep in mind that this simple calculation does not take into account other outlets for selling. At in-person events or through your private website, you would only pay for printing and shipping but not distribution costs for your paperback and hardcover books. Your profit per print book would be around $16 to $22, as your printing costs would be about $4 and $8 respectively.

You can't control what price the market will find most appealing for each format of your book, but you can play with pricing to boost sales and draw exposure at strategic intervals. It makes sense to price your book at its lowest when it is on preorder and shortly after launch. That is when your book will have the least amount of social proof and exposure. You can employ a scarcity tactic by advertising your book as available for a limited time at these artificially low launch prices. Visitors who are interested in your book but unsure about purchasing it will be more likely to do so if they think they will have to pay more at a later date.

Readers may be more willing to risk their money on new releases with few positive reviews if the price is low, such as only 99 cents for the e-book or $9.99 for the paperback. Your social connections will also be more willing to purchase your book at these low launch prices, which will help it move up in Amazon's sales rankings. They will then be able to leave verified purchase reviews, which you'll soon learn are vital to long-term commercial success on Amazon.

Months will go by and your book's social proof will begin to accrue. You will gain reviews and exposure through third party sources. You can gradually increase your book's retail price until you find market equilibrium. Market behavior will always vary. If you notice a dip in your book's ABSR number from uncharacteristically low sales, you can experiment with temporarily lowering the price to 99 cents, $2.99, or some other discounted amount and see if it creates a swell of purchases. Amazon shoppers often add books they like to their wish lists, so they'll receive email notifications when there is a price drop.

No matter how you set the retail price, Amazon will sometimes discount a book if it has a history of selling well. When this happens, the price discount is taken out of Amazon's share of the royalties. You will still earn the same amount of money as though your book were priced at $19.99, even if Amazon discounts it to $14.99 for their customers.

Free E-Book Promotions

You will also have the opportunity to run your e-book for limited free promotions through Amazon's KDP Select program. So long as you are willing to sell your e-book exclusively on Amazon for 90 days, you will be able to run discounted Kindle Countdown Deals for up to five days of free promotion during your 90-day enrollment in the program. After this period, you are free to either re-enroll in KDP Select or list your e-book on other platforms. Note that KDP Select's exclusivity requirement does not apply to the physical or audiobook formats of your book, so you can still sell those on your own site or through other distributors.

A free promotion is one of the best ways to get instant visibility for an unknown author. It might seem counterproductive and cannibalistic to give away what you were hoping to make royalties from, but it can pay off in the long run. Almost everyone who finds and downloads your e-book during a free promotion run shortly after its launch will be someone who would never have been a paying customer anyway. Short-term free promotions of what seem like highly valuable books quickly get spread around the internet on book groups, review sites, and forums. All this word-of-mouth equates to huge exposure your book otherwise would not have had.

Retailers refer to free promotions like this as loss leader pricing. They believe that if they give something away for free or sell it for lower than their wholesale cost, the money they initially lose will be compensated by other sources of profit the promotion generates. In the case of your e-book, you won't be losing money through your free promotion because you incur no cost of production for each unit sold (not counting any money you pay for promotion during this time). What you gain is the opportunity for thousands of members of your target audience to learn who you are and recommend your book to their friends.

As a bonus, the hardcover, paperback, and audio formats of your book will still be fully priced while your e-book is on free promotion. With the increased traffic to your Amazon listing during the free download period, it's almost inevitable that some of them will be interested enough to purchase your book in one of its other paid formats. If you have other books, visitors to your listing might be interested in seeing what else you've written. Even after the short free promotion ends, increased traffic will continue to spill in, some of which may convert into paying buyers. With proper coverage from social media groups and email newsletters that publicize free e-books, it's not difficult to get into the top 100 of all free Amazon e-books during a one- or two-day free promotion. These thousands of free downloads will have a large influence on your book's ABSR, which means more continued visibility. I've included a partial list of these types of promotional outlets for free e-books in the back matter of this book.

Summary of Chapter 11

The way your readers perceive you as the author affects their willingness to purchase and read your book. Your author photo and bio should be tailored to shape the public reception of your work. Write your bio in a way that convinces readers they should care what you have to say about your subject and also makes you seem like an interesting and memorable person.

— — — —

To ensure a successful book launch with lots of exposure and sales, you should begin an outreach campaign while your book is still on preorder in the weeks leading up to its official release. You can reach out to online media platforms like blogs and podcasts that are related to your subject and convince them to review your book, do an interview with you, or share some form of guest content. Distributing a press release about your book will give you the opportunity to get in front of traditional media channels as well.

— — — —

There are many strategies you could use for pricing your e-book, paperback, hardcover, and audiobook. The only way to determine what will optimize your sales and/or profit is repeated market price testing. Each book format and distributor employs a different royalty structure, so you will have to be able to calculate how much a sale of each version of your book is worth to you. This will help you figure out how much you can realistically make per month and how much you can afford to spend on advertising.

CHAPTER 12:

Maintaining Book Traffic and Exposure

A book's launch date may be its introduction to the world, but it's effectively more a formality than anything vital to its lifetime market success. A book launch is an excuse to generate buzz about your recently completed project, which is novel simply because it's new. Any author or publisher who is good at publicity can make a book's launch successful in the short run, but only a unique and valuable message with a creator who makes efforts to keep it visible over time will continue to sell past its first months on the market.

In the months following your book's launch, the nature of your role in its success will shift. Though the hardest and most time-sensitive parts of the process are now over, there are many more processes you must oversee to ensure the plane you've recently made airborne maintains its ascent. The goal now is to get your book's performance to a level where it no longer requires your daily interaction. Only then can you consider the income your book generates to be truly passive, as you will no longer be directly compensated for the hours you trade away.

Though Amazon is presently the ideal hub on which to launch your book and serve as its primary online listing, there are many other outlets you can make use of in due time. Some distribution platforms exist exclusively for one format of books. Some cater only to a specific genre, language, or part of the world. The more platforms on which you list your book, the more exposure it will receive. Exposure means your book will be more likely to find its ideal audience, leading to a domino effect of readership through natural word-of-mouth promotion. It also means you will make more and more money from more and more sales as time goes on and more and more people discover what you've created.

With enough online representation and distribution channels in place, your book will begin to make its way to places you can't even predict. Several times, I've been surprised when someone on one of many social media channels has tagged me to let me know they saw one of my books in a bookstore in a small U.S. town. Amazingly, someone I once matched with on a popular dating app recognized my first name and face from having seen it on one of my books in a store in Jakarta, the capital of Indonesia. I've never been to Jakarta and have no idea why the owner of that bookstore found it pertinent to sell my book there, but I'm not one to look a book horse in the mouth.

Most times, I'm not even aware which distributor each retailer uses to find my work or what makes them decide to take a chance on it; I'm just happy to have the expanded reach and revenue. You don't even need to rely on distributors if you don't want to. There's nothing to stop you from reaching out in person or online to brick-and-mortar bookstores that cater to indie authors like you. Offer a copy of your book for them to consider adding to their stock or leave a small stack to sell on consignment. Bookstores will be more willing to take a chance on you if you eliminate their risk and your book's presentation is impeccable.

The stigma against self-published authors and print-on-demand books is quietly disappearing, which means your options for expansion increase daily. Independent authors are becoming more established and self-published titles now compete with traditionally published ones for sales in some categories. Even some major publishers are starting to print their books on demand to streamline their production. You just need to be willing to put in the effort after your book has been launched to see how far you can promote its presence.

Accruing Public Book Reviews Online

The long-term success of your book, especially if you are a new author, depends on your ability to generate social proof of its value. Prospective buyers need to see what other people think of your book before they can make a confident decision to spend money on it. In the world of book sales, verified reader reviews on Amazon are the most effective way to convey popularity and approval. In addition to Amazon reviews for e-books, print books, and audiobooks, Audible maintains its own database of reviews that can only be left by listeners who purchased the audiobook through their Audible account.

Reader reviewers are so important to the book buying process that online shoppers often skip past a book's description and scroll to the feedback left by other readers. Why? Because they know that a book's description is engineered by its publisher to generate sales. Reader reviews are supposed to be unbiased third-party opinions. Buyers tend to trust the opinions of people like themselves more than any other source, especially when they are not familiar with the item they want to buy. Additionally, the more positive verified reviews a book has, the more likely Amazon is to cross-promote it in the "Customers who bought this item also bought" and "Frequently bought together" sections of other book listings.

In some cases, just a few glowing or scathing reviews can be the cause of many gained or lost sales. One-star reviews, especially if you receive them early in the life of your book (and before you've had the chance to accrue many positive ones), can be seriously detrimental to your sales–no matter how unfounded the criticism may be. Your only reliable defense here is to buffer your book with many positive reviews so that the inevitable negative ones will only be a few darkened drops in a large bucket of praise.

A high quantity of reviews on your book will attract attention from book shoppers, even if the average rating out of five stars is somewhat lower than books with fewer reviews. Of course, the ideal situation is to have both a high quantity of reviews and a high average rating. To achieve this, you will have to recruit many people willing to read and review your book before and after its launch. Your book's Amazon.com listing will be the primary place to accrue reviews for maximum impact, but other online book retailers also maintain their own review systems that are worth staying on top of. There are even social networking sites like Goodreads that are centered around the sharing of books, and they attract a lot of avid readers who love to rate and review books.

You cannot simply launch your book and wait for buyers to start leaving reviews en masse as they finish reading it. The percentage of readers who post Amazon reviews without being prompted to is far lower than you probably imagine. Most readers do not understand the importance of sharing their opinions for a book's promotion. In my experience, the majority of book reviews only happen when authors and publishers explicitly ask for them.

The average reader will only leave a review under one of the following circumstances:

1. They are prompted to in an emotionally engaging way that makes them think their actions matter.

2. They have such strong emotions about the book they've read that they feel compelled to voice them publicly and resolve their feelings. While this also applies to positive emotions, negative emotions seem to carry more weight.

As an author, you will develop the habit of guiding people who read your book to take 60 seconds to click the "Write a customer review" button on its Amazon listing and briefly jot down their thoughts about it. The request will become second nature to you, like saying your name when introducing yourself. This is the single most effective way I have encountered to generate authentic reviews at any stage in a book's life on Amazon, and many other successful self-published authors concur.

[With that fact in mind, dear reader, would you mind taking 60 seconds to write a short, honest review of *The Influential Author* on Amazon and/or Goodreads when you're done reading it? If you purchased the audio narration through Audible, would it be too much trouble for you to paste your review on the audiobook's page on their platform too? It's extremely important to the ongoing promotion of my work and your help would be highly appreciated. Don't worry; I'll remind you again in the book's conclusion.]

Requesting reviews isn't a perfect system. Even though readers generally want to support the authors they like and reviews aren't hard to write, many of them won't follow through with your request. They get distracted or fail to understand how important such a simple act can be for the success of a book. Therefore, as mentioned, the best way you can ensure your book receives ample positive reviews is to recruit reviewers both before and after launch.

Anyone who agrees to review your book is doing you a favor, so treat them accordingly. Do not pester them to the point that they no longer want to help you or might even leave a negative review out of spite. There is no guarantee that everyone you request a review from will leave a positive one. You must make your requests with the condition that you want honest opinions, whether they be positive or negative. Not only is this required in Amazon's terms of service, but it will make your reviewers feel more appreciated, as though their reviews perform a valuable service for discerning buyers.

You can mitigate the chance that the people you request reviews from will leave negative ones by targeting your prospects well. Focus on people who you have reason to believe will fully appreciate what you have created. There's also nothing stopping you from asking for reviews from only people who have already read your work and stated they liked it. Just be aware that Amazon requires that anyone who receives a complimentary copy of your book for review must disclose this fact within the text of their review. This applies whether you provided them an Advance Review Copy (ARC) before launch or a regular copy any time after.

Reviewer Outreach

So, who should you ask to review your book? There are many viable options. You can contact recognized authorities on your book's subject and ask if they would be prepared to read your book and post a review. If an acknowledged expert on your topic says something good about your book, it will carry extra weight. If the expert has their own site, they may be willing to put their review there too, exposing your book to new eyes and generating backlinks.

You can also seek out avid readers and book bloggers who would be glad for the chance to read your book for free. Anyone who offered their input during your beta reading should be among the first in line to leave a review when it goes live. They may even want to share their praise on their website or social media profile.

Reviewers on Amazon, whether typical customers or part of their top reviewers, often list their email addresses or websites on their profiles. Contact them and ask whether they would be prepared to receive and review a copy of your book. Many services have emerged for self-publishers, offering curated lists of the contact information of reviewers. These services find the reviewers most likely to want to read (and enjoy) your book, based on their past reviewing behavior.

Once you have enough email addresses of potential reviewers, you (or someone you hire) can reach out to them with a simple, short request by email. A few sentences go a long way when worded well. A generic book review request template any author can use might look like this:

Subject: (Name of reviewer), would you like a complimentary copy of (name of your book)?

Hi (name of reviewer),

I'm reaching out to you because you left a review on the Amazon page for (name of the book they reviewed).

I recently wrote my first book, (title and subtitle of your book with a link to the Amazon page), which is launching on (date of your book's official release). It covers a subject that is similar to (name of the book they reviewed), but it focuses more on (something specifically appealing about your book). Early readers have been saying it really (way your book affects readers). I think you might really enjoy it.

To make sure my book performs well on Amazon, it's vital that I get as many authentic reviews as possible for it as soon as possible after launch. Would it be alright if I sent you a complimentary advanced copy? Your honest review on Amazon would be highly appreciated.

No rush on finishing it and no hard feelings if you are too busy or not interested!

Thanks for your time,
(Your name)

Once the responses start coming in, you can decide what format you are willing to send your book in. Electronic formats like .pdf and .epub are free to send, but not everyone likes reading on a computer screen or e-reader. Audio is the preferred choice among certain readers, and .mp3 files are easy to upload to a shared folder. Audible even offers to give its authors 25 free audiobook download codes for each audiobook they publish. These codes are meant to be given out to listeners so they can add the recently published audiobook to their Audible accounts and leave reviews.

You can also elect to send a printed book to a reviewer's address, but the cost of printing and shipping to dozens of reviewers can be substantial. Authors on a budget usually reserve free physical books for reviewers who seem to hold a lot of influence, such as if they have a blog or a YouTube channel relevant to their audience.

There is no guarantee that any of the people you contact for reviews will be interested in following through with your request. Of the hundreds of reviewers you email, fewer than 20% will likely respond. Of the portion who agree to read your book, many will drop off the radar soon after. The ones who finish it may take months to do so. Some may leave negative reviews. Regardless, enough outreach will spread your early reviewers out well beyond your current sphere of influence.

Once you publish, you may be contacted by people offering to get you Amazon reviews for a fee. Unless you can verify they are operating within Amazon's strict review policies, resist this temptation. Amazon has implemented measures to catch and counteract inauthentic reviews, such as requiring that Amazon account holders spend at least $50 on the site to be eligible to leave reviews. Amazon even regularly scans reviewing activity and removes anything that seems suspicious. Though it's unlikely, there is a possibility of Amazon closing your account if they suspect you disobeyed their terms of service by paying for false reviews.

In any case, any reviews you pay for are likely to be of poor quality, consisting of one or two generic sentences in broken English with a suspicious number of exclamation marks included. Shoppers will see through them. Authentic reviewers may even call out your fraudulent behavior with lines like: "I really question the authenticity of all the five-star reviews on here. They are all written in the same style and posted within 24 hours of each other. The book was very short and full of typos and grammar errors. Avoid this scam."

Some authors seek out other authors with whom they can swap reviews. Author A buys and reviews Author B's book and vice versa. Amazon does not allow this and other review swapping tactics, so they actively delete any reviews its algorithm finds in violation of this rule. They may even remove reviews if the same shopper reviews too many books published through the same account, even if they are written by different authors. If you bend the rules and pump your book up with shady reviews, they will eventually be taken down by Amazon, thus defeating your efforts.

By the time your book is published, you should have editorial reviews which you can use to promote it. Positive quotes from reputable sources are valuable social proof that your prospective buyers will need to see in order to take the risk of spending money on an unknown product. You can add these reviews to the Editorial Reviews section of the book's Amazon page through your Amazon Author Central account. They also work well placed strategically on the book's back cover.

Acquiring real reviews for your book is an ongoing process that lasts as long as the book remains on the market. It should always be a part of your marketing plan if you want to maintain sales. Encourage your readers to leave their opinions about your work when they are finished. Leave a short note at the end of your book telling them how important reviews are to your success as an independent author. Engage your social media followers and website visitors and encourage them to leave honest reviews. Just remember that it is against Amazon's terms of service to solicit exclusively positive reviews, require the leaving of a review, or compensate reviewers with anything for reviewing.

As with other forms of social proof, diminishing returns affect book reviews. Your book is unlikely to be taken seriously until you have at least 50 positive reviews. The importance of each new review drops off rather quickly once you get to triple digits, however. Each one thereafter counts for less and less. Only the most popular books with the widest syndication on national or international levels ever acquire thousands of reviews. For most authors, it isn't a goal worth pursuing.

Negative Reader Reactions

No matter what you publish, you will eventually receive some negative or middling reviews. Many of these will seem unfair to you. Nearly every author gets at least one negative review with complaints that could be summarized as "This book does everything its title and description promise it will do, but I wish it were a different type of book instead. Worst book ever." A certain saying about apples and oranges comes to mind here. As unfair as this behavior seems, leaving such reviews is their right as shoppers on Amazon.

The more contrarian to genre conventions your book is, the more confused or disappointed readers and reviewers are likely to be. For my book *Travel as Transformation: Conquer the Limits of Culture to Discover Your Own Identity*, I noticed a divisive trend in the reviews shortly after publication. The people who liked it tended to really, really like it. I was quite surprised when some people started writing that my book was one of the most inspiring they had ever read.

However, on the negative end of the review spectrum were some readers who were disappointed and offended that the book did not do most of the things that conventional travel books are supposed to do. My book doesn't talk about fun foreign adventures. It doesn't linger on any individual country for too long before hopping over to a short series of thoughts and anecdotes about another. It's not even strictly chronological. Despite the fact that *Travel as Transformation's* description showcased its break from travel book convention, some readers presumably saw the word "travel" in the title and supposed they knew what kind of book they were buying. A few of them, in their disappointment, wrote one-star reviews explaining how they didn't like the book because it was not like other travelogues and different from what they thought a travel book ought to be. Misunderstandings like this are part of the risk you take on whenever you choose to say something bold and new.

The ways readers can take umbrage with your message are endless, and many of them will seem immoral or unfair to you. It may drive you a little mad when a reviewer complains about something blatantly untrue about the content of your book, seemingly having skipped over integral parts of your book and thus missing the point completely. Do your best to avoid the temptation to publicly respond to these inaccurate reviews with page numbers and direct quotes from your book that counter their accusations. You will only make yourself look petty and unprofessional. It looks much more impressive when your fans jump to your defense than when you must spend your own time sifting through every comment made about your work to stand up for yourself.

All other things being equal, an unhappy reader is much more likely to leave a book review than a happy one. You can't foolproof the expectations of every person who picks up your book. No matter how you position your message, target your advertising, and price each format of your book, some readers will always be disappointed with what they get. If you do not prompt your happy readers to share their thoughts about your book, the unhappy ones will create a lopsided negative impression. You will be at the mercy of a disproportionate but vocal minority. Take preemptive measures to protect your book's image by frontloading its Amazon listing with reviews from advanced happy readers.

Some self-published authors are shocked when their first book accrues a large number of one- and two-star reviews for issues like minor formatting or grammatical errors. Some readers are so disappointed by these mistakes that they don't even get around to assessing the meaning of the book's message. They jump right to the Amazon page to vent their frustrations and warn other readers.

There is nothing unfair about these types of negative reviews, however pedantic they may seem. The reviewer's basic expectations of quality were not met. But consider if the people who write bad reviews because they are disappointed by grammatical errors would instead post good reviews if there had been perfect grammar? Disappointing people is a lot easier than keeping them happy. Upset readers are often unforgiving. Satisfied readers may be content to keep their happiness to themselves. Not only are unhappy readers more likely to voice their opinions, but negative reviews also have more influence than positive ones.

Counterintuitively, a small number of negative or middling reviews can sometimes be a good thing. Not everyone is going to think your book is perfect, and smart shoppers know this. If all your book's reviews rate it five out of five stars and are filled with hyperbolic praise, buyers may be skeptical.

They'll think that your reviews have come from friends or paid reviewers. It's better to have a mix of five- and four-star reviews with the occasional three- and two-star review thrown in from someone who just didn't get everything they wanted. Your book's sales may not even be hurt by one-star reviews if the logic behind them is biased, the complaints are incomprehensible, or it is clear they have been left by someone from an inappropriate reader demographic. Discerning shoppers will know to ignore them.

Verified Purchase Reviews

Although anyone with an Amazon account that meets some minimal activity requirements can post a review on any product, not every review carries equal weight. Amazon indicates at the head of every review if it comes from a Verified Purchase, which only happens if the reviewer purchased the item through their Amazon account before writing their review. Besides creating a stronger impression for shoppers, Verified Purchase reviews also have a greater effect on the Amazon Bestseller Ranking (ABSR) system and search algorithms.

However, it's not a complete waste of effort to gather reviews from people you have given physical or digital copies of your book to. Having many unverified reviews still greatly helps your listing gain visibility and convince shoppers to make purchases–just not as much as the same amount of verified reviews would do. You increase the chances of your reviews being verified by gently letting your reviewers know how important it is for your book's early success that they purchase the e-book from their Amazon account before reviewing. Fortunately, Kindle Direct Publishing (KDP) allows you to price your e-book as low as 99 cents. If someone who has read your book is willing to click the "Buy now with 1-Click®" button and cough up less than a dollar, their review will count as a verified purchase.

Remember the free promo days that come with enrollment in KDP Select? For up to five days per quarter, you can set the Kindle version of your book as a free download. This creates a lot of visibility for your book and has the added benefit of counting free downloads as purchases. Anyone who downloads your e-book while it is on free promotion will be eligible to leave a Verified Purchase review. Because of the limited window for which you can make your book free, getting all your reviewers to download it at the same time takes some coordination, but the results are worth it.

Helpful Review Votes

Amazon allows its users to vote on the "helpfulness" of each review, ensuring the most appropriate ones become the first ones shoppers see when they visit a book's listing. This feature can either help or hurt your book's presentation. Even if you receive only a single negative review, but it's long, detailed, and entertaining to read, shoppers may deem it more useful than the hundreds of short, generic positive reviews you accrue. So, that one scathing review from a reader who took offense to every idea in your book and felt compelled to voice their vitriol may show up at the top of your book's reviews and be read by every visitor to the listing.

If shoppers see negative feedback before they have a chance to consider all the positive things the majority of other reviewers are saying, they may decide to move on. That one negative review could become the cause of many lost sales. The only way you can counter this danger is to encourage your readers to leave long, detailed positive reviewers before any haters have a chance to dominate the public perception. You can also ask your fans to mark certain positive reviews as helpful and negative ones as unhelpful.

As a result of my pre-launch reviewer outreach efforts, almost all the early reviews I received for *Brand Identity Breakthrough: How to Craft Your Company's Unique Story to Make Your Products Irresistible* were five stars and worded to be highly supportive. However, the review that got the most attention from Amazon shoppers (and more than 50 "helpful" votes within a few months after launch) was a lengthy four-star review left by a serial entrepreneur and frequent Amazon reviewer.

At nearly 700 words long, his review begins by saying that the title of *Brand Identity Breakthrough* is a misnomer. He doesn't consider anything in the book to constitute a true "breakthrough"—just valid, tried-and-true advice about positioning, differentiation, targeting, brand personas, and so on. He thinks the book's focus is too broad and that I didn't include enough practical advice to complement all my poetic musings about the purpose of business. The reviewer (being decades older than me and more experienced in business) even points out a few oversights I had made with some of my claims about the history of marketing.

The reviewer then, however, goes on to emphatically state that despite these minor shortcomings, he considers me to be an excellent writer and *Brand Identity Breakthrough* to be a valuable overview of essential marketing and sales functions that could mean the difference between success and failure for entrepreneurs who lack a traditional business education. Because this review lacks the positive hyperbole and vague praise commonly received from the friends of self-published authors, it is given greater credibility by discerning book shoppers. The high number of helpful votes it has received is proof of this.

Amazon now shows this four-star review before all others. It has helped my first book stand out as legitimate reading material for serious entrepreneurs—not just another hastily published regurgitation of tired ideas. This is the kind of "good but not perfect" review that all books could benefit from. They are much more likely to receive "helpful" votes from shoppers than reviews that are short and offer little useful information about the quality of the book or what readers can expect to get from it.

Generating Ongoing Readership

Everything that happens before and during a book launch is focused on short-term influence. It does not necessarily affect what goes on in the long-term life of your book. With as much effort as you have already put into making your book visible for launch, further exposure is required to sustain sales in the months and years to come. Do this by keeping your book ranking highly in Amazon's search index and subcategory rankings. You can also run ads within Amazon that draw attention from other successful books similar to yours.

When you advertise any product online, there are a few different structures by which you can be charged for the opportunity to get your product seen, clicked on, or purchased. The most basic is a flat fee for a certain scope of exposure (e.g., $500 to run a banner ad on a website for one month). The price remains the same no matter how effective or ineffective the ad is. You're simply paying for the space it occupies, usually denoted with a given number of pixels.

Superior to flat-fee advertising is advertising that uses some form of performance metric to determine its cost to the advertiser. In the online world, this can be done a few ways. The price of an ad can be based on the number of people who view it, a metric commonly referred to as the number of impressions. You may see this referred to as cost-per-mille (CPM), with "mille" indicating 1,000 impressions.

Alternatively, an ad can be priced based not on the number of people who see it, but the number who actually click on it. Referred to as pay-per-click (PPC) or cost-per-click (CPC) advertising, this type guarantees at least a visit to your book's listing on Amazon. Advertisers compete for limited ad space on a platform by submitting a bid of how much money they are will to pay every time someone clicks on their ad. The highest bidder gets their ad run and is billed every time a click comes through. If the advertiser has a smart PPC strategy and access to their ad analytics, they will be able to track how often a click turns into a sale and how much profit they get from each sale. Therefore, they will know how much they can afford to spend on each click to break even or turn a profit.

There are many platforms that offer PPC advertising in one form or another (such as Google and most social media sites), but few of them are relevant to booksellers. As noted previously, people who search for a term on Google, even if it's the title of a book, aren't necessarily looking to buy books. It just doesn't make sense to run PPC ads there or anywhere else not tailored to readers and book buyers. Some forums and membership sites offer fixed-price and PPC advertising to their visitors, which can be valuable places to advertise if their audience overlaps with your book's target readers.

With PPC, you're only paying when a customer is interested enough to read your book's Amazon listing. You are less likely to waste money on ads that don't convert. Any impressions you receive that don't result in clicks will effectively be free advertising, resulting in potentially tens of thousands of book browsers being exposed to your book's cover, title, and a short sales pitch.

As a rule, people need repeated exposure to concepts or products before they can be convinced to investigate them further. Seeing your book show up, again and again, may eventually make a shopper curious enough to check it out. Exposure in this form may complement others, such as having heard about your book from a friend or having read an article about it. If one of your book's PPC ads receives 10,000 impressions and only a single visitor, you will have received a lot of exposure for the price of just one click.

Finally, you can pay a commission on the basis of not just impressions or clicks, but actual sales. For this to work well, you'd need to find an individual or organization willing to take the risk of producing no or low sales for your book. They would need to be able to optimize their approach so that they earn as many sales commissions as possible. Unfortunately, it's difficult in most situations to be able to accurately track how many book sales are generated on Amazon by a specific advertisement or advertiser. Commissioned sales strategies work best for expensive, big-ticket items where personal contact is made with a salesperson and it's clear where sales are coming from.

If you see a spike of 100 more books sold than usual, you won't necessarily know who caused it for you. One solution is to sell your book privately on your own website and implement coupon codes assigned to different salespeople. Their customers can input these specialized codes when they purchase from you to save some money and inform you of where they came from. Alternatively, you can allow institutions to sell your book on their own sites, collect payment and orders on your behalf, and then turn it all over to you for fulfillment (minus the agreed-upon commission amount). This is a lot of responsibility to place on a third party, so choose your representatives wisely.

You're free to experiment with as many forms of advertising on as many online platforms as you can identify as relevant to your readership. However, if you're unable to track the effectiveness of your ads, you risk wasting a lot of money. You could actually spend more money on advertisements than you make in total book revenue. Obviously, such spending habits are not sustainable. You need to look at your book as a business with rules that govern its ongoing existence.

Amazon Advertising

The best place to advertise your book is directly on Amazon itself. On there, visitors have a history of making similar kinds of purchases. Amazon makes promoting through them easy with its internal marketing platform called Amazon Advertising (formerly known as Amazon Marketing Solutions or AMS). Through Amazon Advertising, you'll be able to create PPC campaigns for your book from keywords you select, ones it suggests, or even specific books or subcategories you think would be most appropriate for catching the attention of buyers.

Like all forms of keyword marketing, if your Amazon Advertising keywords do not match what your target readers typically type into Amazon, the advertising algorithm will never show your ad. The opposite problem is choosing Amazon Advertising keywords that are too competitive, making it prohibitively expensive for your ad to get any visibility.

Amazon Advertising offers a handful of automatically generated keywords you can use for your ads, but don't expect many sales from them. For sustainable returns, you or someone you outsource the task to will need to experiment with many of your own keywords. Keyword experimentation can cause you to lose money on ads that don't produce enough profit from sales to cover click expenses. This is part of the startup cost of success as an author-entrepreneur. You shouldn't attempt to run PPC ads until you have some steady book revenue coming in or some funds you have put aside for this specific task.

You might be surprised when some of the keywords that produce the most sales with the fewest clicks will seem utterly unrelated to your book. Marketers can't always explain why the market does what it does. They just observe its behavior and try to make it work in their favor. With enough tweaking, you will eventually end up with at least a handful of keywords that consistently produce more than what they cost you. These ads could become your most reliable sources of new readers well after launch.

Paying to advertise your book can make it appear at the top of Amazon's search results for competitive keywords. However, your book's ad will carry a "sponsored" label to distinguish it from the organic results. The keywords you use for sponsored ads should be phrases that your target audience is actively searching for, such as general descriptive terms (e.g., "budget travel" or "relationship advice"). Your PPC keywords can even be the names of related authors or their book titles (e.g., "Men Are from Mars" or "John Gray"). You can even see some success with common synonyms and misspellings for your terms.

The "Customers who bought this item also bought" section of your book listing is a valuable resource for determining what your readers' preferences are actually like, not what you've speculated them to be like. The authors and titles that show up here are generated by real purchases your readers have made, indicating trends in preference. It's reasonable to assume that these books are an ideal starting place for running PPC ads on Amazon if you want to see results.

When you identify books that are similar in tone or purpose to yours, you can check what shows up in their "Customers who bought this item also bought" lists. This tactic will give you dozens of ideas for where to promote that you otherwise would not have considered. This type of research is a viable way to discover and take advantage of the market ecosystem your book will be entering. You can do the same with books ranking well in subcategories related to your topic and Amazon's "Hot New Releases" section. Select these books and others like them as specific targets to run your Amazon Advertising ads on instead of relying solely on keyword searches, which will likely have much broader results.

Monitoring PPC Ads

Tracking the success of your ads can be a little convoluted. The Amazon Advertising dashboard will show you how many impressions and clicks each ad receives, the aCPC ("average Cost Per Click"), the total amount spent on clicks, and the total sales revenue generated. Together, these metrics give you enough information to strategize with your ads by determining which ones are providing the monetary return necessary to justify their existence.

It's important to remember that the Estimated Total Sales metric Amazon Advertising provides tallies the gross revenue of an ad (e.g., the total retail price of all books sold from a particular ad). Your actual royalties will be less than this. Hopefully, you have priced your e-book between $2.99 and $9.99 to take advantage of the 70% royalty rate. You will also need to factor in any additional delivery fee KDP tacks on (such as if your e-book is a large file with many pictures) and tax withholding if you are in a country that requires it.

The ACoS metric on the Amazon Advertising dashboard stands for "Advertising Cost of Sale." It gives you an instant indicator of your ratio of spending to earning with each ad. If you are making 70% royalties from your sales, you need your ACoS percentage to be less than 70% to be turning a profit. Anything higher than 70% means you are losing money because too many people are clicking without making purchases.

PPC ads for your book work best when you offer as many opportunities as possible for people who click onto your listing to make a purchase. This is just one more reason you should have your book available in every format (e-book, paperback, hardcover, and audio) before you advertise. The fewer the number of clicks that don't result in a sale, the less money you will waste on advertising. You will have a higher number of total sales and a higher profit margin by converting the optimal amount of clickers into buyers.

If you have the patience for it, you can track the clicks, impressions, and expenses of each ad at the same time every day to see their change and trajectory. Monitoring your ads in this manner quickly becomes a full-time job though. Making adjustments too frequently also doesn't account for delays in the analytics Amazon reports to you or exceptional market behavior that is not indicative of the general trend. Only a long-term view of your ads' performance does that. It makes more sense to check your ads every week or month and cancel the ones that aren't turning a profit than to try to micromanage them daily.

It generally isn't a good idea to begin running PPC ads for your book right after launch. You should first ensure the book gets ample visibility and sales from other sources. PPC ads work best when you have many positive reviews and a high average rating on your book. This information is displayed on all your sponsored ads, along with the book's title, cover, and whatever ad copy you decide to run with it. If you run ads before you have many positive reviews (or worse, when you have only negative or middling reviews) most of your budget will be wasted because few visitors will complete purchases. Social proof is vital to the success of an advertisement.

While PPC can be a very effective form of advertising for bringing in thousands of new sales over time, it can also be very expensive. Even if you turn a profit, it won't be as much of a profit as if you hadn't had to pay for the clicks in the first place. When you calculate your book royalties each month, you'll always have to subtract whatever amount you spend on PPC ads, which could be many hundreds or even thousands of dollars.

Unpaid Amazon Traffic Tactics

To get free traffic to your book listing, you'll either need to bring in visitors from outside Amazon or manipulate Amazon's search directory to your advantage. You should already have done some research on tactical search terms to include in your title and book description. Now you need to understand how Amazon decides which books to show first when a reader searches for them.

Every time a shopper clicks on a book listing after searching a phrase, the domain URL of the listing will be extended to include the phrase that was searched. If the shopper searched for the term "dog training," the listing they click on will contain "keywords=dog+training" at the tail end of its URL. This is how Amazon tracks the behavior of its shoppers with its search function.

When a listing is clicked on and a purchase made, the Amazon search algorithm learns that listing is a relevant result for that search term. The listing will then rank higher when other shoppers search the same term. If a listing is clicked but not purchased after searching a term, the Amazon search algorithm learns the opposite: that the product clicked on is not a good fit for what shoppers are looking for with that term. The search ranking for that listing with that term will go down.

Understanding how this keyword tracking works, you can subtly manipulate it to give your book a short-term visibility boost after launch. When you share the link to your book with people whom you are sure will purchase it, you can apply a keyword you want to rank for at the tail end of the URL. When your customer clicks the link and buys your book, it will temporarily improve your Amazon search ranking for that term. This will then make it more likely that other shoppers who search the same term will see your book in their results and purchase it (if it meets their expectations).

This customized URL tactic is not a permanent solution, however. If you succeed in temporarily ranking well for a term that does not match what Amazon searchers are looking for, they will not purchase your book. Your high-ranking spot will quickly be overtaken by another listing that better caters to the market demands for that search term. Clearly, sharing a custom URL also will not work in cases where you cannot be sure the clicker will make a purchase, or else you will only be hurting your search ranking.

For more general link-sharing tactics, use a shortened, affiliated-linked URL. Through the Amazon Associates program (www.affiliate-program.amazon. com), you will earn up to 10% of the retail price of any product you've created a custom link to (as well as from most any other products purchased within 24 hours of clicking on your affiliate link). Note that this affiliate fee is in addition to the royalties you earn as the publisher of your book. It's just a convenient way to earn a little more money through the act of sharing your book link.

Foreign Book Markets and Translation

The universe of readers who might love your book does not end with those who are immediately available to you on Amazon, through other distributors, or even within the confines of your nation or language. There are more than seven billion people on Earth. Any additional fraction of them that you can tap into as readers for your book will contribute significantly to your success as an author. Once your book has achieved a respectable level of success in your domestic market, it's time to start thinking about its potential in foreign markets.

You've already created a significant foreign market presence just by publishing on Amazon, whether or not you know it. There are 13 Amazon regional platforms where your book will be made available for purchase just by including them as sales channels in your KDP back office. You can view your book's listing on each regional sales channels to monitor its presentation and performance:

- United States (amazon.com)
- United Kingdom (amazon.co.uk)
- Germany (amazon.de)

- France (amazon.fr)
- Spain (amazon.es)
- Italy (amazon.it)
- Netherlands (amazon.nl)
- Japan (amazon.co.jp)
- Brazil (amazon.com.br)
- Canada (amazon.ca)
- Mexico (amazon.com.mx)
- Australia (amazon.com.au)
- India (amazon.in)

Other large markets like China, Russia, and almost all countries in Central and South America (except Brazil and Mexico) don't have access to the KDP platform, so you can't sell your book through Amazon in these places. Amazon does operate in China (amazon.cn) and Singapore (amazon.com.sg) but doesn't currently offer self-publishing in these regions.

Each local Amazon platform caters to a distinct audience. Thus, each maintains its own user reviews and ABSR system. You will receive your royalties from each Amazon domain in its local currency, which will then be converted to dollars. You can monitor how many copies are sold and royalties generated on each platform through one convenient KDP interface.

There are layout and presentation differences between each platform, as Amazon wisely figured out that online shoppers have different preferences in different parts of the world. Unfortunately, this means all the work you've done gathering reader reviews and driving traffic to your US Amazon listing won't have much influence on other regional versions (with the exception of the fact that they will sometimes display the .com reviews alongside any local reviews garnered).

There are some unique market advantages to selling on Amazon's regional sites. Compare the roughly five million Kindle e-books published on Amazon's .com site to the 500,000 in German, 240,000 in Spanish and

French, and 200,000 in Italian. The lower competition makes it easier to become a bestselling author in France, for example, than in the United States if you translate your book in French for Amazon.fr.

There are, however, often fewer readers in countries outside the United States. There are roughly one fifth as many people in France as in the US (70 million versus 330 million). This doesn't mean you will have five times fewer sales in France than in the United States though. Reader habits in France are different than in the United States. No author or marketer can control or predict how every variable will influence their sales on the international market.

If your book is written in English, you are already operating in the language with the highest market viability for self-published books. You may be surprised to realize how many countries English readers can be found in. There is an aggregate audience of 1.5 billion English speakers (about 20% of the world's population) in the United States, Canada, the United Kingdom, Australia, and many countries where English is not even an official language. 11 of India's 29 states have adopted English as an official language and approximately 10% of its the total population (about 120 million of 1.2 billion Indians) speak English as a first or second language.

Foreign Publishers

If your book sells well on the U.S. market, you may receive emails from overseas publishers interested in purchasing its foreign translation rights. Such offers will come with a flat fee, a small percentage of royalties from sales, or a combination of both. Knowing the royalty percentage and the selling price for your book, you can calculate how many copies need to be sold to earn the same amount as a one-time payment. Be aware that the retail price of books in a foreign market might be less than what you are used to selling your books for at home, thus they will require more sales to achieve the same profit.

Throughout *The Influential Author*, I have argued the merits of self-publishing, so long as you are in a position to refine, launch, and promote your work. However, handing these responsibilities to a publisher may make a lot more sense in foreign markets you know nothing about. Do some rudimentary research on any foreign publisher that approaches you to determine their track record of success with translated titles. You don't want to get involved with scammers or newcomers who won't represent your book well. If they are offering to compensate you with a percentage of royalties, you will need some assurances that they have a competent sales plan and you will be able to collect your royalties from overseas.

After signing an agreement with a foreign publisher, you won't have much input on the book's preparation. Unless stated in the contract, you won't be able to make any decisions about translation, cover, formatting, or anything else before it shows up in foreign bookstores. This is probably for the best. Local publishing houses (should) have a better understanding of local market preferences about presentation and promotion. These cultural differences are beyond the intuitive understanding of a foreigner who has not spent years studying the local book market. What looks strange and unattractive to you might match what Indian, Chinese, or German readers are expecting.

Before foreign publishing, consider the possibility that your subject matter or writing style, by their nature, might be attractive exclusively to American English speakers, making it wasteful to invest in foreign translation and distribution. A book about American history or that offers advice about specifically American things might not ever be able to find a foothold overseas.

Working on Your Own

If you decide to pursue translating and publishing your book in a foreign language on your own, there are many new variables you will have to consider. Effective translation is a complex process, and the nuances are different for each language. There are over 480 million native Spanish speakers in more than 20 countries, making it the second most spoken native language in the world (after Mandarin Chinese). There are, however, substantial differences between European Spanish (also called Peninsular

Spanish) and the Spanish of the Americas, as well as many different dialect areas within both Spain and Hispanic America.

For instance, the verb "to drive" in Latin American Spanish is "manejar." In Spain, you'll hear people use "conducer" to indicate the same action. But Spaniards will also use "manejar" as the verb "to manage," like in the phrase "manejar el negocio"—to manage a business. Less innocuously, a common word in Castellano (another name for the type of Spanish used in Europe), "cojer" ("to take"), has a crude sexual connotation in parts of Latin America. It has roughly the same meaning as the f-word in English. Obviously, you don't want to confuse these terms in your book's translation.

Besides numerous vocabulary differences, there are inconsistent grammatical quirks within languages that cannot be ignored. There are entire forms in which to congregate verbs that are practically non-existent in Latin American Spanish but common in the European variant. If you learned Spanish in an American high school, you were probably never taught the vosotros form (used in Spain when addressing more than one individual in the second person perspective—just like the slang contraction "y'all" in English). The people who designed your Spanish curriculum decided your proximity to Central America made it most pertinent for you to learn Latin American Spanish, which lacks the vosotros form. Students who learn Spanish in Europe are taught different grammatical rules because they are closer to Spain.

So, before hiring Spanish translators, you should have a clear vision which type of Spanish will appeal most to the readers you are targeting. If you want to publish your book in Spain, you should hire translators who work in Castellano. If you want to enter Central and South American markets, you should translate your book using Latin American Spanish. Otherwise, you might harm your author brand and lose sales in the long run.

The Chinese language poses similar translation problems. Chinese is infamous for having hundreds of complex dialects. However, for publishing purposes, there are two languages to consider: Simplified Chinese (prevalent in mainland China) and Traditional Chinese (prevalent in Hong Kong).

The goal of translation is not simply to replace words in one language with their equivalents in another. It is to deliver the same idea in the way it will be best received by its foreign audience. Even if you have a high command of the language you want to translate your book into, you probably shouldn't translate it on your own. You should play a role in clarifying your intended meaning for your translator, but it is best to leave the actual translation work to someone familiar with the nuances of conveying meaning across both languages.

Foreign Titling

Even the Russian translation of the title for *Brand Identity Breakthrough* presented a conundrum. There is no equivalent for the word "breakthrough" in Russian that would work with the term "brand identity" (which is not a concept Russian-speaking audiences would be likely to recognize anyway). After examining about a dozen possibilities, my translator decided to move forward with the Russian title *Revolyutsiya Brenda* (Революция бренда), which translates directly to "the brand revolution." It might sound different to English speakers, but Russian audiences are more likely to understand this title the way *Brand Identity Breakthrough* is understood in English. Meanwhile, the Spanish title for the same book became *Desarrollando la Identidad de Marca*, which translates to "developing the brand identity."

Similarly, the Russian title for *Travel as Transformation* became *Puteshestviya Kak Sposob Izmenit' Sebya* (Путешествие Как а Способ Изменит Себя), which means "travel as a way to change oneself." The Spanish title was *Viajar para Trascender*, meaning "travel to transcend." Through repeated testing, both of these were deemed more appropriate for the cultural contexts in which they would be presented and promoted.

Foreign Proofreading

Unfortunately, many translators who claim to be professionals don't have the relevant education or experience to perform at the necessary level for retail book publication. You can test the abilities of your potential translators by sending them a few paragraphs of your book to translate. If you need it, get help from a native speaker of the language to assess the quality of their trial translations. Ask them to evaluate the quality of the translations both grammatically and stylistically. Has the meaning of the message been preserved? Will a foreign audience have trouble understanding it? Is the original voice still present?

No matter who you hire to translate your book, showing the work to another party for proofreading is essential. Aside from just typical human language errors, your translator might have misunderstood the original message in some crucial way. There are always many ways the meaning of a phrase or sentence can be conveyed. When translating my first book, *Brand Identity Breakthrough*, into Russian, I ran into hundreds of situations where the first draft of the translation didn't convey the message I intended. They required several new read-throughs by other translators to correct.

Foreign Marketing Challenges

Marketing to foreign readers in foreign markets presents foreign challenges. Not knowing the language and being unfamiliar with the culture makes promotion more arduous and less efficient. You may need to have your promotional materials translated and proofread, assuming they will even be appropriate for readers in other countries. You will need to learn what each foreign audience that you target prefers to read and in which formats. You will need to understand their motives, habits, and responsiveness regarding your unique message. Even cover design preferences can vary across countries.

If you are totally unfamiliar with the foreign market you want to enter, it's good to have an insider—a local expert—to guide you. Unless you regularly surf Russian websites related to books, it's unlikely you would know about the largest social network of books in Russia, livelib.ru (an analog of goodreads. com in the United States). The knowledge of this kind of website will be crucial to your promotion in any Russian-speaking countries. Without insider familiarity, you would not even know where to even begin looking.

With over 1.4 billion people, China has potentially the largest reading audience in the world. However, disseminating ideas in China presents a unique legal problem. Due to rampant government regulations and censorship, all Chinese books go through a tedious approval process by the state. If your message is deemed to be politically correct, you will receive a number that allows your book to be published. This number is analogous to an ISBN and is given only to publishing companies, not to individuals. Only Chinese citizens can run publishing houses in China, and no foreigners are allowed to enter the market directly. Therefore, an author who wants to be published in China must work with a local Chinese publishing house.

Summary of Chapter 12

Reader reviews on online book platforms (particularly Amazon) are crucial for sustained sales. They enhance the effectiveness of all forms of exposure you generate. Accruing dozens or hundreds of positive reviews over time will require you to recruit reviewers or encourage your readers to leave reviews when they have finished reading your book. The process is complicated by Amazon's "verified purchase" system and strict rules about how shoppers are allowed to leave reviews.

— — — —

There are many ways to encourage new traffic to continually flow to your online book listing. However, most platforms that offer performance-based advertising with metrics are not specifically relevant for authors selling books. Fortunately, Amazon offers its own native price-per-click advertising that can be targeted by keywords, subcategories, or specific book listings. You can also manipulate how your book appears in Amazon's search results to encourage more unpaid traffic to end up at your book's listing.

— — — —

There is an entire world of viable readers beyond the exposure you will receive with your book on Amazon.com and other English-based book retailers. Amazon will also publish your book to its 12 other regional platforms, and there are countless others who can discover you independently or through a distribution aggregator. You may choose to translate your book into strategic foreign languages. You may even be contacted by foreign publishing houses who wish to buy your book's translation rights.

PART 7:

REWARD

CHAPTER 13:

What Happens When You Publish a Book

If you've followed the advice of *The Influential Author*, you should be at the end of your long journey to create a remarkable book and introduce it to the hungry online market. You should feel a healthy amount of pride for even having attempted to understand the strategies for creating, publishing, and promoting a unique collection of knowledge such as yours (without letting self-praise go to your head). Now that your primary publishing tasks are done, you are in a position to reflect on what has so far transpired, what comes next, and how to make the most out of it in both the near and distant future.

The work of authors and publishers does not end with the launch of a book. It just begins to take on an increasingly passive role. No great and pressing efforts should be required past this point. The minor changes and tight deadlines have all been handled. Your focus now will be to start optimizing the rewards that writing a book makes available to you. With time, you will learn how to recognize and harness every good thing your book brings into your life. But first, you need to be prepared for the thoughts, feelings, and issues you will encounter once your book is out on the open market.

Your life, from within and without, will change now that your book is complete and for sale. The opportunities your book will create are potentially quite vast and impressive, but only if you know how to recognize and use them. You started this journey with your own ideas about why it would be worth the patience and labor to get where you are now. Therefore, you will be the judge of whether your book accomplishes what you set out to do.

Most likely, you wrote for some combination of the following reasons:

1. Existential fulfillment and self-investment

Writers write firstly for the internal satisfaction that comes from the expression of their deepest and most sacred thoughts. They experience uniquely meaningful relief when, after struggling for so long to find the right words, they can finally articulate what has been on their hearts and minds for a great while. For some people, writing to express meaning is the only way to stay sane and force themselves to grow as individuals. They are their own greatest teachers.

2. Social impact and reception

Every self-aware person pursues purpose in the world around them in one form or another. On some level, all people need to believe that their words and actions mean something in the grand scheme of events beyond the confines of their own lives. After a while, telling ourselves a story about what our lives mean isn't enough; we need to witness the consequences of our meaningful actions to reap their full emotional rewards. When a writer shares their wisdom and ideas and sees how they affect the way other people think and live, their cathartic release is elevated to a new category of fulfillment. This kind of influence is difficult to achieve without the aid of technology and willingness to put oneself on the world's stage to be judged.

3. Ongoing passive financial return

Finally, there are important practical rewards for writing and publishing. The marketplace for nonfiction books has risen to a prominent level of democratization for producers and consumers alike. It is easy now to provide for the material necessities of life through the same activities that bring life meaning and purpose. A published author can accumulate wealth in direct proportion to the value of their message and ability to spread it. If you've never earned money in a passive or entrepreneurial fashion before, you will soon learn how much doing so can improve the way you live and work.

To reap each of these categories of reward, you will need to stay sharp and on top of all things related to your book. You'll soon learn many new things about how your book will come to affect you personally, interpersonally, and financially.

Existential Fulfillment and Self-Investment

For as long as I can remember, I have been seeking a rightful place to occupy in the world. I have lacked creative, rewarding outlets through which to apply what I perceived to be exceptional faculties. The need to forge my own path in a world that seemed not to have one prepared for me pushed me into a rampant exploration of my options for purpose early in life. Wandering soon evolved into entrepreneurship and education, both of which tested my ability to organize reality's elements in my favor.

Until recently, I did not really understand the logical end of the path I had been paving for myself. Now, at this still-early juncture in my authorial career, I know my motivation, such that I can project into the future what new books I will someday write. I am intimately aware of why I will persist in writing and publishing for reasons beyond the practical rewards of additional income and recognition. Writing *The Influential Author* has helped me gain even further clarity on this issue.

I believe now that organizing important information is one of the most meaningful ways I could spend my time. Writing and sharing my thoughts allows me to apply my natural faculties through the filter of my unconventional life experiences. Each new book I write refines my abilities and increases my options for expression. Writing books I know will be published for public consumption forces me always to be growing as a thinker, communicator, and human.

I began writing books as part of a personal experiment in marketing and communication. It has since evolved into a desire to show the world the many un-obvious truths I see about the how important things work. The more I write, the more I realize that there are powerful ideas and perceptions at work within me. They will not rest until I take the trouble to arrange and present them for public validation.

Authoring meaningful books is rewarding for me because of the way I interpret the state of human civilization on this planet. When I look around me, I see a world shaped by the consequences of chaos and inefficiency. I know that much of it could be eliminated by better human thought and action. I know that if we could all reason more clearly and operate with more accurate premises about reality, we could live much better than we do. Each philosophical contribution moves us (and those who will come after us) a little bit closer to a more ideal state of living on this planet.

I know it is not within my power to make the better world I imagine snap into existence as quickly as I can imagine it. Reality has its immutable restraints. Human beings operate with laws for their behavior, no different than a ball rolling down a hill or a pendulum swinging in a grandfather clock. I cannot make anyone break these rules in their life, even if they wanted to. I can only contribute to the causal factors that will eventually result in obvious changes.

I know now that my journey into influential authorship has only just begun. The book you are reading is only the most recent step I have taken in the pursuit of personal meaning. If by writing *The Influential Author* I have provided the tools and inspiration necessary for some would-be communicators to share their knowledge in an effective, profitable, and sustainable manner, I will have earned for myself a sense of personal meaning.

Through writing and publishing, I clear new spaces in my mind. I can better observe and analyze without the baggage of outdated knowledge to slow me. I can look back on some of what I wrote in my first books and scarcely even remember thinking or writing them. I am continually surprised by the wording and ideas that were so prominent in my mind at the time of writing. Getting them out in paperback serves a similar function to an external hard drive for my computer. In a manner of speaking, I now have multiple minds that belong to me with copies circulating the globe.

Clearing space in the mind creates an incentive to fill it with new, valuable ideas and experiences. In that manner, writing can be a powerful ally for the man or woman concerned with rapid, lifelong personal development. When you lack teachers to show you how to refine your knowledge or what to learn next, your drive to continue writing may be what carries you to your next station in life. Your understanding of yourself will evolve just as quickly as your understanding of how to interact with the world.

As long as I keep writing, I will have to keep evolving my knowledge and abilities. I will not allow myself to fall into the trap of writing the same book and recycling the same knowledge time and again. If I want more material for my next books, I have to keep exposing myself to more meaningful life experiences. I have to keep refining my understanding of the experiences I've already had, looking for a deeper truth to their place in my life.

The hours and mental strain required for each book's creation will always be worth it, so long as I am writing something true to my core values and beliefs, fame and financial reward notwithstanding. People who never create anything new never get to appreciate the effects of this kind of self-investment. When you create something that represents you, you build up your own sense of identity a little more. It can do wonders for self-esteem and confidence.

Respect My Authority

Promoted well, the message of your book becomes a lasting part of your public and private identity. The knowledge you worked so hard to organize on the page should hold greater significance for you now because it exists in a form the world can consume and allow itself to be affected by. Accordingly, you should be ready to represent yourself as the progenitor of what you've undertaken great struggles to articulate. You aren't no one anymore. You stand atop an epistemological platform. The opportunities yours creates are unique to your circumstances and only as limited as your imagination.

The first change you might notice after you release your book is how differently some people will treat you when they discover that you've written a book. Being a published author is a status that still carries significant weight around the world, among all social classes. In some situations, the social authority a book bestows on its author is roughly the same as a PhD in my estimation. Many non-authors carry the assumption that only experts ever write tens of thousands of words on bound paper and charge a retail price for it. They don't realize the doors are now open to anyone. Use their presumptions to your advantage so long as you can do so ethically and accurately.

If you are not careful and especially self-aware, the heightened recognition you receive from your first book may go to your head. Avoid the temptation to think too highly of yourself due to the cultural image that authorship imbues. Capitalize on your increased social authority when it is useful for your goals, but always do so with a sense of humility and respect for your new social responsibility.

Within a year of publishing my first two books, I had leveraged my social status as an author to achieve many accomplishments which were unprecedented in my life. By that time, I had adopted the habit of keeping paperback copies of my work with me almost anywhere I went, usually tucked into my laptop bag beside my computer, which I conveniently also always needed with me to be able to work on what I was writing next. I would then sell, give away, or simply show off my books whenever I spotted the opportunity to use them for social leverage.

Examples:

- I have always loathed flirting and cold social openings with attractive strangers. My books have given me opportunities to start meaningful conversations on subjects I care about when I desire to get to know someone new. It's far better than struggling through awkward small talk and the contrived rules of pickup artistry in a vain attempt to trick a pretty face into handing me her number.

- As a world traveler, I cross a lot of international borders. This sometimes entails getting delayed to be questioned by border agents about the nature of my identity and what I intend to be doing in their country. If I have a copy of one of my books in my carry-on bag, I can show my interrogators that I am a "world-famous" author with my full name and headshot on prominent display in a professional-looking publication. Suddenly, I will begin to be treated as a high-status individual who is not only welcome but encouraged to be within their borders.

- When applying for citizenship in another country, I attended a mandatory government interview pertaining to my character, profession, politics, and the value I would bring as a registered member of their nation. During this interview, I used *Brand Identity Breakthrough* to position myself as someone of high entrepreneurial value and international fame who would contribute to the business culture of their developing economy. My application was accepted, even though I later learned that most other applicants of a similar age and background to me were denied. Of course, it's only appropriate that I used a book about branding to help me establish my own personal brand.

- I've received free food and accommodations at some hotels and restaurants around the world when the staff learned I was a published travel author. I assume they hoped that I would write something positive about their establishment on social media, in my (nonexistent) blog, or in my next book. I have no moral qualms about letting them persist in these premature assumptions.

- Because I've now translated my books into Spanish and Russian, I've had increased opportunities to connect with local people throughout Latin America and Eastern Europe that language barriers might otherwise have prevented. In my ancestral home of Armenia, I was able to get the Russian versions of my books listed in local bookstores, catching the attention of community leaders and entrepreneurs who wouldn't have been able to digest my message in English. I became known around certain parts of the country as the eccentric author from America.

- In my work related to personal development coaching, my books have played integral roles in convincing prospective clients that I am the ideal person to work with. My approach to personal growth is complex and unique. Understanding my paradigm takes a lot more exposure than most other coaches who offer only mild variations on a generic theme of self-empowerment. Books allow for the opportunity of lengthened exposure.

- *The Influential Author* serves a similar purpose regarding my work with Identity Publications, where my task is to help prospective authors write and publish a certain caliber of book. By the time you've reached these final chapters, you have read many hours' worth of my words about my philosophy of influential authorship. You should be crystal clear about whether I am the person you want to work with to create and publish your book.

- I semi-regularly receive emails and social media tags from readers, most of whom just want to mention how much they like one of my books. Some of these people go on to become meaningful friends, clients, or professional associates. If your motivation to publish is centered around your profession, your book will serve as a glorified business card to make connections with.

- When recruiting beta readers on online forums for *The Influential Author*, some people who responded to my requests recognized my name from my other books they had already bought and read. Because they liked my writing style and unique brand of insight in those earlier cases, they were eager to engage in a dialogue with me about writing and self-publishing. It was notably easier to find high-quality beta readers this time around, and part of that is because I'm now somewhat acknowledged as a source of information worth listening to.

When you understand the potency of social authority, you will realize that publishing a book is about so much more than the content itself or the royalties generated. Publishing a book is about elevating the way the world sees you so that you can operate with greater influence and leverage within it. The more you write, publish, and promote your books, the more social power you will accumulate. The more social power you accumulate, the more creative ways you will discover how you can use it. The world works quite differently when strangers naturally assume they ought to be listening to your knowledge and opinions . Always remain aware that with great social power comes great social responsibility.

Elusive Rewards

Writing books can offer you a sense of meaning unlike anything else you might have accomplished in your life so far. However, purpose and meaning can also be rather fickle rewards. The book you need to write today might not matter so much to you in a few years' time. Perhaps you will have moved on to new interests then. You may not even remember the hours you spent perfecting your words about something that once dominated your mind. Only time and publishing experience will reveal more of the concepts that will bring you sustainable internal reward.

Each new book you begin writing is a chance to improve your powers of outlining and articulation. Each successful publication should get you closer to the highest meaning you are aiming for, just as publishing *The Influential*

Author has been a major push forward on my path as an organizer and promoter of unique values and influential ideas. You only need to have the endurance to make it through the missteps and mundanities of the process.

I can predict many of the properties the next books I will write will have, but the details still elude me. Until I am ready to put my broad ideas down on paper and start chipping away at them, I will not know their ideal form. I can also predict that somewhere along the way I will be struck with new inspirations I cannot currently fathom. I only know that each new book I write will add to my personal sense of a meaningful life and identity.

Social Reception and Impact

Every person on Earth, in some way, shape, or form, identifies themselves by their effect upon the world as they perceive it. It is in our nature to seek a greater-than-personal sense of purpose by doing things that are not limited to our own lives or observations.

When you write a book that matters, you do so partially with the goal of influencing as many of the right people as possible to think and live differently. If you have targeted your book and presented your message well, you will begin to see the effect you intended take place in people, in places, and in ways you never even presumed. Beyond the satisfaction of knowing that your work is making a difference in other lives, you will also see these effects reflected on your own life.

For the modern man or woman, there are more ways than ever before to create something that will last long after their ephemeral life has ended. With the aid of technology, they can reach beyond their ordinary limitations to create things past generations would have only dreamt of. Some creators focus their ambitions on erecting long-standing physical structures. Others design new systems, narratives, and symbols to represent some great meaning they care for. The vainest of men and women pursue fame as the highest end—to cement their names and faces in the memory of the collective, if only for a while.

Publishing a book that represents your deepest thoughts and values may be the most important thing you ever do. As an author, you will have left the best parts of yourself behind for present and future generations to learn from. When they read your message, they become your intellectual progeny. Because your book has captured the uniqueness of how you think about the things most important to you, it represents a prolonged snapshot of the internal monologue that defines you. Your readers, no matter where or when they are, get to converse with you for the rest of eternity.

You cannot foresee right now the result of the butterfly effect you have set in motion by publishing a unique perspective on reality. Historically, the right ideas have changed the course of individual lives and global societies, so long as they were viable for reception among their populations. They have offered instruction, hope, and meaning to people seeking answers without end. Your book constitutes a psychological legacy, one primed to spread almost anywhere humans will derive meaning from it.

Your message may help someone acquire a powerful form of mental or emotional resolution they have been seeking. That person may then be able to move forward in some critical area of their life that had been preventing them from using their gifts and feeling their emotions to the fullest. Therefore, everything positive that person accomplishes thereafter will be a direct result of the influence your words imparted to them when they most needed it. You will never know how far this outwardly branching influence will reach, but it does not have to end with your death. Your book will surpass the natural boundaries of your life.

The influence your message has on the world is not fixed. Some influences stay with a person all their life. Others come and go at different stages of their development, depending on when they are needed. What any given culture is craving most at any time will change. Many of the people

361

who need most to hear what you have to say will not know what they need. Only when the reader becomes ready will the right book appear. If the world or an individual is not ready to hear what you have to say, the meaning of your book will be lost.

Influence Overwhelm

Once the people your message touches the most begin to reach out to you to share their gratitude, you may not know how to respond. Strangers will begin talking about the collection of personal thoughts you worked so hard to craft as an entity unto itself. A little piece of you (perhaps what you consider to be the deepest, most authentic piece of you) will have become a product for the public to pass around and discuss. Each of them will be forming ideas about you that you cannot monitor or control.

For shy or introverted individuals who never wanted or expected to become a figurehead for their values, a sudden influx of praise can feel intimidating. When you earn the adoration and respect of even a single reader, their expectations about you may surpass what you are able or willing to live up to. If many, many people begin talking to or about you in a specific way, it will create public pressure to be the icon others now see you as. This is just one of the reasons why it is crucial that you write about topics and in a tone you can comfortably integrate with the person you want to be in the world.

The first time you hold your printed book in your hands or see its listing go live on Amazon may be when you begin to understand the public effects of being an author. You cannot necessarily go back to the silence and anonymity you may have known before. For better or for worse, some part of the world will know you first and foremost as the author of the book you have created. With that association comes responsibilities and expectations. The greater the depth of your message, the greater your responsibilities may be.

Influence Resistance

No author can expect a universally positive response about what they have produced. There will always be some resistance, and its effects reach far beyond the occasional negative online review. Every message of substance carries the potential for misinterpretation or offense. For every reader who strongly agrees with you, there may be 10 more who strongly disagree with you. If your point of view is controversial, expect people to form biases about you and the content of your book without even bothering to read it. The title, description, or reputation of your work may be enough to earn their condemnation.

As Thomas Paine (clearly one of my primary ideological influences) wrote, "He who dares not offend cannot be honest."

Whenever you voice strong values, you open yourself to the possibility of ideological conflict. Complete strangers who should have no reason to care about your values or personal affairs will take it upon themselves to antagonize you for daring to speak your mind. You cannot spread your ideas if you are not willing to offend anyone. If your message challenges what people believe, there will be some people who take umbrage with its very existence. To undertake the effort of writing, publishing, and promoting a meaningful book is to make a bold statement about yourself and your values. Bold statements garner strong emotional reactions, favorable and unfavorable alike. The more important your message, the more it may upset readers who disagree.

It is normal to face resistance from your peer group (the people who know you to be a certain way) when you set aspirations for yourself beyond the limits of their comfort. They may prefer the version of you that existed before you ever expressed yourself in such a public and confident manner. They will not necessarily appreciate your new role as author and figurehead for a subject that matters more to you than the innocuous identity you once embodied.

Human beings tend to define themselves by what they can observe, relate to, and replicate within their micro-social environments. Because their sense of identity is constructed by how they perceive their social order to function, they may resist anything that challenges how they have come to believe the world must work. These artificial limits include what they perceive you to be capable of. So, an individual's progress into a new domain of life sometimes requires the loosening or letting go of old social connections. Do not let yourself allow others to dictate what you can do or become.

Your book represents an opportunity for a rapid acceleration of purpose and social standing. Quick gains bring with them the possibility of equally quick losses. The outcome of a life is the result of many cycles of targeted creation and destruction, just as it is with the process of writing and editing a book. You must know what you want and are willing to give up to get where you are intent on arriving. Prepared with this self-knowledge, your ascension will be much smoother.

If at any point you cease believing in your ability to be an author, you will sabotage your own success. You will no longer write with the same passion or purpose. You will no longer produce efficiently. When you finally complete a book, you will not promote it as you should. It gets easier to maintain confidence when you have multiple books to your credit, but it can be hell for some people who have a history of anxiety to get their first book off the ground in the face of social resistance.

Author Envy

As you may have already learned during the beta reading and outreach stages of publication, even your fellow authors can be a source of great scorn toward your book. It's not hard to understand why. Some self-published writers have poured years of their lives and the depths of their emotions into their work. Yet, few of them ever receive any respectable level of economic success or even social recognition for their efforts. This causes some authors to adopt mentalities of victimhood, as though their books were magnificent, but the world lacked the palate necessary to appreciate them.

Any artist who takes their work (and their ego) too seriously is subject to extreme envy. They become easily threatened by other artists in their field who hold big aspirations or achieve success without failing in the same ways they have. Veteran self-published authors may especially hate newbies who appear to know more than they do about writing or publishing. To save face, they may attribute your success to luck or marketplace trickery. They must continue to see themselves as victims of circumstance beyond their control.

Ambition is often punished by the unambitious. Giving a voice to your values can upset creators who lack the courage to do the same as you have and earn the same accolades you have earned for yourself. Even just learning that you plan to write a book is a potentially triggering event for such fragile egos. For many failed creators, prognosticating the failure of someone else provides a hint of the same emotional reward as achieving success for themselves. You cannot let this form of professional resistance slow your production or release. You cannot let yourself become like them.

There's an inverse relationship between an individual's self-worth and the offense taken at others' expressions of self-worth. Crab mentality is the social phenomenon that keeps subcultures of people enslaved to each other's psychological limits, like angry crabs trapped in a barrel who cripple each other with their claws to prevent any other crabs from climbing out to freedom. When confronted with individuals who are capable of ascending to higher tiers of social operation, those who stand to be left behind will fight to maintain their mediocre status quo. Nothing ever changes unless the aspiring author is convicted enough to break through the social resistance.

Such is the origin of the phenomenon of trolling: those who cannot assert their own identities through proactive means attempt to destruct the assertions made by others. If they cannot attain the objects of their desires, no one in their social class ought to either. Ordinary people will sabotage the ambitions of their brethren in a heartbeat if doing so provides just a little validation for their own perceived failures. You are going to piss someone off with your writing eventually. If you don't, you're not doing it right.

Just as the positive reactions to your work can improve your morale, the negative ones may dismantle it. If you do not take psychological precautions against peer ridicule, you may even start to believe the babble others heave at you. Imposter syndrome occurs when you begin to question the efficacy of your own accomplishments for no reason grounded in reality. Even if you believe in your message for reasons entirely your own… even if you receive evidence of the positive reception of your book… you may come to disregard these factors and let the nagging voices of a few vocal haters corrupt you. You may come always to feel disappointed no matter what happens to you and your book.

Unknown Destiny

My early success with books has given me the confidence to keep writing, but I do not know exactly where the road will take me. I see that some of the perspectives I hold are underrepresented in the world. Some of my ideas are more elaborate, accurate, useful, or advanced than what people commonly believe about reality. I can predict that my paradigm will continue to evolve in this manner as I get older and acquire more meaningful life experiences. The same ought to be true in your life, but in ways that are unique to your temperament, memories, and values. When you embrace this truth about your life, writing books will be seen as an opportunity to make real what was once only imagined within you.

I'm still quite early in my writing career. I do not know what will become of the technology or marketplace that have thus far made my modest success as an independent author possible. I don't know what new inspirations I will receive that I feel must be shared with the world. I only know I see a long road of opportunities for what I can become if I continue to refine my knowledge and abilities as a communicator. I know from the positive feedback some readers have already sent me that there is great, untapped potential to continue changing minds and lives with the ideas I promote.

Someday, I may find a better medium than books through which to create the influence I desire. Whatever new methods I adopt into my knowledge empire, they will not negate the groundwork I lay here by writing about my passions. If I am clever and wise, I will be able to leverage the influence of my philosophical seeds here into something better yet still unknown to me. Until then, I will continue to write and publish the most important books I am able to with my present acumen. I will experiment with ways to arrange my ideas that will contribute something of unique value to the world.

Ongoing Passive Financial Return

As much as you may have been motivated to write your book as an expression of your deepest thoughts or to deliver a potent message to other people, you (literally) cannot afford to neglect its entrepreneurial requirements and rewards. At all times, you should be aware of how much your book is selling for at retail, how much of its price counts as revenue for you, how much you are spending on various forms of promotion, how sales rise or fall as you change pricing, marketing, or presentation strategies, and so on.

If you fail to tend to the responsibility of your book royalties, you could actually end up losing money each month that your book remains on sale. You might not even notice your losses until it is too late if your accounting is disorganized. If, on the other hand, you experiment with many approaches and pay attention to what consistently works for your book, you stand to gain access to a totally new type of lifestyle. Soon, you will discover how passive income can be a complete game changer for people who are used to always having to work harder and harder to earn more money.

Most people have never experienced the unique feeling of freedom and security that accompanies knowing money is going to show up in their bank account every month without them having to do a single thing to acquire it. Passive income, which is money made in an ongoing manner from something already produced, can completely change how you think of your life and the fruits of your labor. It can release you from the chronic stress of always having to trade valuable hours of your life just to earn enough money to pay the bills. For some people, this is by far the most practical and consequential reward of publishing a successful and influential book.

Because its nature is cumulative, passive income quickly becomes an addictive pursuit. $1,000 per month recurring revenue seems life-changing to many people, whether it is an exclusive source of income or a complement to several others. Soon, however, comfort tends to give way to the desire for surplus. Can you picture how your life would be different if you knew $5,000 would be yours at the end of each month without sacrificing any of your time to earn it? What about $10,000 or more? It seems premature to dream so big so early in an author's career, but these numbers are not outside the range of earning possibilities for a single successful book or the combined royalties of many books published over an author's lifetime.

With passive income as your goal, your professional focus will shift from a daily grind and 40-hour workweek to a systemic overview of your earning capabilities. You will begin to think of your finances not in terms of one-time sums earned for labor performed, but as scalable patterns that you can predict and influence. This is how good entrepreneurs perceive the consequences of their creative efforts. Only someone with a long-term perspective on their rewards and the ability to delay their gratification for a while can ever live this way. Thinking in terms of passive income constitutes a fundamental shift in monetary psychology.

Passive income isn't just about being able to live a more comfortable life. It plays an important role in supporting your writing habits too. When you see how the revenue from a single book can transform your financial life, it gets a lot easier to justify dedicating more of your time to creating more books. Authorship is then no longer just a hobby, passion, or calling. It is a wise investment in your wealth, time, and future. Writing becomes a career you can scale throughout your life to heights that are difficult to achieve through traditional employment.

My version of success involves my books becoming thriving organisms unto themselves, not full-time jobs that require my constant attention to keep their place in Amazon's rankings. I don't want to have to fear that they will drop off the public radar at the slightest change in market conditions. Knowing that my creative works will survive without my intervention frees my time and effort to be applied to other creative endeavors, such as writing my next books or simply enjoying the leisure time my labor has earned me. The unique value of passive income is that it remains immune to the other circumstances of your life. Passive income isn't really passive if you have to keep working to maintain it.

Content Repurposing

The next logical step after learning to see your book through a systemic lens like this is to learn to look at the potential of your entire career as an author in a similar way. The more books you publish, the more you will learn about how to make each one successful. You will discover new tools and resources to hack your way to greater recurring revenue. On top of that, your new books may complement your old ones by expanding your author brand. Anyone who likes your new work has good reason to check out what else you have written, even if your other books are on unrelated subjects. Soon, you may find yourself splitting your daily productive hours between writing, editing, and promoting your various messages.

Beyond seeing your authorial career as its own independent system of passive income generation, you can branch out into other related forms of media. With all the effort required to write a book that matters, you have a powerful incentive to make the intellectual property you've created count for everything it can. With some adjustments to prepare your content for new formats, you can expand the reach and accessibility of your message. With each additional medium that you prepare your message for, you also create the possibility of new streams of financial income or exposure for your existing ones.

I've already discussed the promotional opportunities afforded by breaking sections of your book content off and editing them to work as standalone articles for online guest posts. You can use a similar tactic for a platform you own, such as your blog or social media profiles. This is a good way to rapidly build up a library of proprietary content that is available online to anyone who wants to learn more about who you are and what you're all about.

If you host a podcast, you can apply a similar approach to come up with episode topics and outlines. Depending on what online mediums you want to occupy with your message, you can do the same with informative videos, email newsletters, or colorful infographics. In fact, there's nothing stopping you from turning each chapter or subsection of your book into a blog post, podcast, video, newsletter, and infographic all at once, so long as you determine them all to be appropriate for your audience and a wise investment of your resources.

Even individual sentences or paragraphs can be copied and pasted as short posts to your various social media profiles. By picking out enough gems from your body of work, you will have ample content to populate new or preexisting social media platforms and create the appearance of a robust online identity.

With each new form of repurposing, you increase the possible spread of your audience. When an online browser finds your content presented in one of its other forms, they may develop an interest in purchasing the book or getting involved with you in another way. Repurposing your book content also makes you show up in more and more places around the internet, improving your reputation and appearance for anyone who might decide to look you up when evaluating whether to buy your book.

Online Courses

Of the many other ways you could repackage your message into a new type of product, online courses are perhaps the most rapidly growing in popularity. For students who regularly enroll in them, online courses created by independent educators offer a favorable alternative to traditional learning environments. Online courses are more affordable than higher education, and they generally don't carry any arbitrarily imposed barriers to entry. Yet, the quality of education they provide can be just as good or better.

The simplest way to create an online course without investing thousands of dollars into design and production is to pick out all the parts of your book that will translate well into the new format. Examine which elements of your message can be translated into a step-by-step process, lecture, or easy series of instructions. You should also reconsider the parts of your book you didn't fully develop because you felt the medium of long-term text would not accommodate them. These sections may be more appropriate for your online students.

When you build your course, you'll have the opportunity to enhance the meaning of what you've written from the market feedback you should have since received about your book. If your book has been for sale for months or years, you're likely to have realized several ways in which it could be made better. You may think of new sections worth including or old ones worth expanding. Your knowledge about the subject may have grown. Your course offers an opportunity to enhance what you already have.

Repurposing your book into an online course will take some work, but not nearly as much as writing the book itself did. You already have most of the creative work done. The rewards to your bank account and brand can also be large enough to justify the extra effort. Since you have already divided the message of your book into independent chapters or subsections through outlining, writing, and editing, it should be easy to envision how each unit might work as a module of a course.

However, you'll probably need to modify your existing book content to some extent to make it ideal for inclusion in your course. People generally don't want to learn the same way from a human instructor as they do from a static book. All other things being equal, the tone of a course should be more casual and inviting than a book. You should remove or gloss over details that work well as plain text but are a pain to listen to someone talk about. You may, conversely, want to add more personal stories, anecdotes, and personality that you may have chosen to leave out of your book.

There are a few tried-and-true presentation styles for online courses. You can use points from your book and create slides, then film or record yourself going over each one charismatically. This is usually the easiest approach, as it doesn't require much additional writing or formatting work (and improvising speech about familiar subjects is easy for most people). You can make "talking head" style videos of yourself from the shoulders up talking about your materials. You can record screencasts of your computer screen to show your students an example of something you want to explain. You can conduct in-person or online video interviews with experts or show off people as case studies for your material.

Once you've created your online course, you can start to market it to the audience you've cultivated for your book. Put a link to your course at the end of your book or promote it to your email list. There are many online course platforms, such as Udemy or Coursera, for independent educators to publicly host and sell what they create. Students who independently find your course on these platforms may also decide to head to Amazon to buy your book. So, just as selling your book can lead to course sales, selling your course can also lead to book sales.

Derivative Services

Another way you can repurpose your book content is with derivative services you presume readers may need when they finish reading. If you want to work as a coach or consultant about your subject, your book will generate clients who are uniquely qualified because they will have already digested a large amount of your unique value. They will know what you offer and will have decided it is what they desire. If readers love your unique philosophy and personality, it only makes sense that they might want more of your help. You can make up your own mind about how you feel about my philosophy, personality, and ability to help passionate people write, publish, and sell nonfiction that matters.

If you are already working as a coach, consultant, speaker, or thought leader of any kind, your book will act as proof of concept for your promises. If someone is unsure about paying high fees to work with you, reading your book may be the leverage that converts them. Even if they don't read it, knowing that you have even written a book and that other people like it might be all the social proof they need.

Summary of Chapter 13

Publishing your book and knowing that your ideas extend beyond the limits of your life should give you a uniquely powerful sense of purpose and meaning. By putting your name and face on what is important to you, you have also invested in your identity and created many new opportunities for yourself. Depending on the nature of your book and how you present it, authorship may open the door to new tiers of lifestyle and identification.

— — — —

If the information contained in your book is important to your readers, it will affect their thoughts, emotions, and actions in irreversible ways. Some readers may praise you for what you have dared to communicate; others may deride you. Other authors may be jealous of your ambitions or success. Negative social reception may hurt your morale if you are not prepared to process it appropriately. Alternatively, positive reception may inspire you to write more and more.

— — — —

A self-published book, if managed well, becomes a renewable spring of income from book sales that may sustain or grow over time. As well, the existence of a book can create countless other financial opportunities for its author. If you take authorship seriously, you can look at it as through the lens of a cumulative, lifelong career path that offers more and more recurring revenue with each successive book you write. The increased freedom and incentive that passive income brings will make it easier to keep writing.

CHAPTER 14:

Your Destiny as Author and Publisher for Life

The time has come to reflect upon what brought you here and where it will next bring you. Though by publishing a book you've taken your first steps into a much larger world, you cannot yet see how large this world really is. You should recall why you began this journey so long ago and the new person you have since become by seeing it through to this first major milestone. Reflect so that you can understand what has transpired so far and what it all means for your future as an author, publisher, and public embodiment of your values.

Reflection is necessary for every author because no two authors' circumstances are equal. No two writers are coming from the same origin or heading for the same destination. Trajectories can reset at any point in the journey with new revelations about what is possible or the achievements one desires. Everything you thought you knew about writing a book and experiencing life as a published author should have radically transformed on your path to arrive where you are now. Where you think you are heading next should also have shifted through the perspective of your present accomplishments.

In the months and years following publication, you'll experiment with how to position your book in your life so that it will accomplish the greatest possible good for you, according to your subjective evaluation of what "good" means. You'll no doubt also realize that there are ways in which it underperforms for you, leaving you wanting it to accomplish more in some important regard. These revelations will affect how you choose to go about planning your next publications, for they will have shown you more of what is possible through publishing (and, perhaps, what is not as easy to achieve as you assumed).

The choices you will make as a lifelong author will change with new trends in the industry. Self-publishers exist in the middle of two halves of a dynamic market: the market to produce books and the market to consume them. When factors change on either side of this interaction, the author must change with them or risk their efforts all going to waste. Where the demands of their readers intersect with their ambition to produce meaningful communication is where they will find the ever-moving target of their creation. With a wider perspective than just focusing on the book or its pages that are right in front of them, they will plan and adapt as needed to stay within the narrow window of success as independent authors.

Assessing Book Failure and Success

For artists and entrepreneurs alike, no measure of success is ever guaranteed. As a self-published author, you embody both roles.

I've written *The Influential Author* with the hope that if you follow my advice and play to your strengths, your book will almost certainly find greater success than the majority of self-published books by authors who only ever half-heartedly tinker with the process. My goal from the start has been to provide a practical and philosophical overview of how and why to form and disseminate valuable ideas through the medium of books. However, it would be impossible for me to tell you exactly what you need to do and how to do it to find the version of success you desire. There will always be strategic decisions you will have to make on your own, based on your message, goals, and audience.

Under ideal circumstances, adapting the guidelines of *The Influential Author* to your situation should produce measurable and sustainable success. As long as there is a sizable audience for your message, your book should eventually begin to grab a chunk of their attention (even if it is only through the network effect generated by one happy reader telling someone they know, ad infinitum). But no matter what you do, book marketing circumstances will never be ideal. There will always be elements to the process you cannot account for, so your success is not a given.

When launching any product into the market, it's possible to commit no discernible mistakes and still fail to get the traction you were hoping for. That is not a weakness on your part. That is the will of the free market, the invisible hand that guides the flow of supplies to where they are demanded. There isn't a direct correlation between how hard you work on something or how much it means to you and how successful it ends up being. Despite what seemingly every modern self-help guru will tell you, it doesn't necessarily matter how much effort you've put into creating your book or how much you've visualized your own success. It may not even matter how much money you have spent on its promotion.

The possibility of failure is always real. Your book might not sell any copies beyond what you cajole your friends and family into buying. Whoever does buy your book might hate it and leave negative reviews on Amazon and Goodreads, dissuading any other readers from making the same mistake they did. Maybe you wrote a great book but didn't do a good job preparing its presentation or targeting the right readers. You might waste your promotional budget in ways that provide barely any return.

Maybe, despite all your hours of hard work and financial capital invested, there just isn't a large audience for the first book you decided to write. Maybe a market exists, but it is disparate and unorganized, making it impossible to target with conventional promotion. You may even need to consider the possibility that your wordsmithing is just not very good or your philosophy is not easily transferable. These and many other factors may contribute to the marketplace failure of your book.

If your book receives disappointing results, you may choose to accept that authorship and publishing are not for you. There is no shame in walking away from something after having made an earnest effort to succeed in it and honestly assessing it not to be worth further effort. It may be wiser for you to place your priorities elsewhere. If you choose otherwise, however, you can use the circumstance of your initial defeat to reflect on your book's poor reception. You can channel your disappointment into motivation to improve. You can find the inspiration to try again, this time circumnavigating whatever errors you may have made before.

Success Metrics

Before you chalk your book up as a total loss, consider that what seems like failure in one regard is not necessarily so in others. Success can be measured in many valid ways, and it's up to you to determine what is most important to you about your book. If you are not keeping track of the all the things your book accomplishes, it's easy to assume that nothing good has happened because of it. Your information will also be biased and incomplete. For all you know, you could be building legions of eager fans or planting brand-building seeds that will sprout in years to come. You don't necessarily even know what to look for and can't monitor it all as it happens.

You might not care much about the number of book royalties you receive. Getting people to consume your message might be more important to you. You may even be okay with losing money on the venture, so long as your work gets out there. For you, success might be more a matter of your ability to use your book as a tool to create other opportunities. If you can use your book as a catalyst for brand leverage, its actual market performance may be moot. The book's mere existence can be a source of valuable exposure for your business or some other organization or idea you care about. You can track the exposure you receive as website hits, email list subscribers, social media followers, sales of another product, or anything else you deem important. These assets can be worth far more to you than audience size and ongoing royalties.

Success may also be a wholly internal state of understanding. The satisfaction that comes from having crafted a meaningful philosophy or a series of useful ideas may be enough for you to feel the work was all worthwhile. To know that you possess the moxie to create a real, meaningful, professional quality book is self-affirming in ways few other accomplishments are. Finishing your book will have required you to hone many skills and expand your knowledge of writing, editing, marketing, product launching, brand building, and more. These experiences may lead to better opportunities to apply yourself toward something else you will find greater meaning and success with.

Learning to articulate your thoughts is a lifelong pursuit. There is no one way or even best way to do it. I can already look back on the respective styles I approached my first two books with and see how I would do them differently if I were writing them today. Each approach I took was serviceable for its book's purpose, but a more refined and experienced version of my mind would have made somewhat different choices in wording and structure for each of them. *The Influential Author* was written to the best of my present writing ability and knowledge of the subject matter and audience. I can only anticipate that some time from now I will look back on these words and cringe with my newly developed perspective on how I could have somehow done them better. Only by committing yourself to writing and improving do you ever gain this awareness. Self-improvement of this type is just one intangible way your first book can be made to serve you.

Some of the effects of success will be available before your book even launches. Others may take many years to activate or for you to fully realize. You cannot know with certainty whether in five years or a decade there will be a surge in demand for your message or someone important will read your book and feel compelled to reach out to you, creating a branch of new opportunities. If your book has been written in a timeless fashion wherein its main points remain valid and its style appealing, you could someday begin reaping the rewards of something you presumed to be long forgotten and outdated. The positive consequences of your book can stay with you for life.

Success Variability

Even for well-written, in-demand books, sales can come and go with jarring irregularity. It's possible that, due to sheer dumb luck or overwhelming promotional tactics to generate massive exposure at launch, your book will see a spike in sales during its first weeks or months on the market. You may prematurely take this as a sign of lasting victory. Then, without warning, the readers who seemed so interested in your book when it was cheap, new, and trendy may suddenly lose their interest. Authors who write on topical subjects should especially be wary of this hubris. When sales drop and stay down with no obvious explanation, you may find it pertinent to begin experimenting with new pricing strategies, book description, or cover design to see if they make any difference.

The opposite phenomenon can also be true. Your book might face slow beginnings, but this is not necessarily an indicator of its lack of long-term viability. Over time, you may be able to build a sustainable, organic following that only grows upon itself with the passage of time. For my books and those by other authors I have worked with, the goal has always been to get them to a state of perennial demand where they will continue to sell with some consistency, organic spikes and dips in the market notwithstanding. I want each book to create some meaningful level of influence without requiring much ongoing author involvement in the months and years after release. It's not worth it to me if I have to be constantly bailing water to keep a sinking ship afloat.

Whatever happens with your book after publication, it's important that you do not jump to conclusions about yourself or it. Only time and experimentation will reveal the ongoing truth about your message's ability to succeed on the open market. Any book by any author can face short-term peaks or valleys in performance. Any product can receive a sudden influx of praise or slander from surprise sources. No one is invincible or irredeemable.

In the long run, it won't matter if your first book underperforms. When you have published a dozen successful titles on subjects near and dear to you, you will look back on your early work as the unconfident baby steps that brought you to your present level of dominance. Your eventual success may even create new demand for your early works that initially failed to gain much market traction. Success is largely a matter of the timescale through which you are willing to evaluate your work. A patient and mature creator knows this truth and embodies the mentality it requires.

Writing Your Next Books

If your book has turned out the way you hoped, you'll probably be eager to get started on the next one. You'll have discovered a potent outlet for influence, meaning, and financial reward and will not want to delay taking advantage of it.

Writing additional books is your opportunity to create a vast body of work that represents your entire range of values, interests, and opinions. Done well, it is one of the smartest investments you could make in your future and public sense of identity. Publishing more works will also improve the performance of your first one, as each new happy reader has an incentive to explore the other titles you've written. Even if your next book is on an unrelated subject, its readers may like your approach and style so much that they take in interest in everything you write about. It's easy to become addicted to someone's personality somewhere in the course of reading tens of thousands of their words.

Before you start your next publication, reflect on how the existence of the first one has affected you. Introspection will help you determine where to go from here and what you ought to write next. You may decide it is wisest to repeat the steps that brought you success with your first book, this time with a superior understanding of how the process works and what you are capable of. If you feel brave enough, you may decide to try something totally different so that you will expand your knowledge of the possibilities of publishing.

Each new book you produce will give you greater insight into what you can do and how the world responds to your ideas. In time, you will unlock deeper and more meaningful arrangements of the information swirling around in your head. You will also find places to store the new facts and experiences you take in with the passing of days to come. Your skill for organizing your thoughts will improve to the point that it becomes intuitive. Soon, you will begin tapping into new ways to turn your lifetime of unique experiences into effective conversations. The struggles of the writing process will not always be so hard on you as they are now because you will optimize the transmutation of images into words.

In time, you may even grow comfortable working on multiple books at once. Full-time authors have learned to begin a new book outline the moment inspiration strikes them. What begins as a single good concept or a disorganized collection of phrasings will turn into something organized and worthwhile, but only if you store it somewhere you will be able to return to it when the time for expansion and refinement comes. Then you will morph your isolated musings into something resembling a cohesive framework of ideas that work as the outline for a new book.

At the stage of authorship I currently operate in, I have found it most productive to divide my hours among several related tasks for the multiple books I am producing for myself and others. On any given day, I may be busy drafting one or more books, editing some others, and promoting those I've recently released for myself or the authors I work with. Patchwork progress, even if it's just a paragraph at a time, ensues until my vision is clear enough to bring one of my working drafts into publication. Working on more than one book at a time in this manner usually means you can't predict exactly when or even in what order each one will be done. You just keep chipping away at the one that holds your attention the most until your attention fades or the book is finally ready.

I got the idea for *The Influential Author* almost a year before it was published. Shortly after, I had a working outline of most of the major points I knew I would need to cover. Then, I arranged those many points into seven major sequential categories that became this book's seven sections: Philosophy, Strategy, Creation, Refinement, Presentation, Promotion, and Reward. From there, it was simply a matter of chipping away at it by filling out each point with all the necessary details, rearranging concepts and adding new ones as needed throughout. All things considered, I think I made pretty good time.

However, nearly a year before I even had the idea for *The Influential Author* I had begun working on another book called *The Exceptional Individual* that I plan to be ready to launch a few months after this one. At less than the half the length (about 50,000 words compared to about 130,000), you'd think this book would have been much quicker and easier for me to write. In an ideal world, I would have launched it before even beginning working on *The Influential Author*—but an author's process is never ideal.

It was because I had to keep expanding, rewriting, and rearranging nearly every chapter of *The Exceptional Individual* that its production took so much longer than expected. This was further complicated by the fact that the book is written in a deep and dense, simultaneously intellectual and inspiring style. Every single sentence had to be given careful consideration about its wording or risk losing the intended meaning, either on its own or in the context of the other sentences around it. I couldn't just write the first thing that came to mind and leave it at that.

Other practical factors related to the release of each book also became apparent, leading me to the realization that it just made more sense to focus on finishing and publishing *The Influential Author* first. Even still, I found the time to frequently return to editing *The Exceptional Individual* while focusing my efforts here. I also had the inspiration for two more nonfiction and two fiction books while all this was happening. I have since created loose outlines for each one and a fair amount of first draft content for one of them. In the coming months, I'm sure I will have more insights about which ones to finish first and how.

If you think it sounds too complicated to be actively writing and/or editing more than one book at the same time, you're not alone. Most new authors hardly have the wherewithal to see even one book to completion. Depending on your writing habits, however, jumping back and forth between different drafts may actually be less strenuous than forcing yourself to focus on only one. Working this way gives me a lot to keep in mind, as each stage of production requires input from different faculties. That's part of the appeal for me. It keeps things from getting boring. There will always be plenty of work to challenge me as long as I remain an author.

You can't keep writing if you can't think of what you want to say next. Arguing with yourself about the same subject for hours on end can quickly drain your ability to think creatively about it. When you notice yourself slowing down in one conversation, switching to a new draft requiring a completely different train of thought may temporarily refill your creative juices. You can always switch back when you find the muse you need to continue with what you were talking about in your other book.

As you know by now, writing and editing tax different faculties in the brain. One works through creation and the other through destruction. If you try to do only one without the other in all your productive hours, you will see diminishing returns for your efforts. So, when you tire of thinking of new things to say, switch over to a document that is already too long and needs to be trimmed. Finding ways like this to differentiate how you work on your books can make you a more productive author.

Digging in or Branching out

Your second book can be something related in subject to your first one, or it can be completely different. It depends on what you feel compelled to say and what you are trying to accomplish by writing more. You can even write your second book as a companion piece to the first, filling in the gaps that were present in your earlier publication or taking the same themes and expanding them in a new direction. If your first book approached its subject with a mostly philosophical tone and angle, perhaps it warrants a follow-up volume that focuses on the practical application of the concepts you introduced. With this approach, your books can work either as complementary standalone pieces or as sequential parts of a numbered series.

When you understand enough of your own writing habits, there's no reason you can't expand into the domain of fiction too if that's where your ambition takes you. Although the functions of fiction and the faculties required to create it are not quite the same as those of nonfiction, much of the writing, editing, publishing, and marketing knowledge you've acquired will still apply. By the time you've mastered nonfiction writing and marketing, you will know more about what it will take to be a successful fiction author than most of the novelists who simply throw their books up on Amazon and wait for the royalty checks to start coming in.

There is always a danger of letting your first book's performance dictate your next creative endeavor, whether you found the success you desired or not. If you have a smash hit on your hands, you will naturally be tempted to replicate as many of the same steps that worked for you the first time as possible. If you are scared of stepping away from what you know works, your originality will soon run dry. Your next book will be only a minor variant of what you've already done. In this way, early success can stifle creativity and become a trap for your vision.

Do not make the mistake that so many amateur authors do by writing the same book over and over or sticking to one rigid style for every subject. You should always be evolving as a thinker and communicator, seeking new plateaus that obviate the shortcomings of whatever your last publication was and however well it sold. Do not let yourself get too comfortable with your identity as an author, no matter how much your readers may love your early work. Becoming a serial author provides an incentive to challenge your knowledge and abilities throughout your life.

If, on the other hand, your first book's performance has been underwhelming, you might assume it is impossible to turn a profit with the subject or style of writing you used. This is an unfair and limiting analysis. There could actually be many overlooked reasons why your book has underperformed. If you felt so inclined, you could even write your second book as an upgraded version of your first and get totally different results than you did before. You shouldn't stop trying to be the author you want to be just because you haven't yet derived how to make it happen. Do not let your initial lack of success teach you the wrong lessons about how to achieve it.

Collective Promotion

Having multiple books will change the way you approach promotion for new and old ones alike. If some or all of your books are written on similar topics (and would, therefore, appeal to similar audiences), you can pair them together when you perform most forms of market outreach. When you connect with book reviewers or various forms of online media, you can offer more than one book you think they might be interested in. This will increase your positive response rate and reduce the time you have to spend promoting each book. Perhaps years from now, when you have many books to your name, you will be able to promote them all simultaneously with one massive campaign.

Through experimentation, you can discover what paid promotional strategies are consistently effective with your work. Then you will be able to apply these tested practices to each new book with a reasonable degree of certainty about how well each one will work. You won't be flying quite so blind as before, so you will waste less time and money.

Managing more than one book at a time presents new challenges and opportunities. You can't always predict which of your books will be the most successful before you expose them to the market. This is especially true if you write on many different subjects and experiment with different promotional tactics for each one. You will also need to consider the prep work that goes into launching each book. If you spread yourself too thin, you will see fewer results than if you took the time to launch each one on its own in sequence.

In time, you'll learn that it doesn't make sense to put the same amount of money or effort into each book because they won't all warrant the same level of investment. The book that you think captures the purity of your soul better than all the others might be the one that consistently sells the worst. If your goal is to make money and get your message out there, you would be wiser to work harder on expanding the reach of the books that are proving to sell more easily to a wider range of people. These are the types of value judgments you will need to make as you build and maintain your paradigmatic empire.

With a long-term view of the books you may someday write, your whole approach to writing might change. An author's lifetime strategy can revolve around launching several books as quickly as possible, then monitoring how the market responds to each. With several months or even years of reliable market data to work from, the author can optimize their ongoing outreach and promotion. They will know which books will be best served with what types and amounts of promotion. This is known by some as the "throwing everything you can think of against a wall and seeing what sticks" approach to entrepreneurship. Failure will not discourage you as it once may have. You will be better able to adapt to the unique needs and nature of each book, as no two can be or should be identical.

Which books become your biggest sellers may end up surprising you. Online sales data may not match your anecdotal experiences of how people respond to your books. My branding book, *Brand Identity Breakthrough*, has consistently outsold my travel and philosophy book, *Travel as Transformation*, across all mediums and online sales channels. The most obvious reason is that branding appeals to a wider audience than an esoteric approach to the nuances of travel does. However, when I talk about my books in person, whether in a formal presentation or casual conversation, my live audience almost always displays stronger interest for *Travel as Transformation*.

I don't know how to account for the discrepancy between what the sales data shows me and how the people in front of me act. Perhaps it is because the people I show my books to have a stronger interest in me, the author, and therefore want to know more about my experiences than strangers on the internet do. Perhaps the concept of my travel book just sounds unique and therefore catches people's attention even if they weren't thinking about buying or reading a book.

It's safe to assume that most of the people who buy *Brand Identity Breakthrough* on Amazon come to the site with the intention of buying a business book (if not one specifically about branding itself). The same qualification does not apply to the live, spontaneous conversations about my books that I sometimes witness. The early anecdotal feedback for *The Influential Author* suggests it will receive a favorable response on the market, but only many months after launch will I be able to assess if this is true fairly. You cannot always trust your own judgment about how to scale your presence as an author. Look for what is consistently true in the sales figures and extrapolate from there. Try not to let your personal feelings about your books get in the way of good analysis.

All other factors aside, the book you write next should be the one you need to write. You should write because you know there is information flooding about in your brain that must be let out. You have strong emotions that you have not yet been able to express, and they are eating you up inside. If you write your next book for these reasons, the creative process will come much easier than if you try to force yourself to communicate anything less worthwhile. Your third and fourth books will follow this same motivational pattern, though what creates the motivation may always be different. The impetus to write, evolve your thinking, and clear the debris from your mind never has to end.

The Unknown Future of Self-Publishing

The Influential Author has not been an easy book to write. As I have striven to strike a balance between timeless philosophical wisdom and timely practical advice, I have had to keep up to date on the ever-changing world of modern self-publishing practices.

During the year I have been writing, editing, and preparing this book for publication, several of the key policies and strategies related to working with Amazon and its affiliated companies have evolved. CreateSpace's print-on-demand platform merged with Kindle Direct Publishing (KDP) to become one integrated dashboard called KDP Print. Amazon Marketing Services (AMS) rebranded as Amazon Advertising. Audio Creation Exchange (ACX) changed the amount of room tone required at the end of each audio chapter file from between half a second and one second to between one second and five seconds. The European Union's General Data Protection Regulation (GDPR) went into effect, causing Amazon to remove many of the email addresses of its top reviewers it had once made publicly available.

Though I have worked to make this book as accurate as possible at the time of its 2019 publication, many of the tactics described herein will change in the months, years, and decades to come (even if the principles of their operation, such as reader targeting, remain inviolable). Though change, as a principle, is predictable, no one knows the exact manner in which changes will occur. The only certainty is progress in some form. Production and market processes do not stay the same if there are better, more efficient ways to reach a goal. Entrepreneurs know they must stay on top of the advancements pertinent to their industries. Yours are now book sales and self-publishing.

Amazon has been the king of self-publishing and online book sales for a while now, but there's no guarantee it will continue to be so forever. Furthermore, Amazon's requirements for self-publishing will continue to evolve, becoming more open or restrictive as both authors and readers demonstrate their desires and capabilities. By the time you read what I have written here, many more factors may have already become relevant or irrelevant to publishing your book. Authors will need to learn new step-by-step instructions if they wish to solve the immediate problems related to preparing their book files for publication submission or taking advantage of the latest book marketing tactics.

A self-published author is an entrepreneur who must remain cognizant of the market's general behavior and required processes. If you take to heart the principles of effective communication and the historical standards set by books so far, you will always have the skills you need to stay ahead of the game and position yourself for greater success than the majority of self-publishers will ever know. Lifelong authorship is not sustainable if you can't make enough return on your efforts to keep writing, so your willingness to adapt is essential.

Improved Perception

In the infancy of self-publishing, print-on-demand books were derided for their lackluster quality compared to traditionally published titles. Whether it was the shoddy formatting, the sloppy proofreading, or poor-quality paper or binding used in production, there was a noticeable difference to the discerning reader. Those differences, however, are rapidly getting smaller and less jarring. I believe that one day soon, calling yourself a self-published author will not necessarily carry any assumptions of poor quality from general readers. In the same way, regular people now consume much of their entertainment from "amateur" online video producers in conjunction with the products of major television and movie studios.

Decreased Costs

As the quality associated with self-publishing increases, authors should expect a general decrease in production costs. Machine labor and distribution methods improve as they are used more and market demand rises accordingly. Although the barrier to entry for self-publishing is already low, authors can expect it to get even lower in the years to come. The price of printing copies of your book on demand or inserting it into far-reaching distribution channels will also diminish.

Increased Activity

With increased general awareness of the possibilities created by self-publishing (and even lower costs to get started), authors can expect the present level of poorly written books produced by half-hearted authors to expand even further. There's no reason to view this as a problem, however. If you are one of the brave few to put real effort and attention into crafting your message and ensuring it meets the standards demanded by the market, you will stand out even more like a diamond in this rough ocean of pages.

Ample Providers

More authors partaking in self-publishing means more companies emerging to cater to their needs. Right now, connecting with the ideal audience for a self-published book requires a fair amount of marketing prowess and a lot of sweat work. It is not well-suited for the lazy author who just wants to write their book and wait for it to makes its way to the right readers. But if there is enough profit in offering services tailored to promoting specific types of books to specific types of readers, it's predictable that authors will eventually be able to pay a reasonable fee to ensure their book shows up where it should for maximum sales and influence.

Currently, most of the promotional services for Amazon books available to self-published authors with modest budgets are generic and widespread. They offer little opportunity to track the results of any marketing campaigns invested in. Plenty of websites will offer to include a self-published book in their email newsletter, social media blasts, or on a dedicated ad somewhere on their site. The problem with these approaches is that they do not display books to curated audiences. These book promoters build big, self-identified lists of "people who like to read free or discounted e-books" or some other ambiguous qualifier.

Some sites go so far as to divide their lists into broad topics or genres of reading material. This is a step in the right direction, but there's no guarantee that subscribers who have self-identified as liking history books, for example, will be interested in your take on a specific set of decades from the perspective of a specific group of people in a specific corner of the world. Reliable book marketing occurs when someone savvy takes the time to craft images and impressions that will catch the attention of a targeted type of mind. If it's not you performing this function of finer targeting, it must be someone else you hire. Expect that in time, it will become cheaper and easier to hire such talent.

In addition to targeting readers with greater precision, time will make it simpler to get self-published authors' books carried by more online distributors, libraries, and brick-and-mortar retailers. Some of this increased ease will be due to the lessening public stigma against self-publishing. Some of it will come into effect as more services tailored to non-traditional book distribution arise in the market to meet the growing demand. Whenever there is a profit to be made, entrepreneurs rush to take advantage of it by catering to the need that caused it.

Spiritual Liberation

To me, it seems inevitable that the increasing availability of self-publishing options will play a vital role in making professions of a creative or intellectual nature the norm for people who have the natural faculties to perform them. In the past, many brilliant young people (who perhaps lacked traditional employment credentials) felt there was little hope of ever being able to earn a living doing something they loved and which made full use of their exceptional abilities. Because of creative technologies, this need not be the case much longer.

I perceive there to be a great discrepancy between the raw artistic and psychological talent found throughout the world and the economic output generated by it. Young, gifted people simply don't understand or can't access the societal mechanics that will allow them to transform their acumen into profitable and rewarding products of their existence. Imagine a world where every stroke of genius from an unexpected source was brought to fruition and its beneficial effects made real throughout the world. That's the world I would prefer to live in.

Complemented by developments in other creative industries and taken to its logical end, self-publishing could transform the way the world thinks about the way knowledge and experience come into play with entrepreneurship. Many people will be able to bypass the need for traditional, often unrewarding employment. Highly creative and intellectual labor is, by its very nature, the type least likely to be obviated by machine labor and automation. Thus, counterintuitively to some, authors will perhaps enjoy greater job security than most of the common jobs that occupy the modern workforce.

As channels and techniques evolve, more traditionally published authors (or those who would have been traditionally published) will feel comfortable doing things themselves or using a trusted consultant to bring their content to market without sacrificing ownership of their work. The greater the respect and demand for self-published titles, the easier it will be to get them carried by traditional bookstores, which in turn will only increase their demand. I hope that by inspiring talented thinkers and writers to produce and publish their original works, *The Influential Author* will play a vital role in helping to expedite this sociological evolution the world over.

Summary of Chapter 14

Even if you do everything right, there is still a chance that your book will not perform well. There may not be a very large audience for the information you have shared. It may just take time for your ideal readers to become aware of their need for your book. Regardless of total sales or profit, there are many other ways you can measure the positive return of your book. These include your internal satisfaction for having articulated your values, your improvement as a writer, the effect your message has on other people, and the betterment of your personal brand.

— — — —

It's unlikely that your creative and intellectual faculties are limited to producing just one worthwhile book. Take the lessons you've learned from the process of your first book and apply them to what you want to write next. You can even be working on many books simultaneously, each at a different stage of production. Just be careful not to let the failure or success of your first book limit your ability to write new books comfortably and authentically.

— — — —

Self-publishing is still a young industry in development. You can predict that many of the complex, inefficient, and expensive parts of the process will get simpler, easier, and cheaper in time. As quality improves, self-publishing will carry less social stigma and attract more authors and readers. Authors who master the process now will be in a position to enjoy more professional success as the industry evolves. Soon, there will be almost no barrier for people with good ideas to use their knowledge to improve the world by producing original and successful books.

Conclusion

"Perhaps the sentiments contained in the following pages, are not yet sufficiently fashionable to procure them general favor; a long habit of not thinking a thing wrong, gives it a superficial appearance of being right, and raises at first a formidable outcry in defense of custom. But the tumult soon subsides. Time makes more converts than reason."
—Thomas Paine, *Common Sense* (1776)

Do not fret too harshly if you perceive that the world is not yet prepared to appreciate whatever message is most sacred in your mind and kept closest to your heart. You should not let that stop you from doing your best to communicate it anyway. The act of formally articulating your principles will anchor your actions to be ever more in line with your intent. That is when purpose and a lasting sense of meta-satisfaction occur: when you know you are being the person you aspire to be.

I've given you all I can manage to give within the confines of these covers regarding the creation and dissemination of influential ideas. Now comes the obligatory part of the book where I try to wrap up and summarize everything the preceding hundreds of pages have been attempting to instill in your mind about writing, publishing, and selling nonfiction books that matter.

Now is also the appropriate time for me to remind you how much it would mean to me if you left a short, honest review for *The Influential Author* on Amazon, Goodreads, or whatever online platform you prefer. I should tell you that the reason why is that I love seeing what my readers think of my work and how it has helped them (or, in the case of negative reviews, receiving constructive criticism I can use to improve as a writer). But by now, you know the most important reason I want you to leave me a review is that ample reviews are essential to my ability to promote my book to new readers and rank highly on Amazon's Best Seller Ranking system.

Next, I'm going to tell you that I've done you the favor of listing links to various tools and services you might find useful at different stages of the book production or publishing process, each of which vary in utility, cost, and quality. You'll find this list in the appendix that follows. Hopefully, you won't mind if I slyly mention that if you'd prefer to work with me as a ghostwriter, editor, publisher, coach, or consultant for any portion of your book's journey, I'm available to assist a limited number of authors each year whose intentions align with my methods.

I even offer a bespoke, all-inclusive conception-to-completion package for aspiring authors that includes market research, outlining, ghostwriting, editing, proofreading, beta testing, designing a cover, formatting each book medium, narrating, writing a description, titling, launching, promoting, and monitoring book performance through my company Identity Publications. If you're curious about learning more about how I work and who I work with, it would be a great idea for you to visit www.identitypublications. com or email me at gregory@identitypublications.com.

What I've presented here may seem like a lot to take in, even if you were already somewhat familiar with writing and publishing before you began reading. To make the most of this information, you should spend ample time planning and in reflection before anything else. Adopt the mentality of an entrepreneur who has been tasked with making sure a unique new product ends up in the hands of the right people. At the same time, you will have to think like an educator whose goal is to ensure the clear and structured communication of their unique knowledge.

Do not feel intimidated by the false idea that you must have a perfect and detailed plan for how every aspect of writing and publishing will go. If that is your outlook, you will probably never even begin. Trust in your ability to reason and solve problems in each moment as you proceed toward completion. So long as your intangible mindset or tangible draft is moving closer to its ideal state, you will eventually arrive there. There is always some type of progress to be made. If you are principled and adaptable in your approach, the many unknown details will work themselves out along the way.

Focus on the long-term, big picture outcome of your struggle toward publication. It is possible through structure, vigilance, and determination to interject the products of your mind into the entropic flow of society. Your life and all its products represent an opportunity to pivot the direction the world had been moving until you arrived. Your thoughts, once articulated, have the power to create exponential change in the way some people think and live. You can offer them better philosophical tools than they had before. You can show them how to act and feel in areas they once felt unprepared for.

If at any point in your life you apply the lessons of *The Influential Author* to a meaningful degree of success (as you define it), I would like to hear from you. My personal sense of meaning in the world depends upon knowing that my actions have impact beyond the immediate satisfaction they bring me. I need to know that what I have created will go on to influence the choices my readers make about how to structure and share their knowledge. The more good you accomplish as a result of reading my work, the greater the sense of meaning it will impart to me.

Besides emailing me directly, you can reach out to me on any of the following social media profiles.

Facebook: www.facebook.com/gregoryvdiehl
Instagram: www.instagram.com/gregorydiehl
Twitter: www.twitter.com/gregoryvdiehl

I wish you well on your journey toward influential authorship. More importantly, I hope you have learned to look at yourself in a new light, to believe in your ability to change the way humanity and its reality operate by being yourself and expressing the deepest parts of your identity. That is the mindset from which all power and influence derive.

Appendix: Resources

Dear reader,

This list is not exhaustive of all the tools and resources available to self-published nonfiction authors. The ones listed here are not all necessary or even advisable for all writing and publishing situations.

Though I have personal experience with many of these, most of the included resources came to my attention through recommendations from other authors. I do not necessarily endorse everything here. Do your own due diligence before purchasing or using anything listed here, especially as these resources (and self-publishing best practices) are subject to change.

I have attempted to keep this list short and appropriate for new authors who don't already have their own preferred resources in place. I have made efforts to avoid including anything unnecessarily or prohibitively expensive. You may still decide it is wiser to accomplish certain tasks on your own or to source your own talent at a lower cost.

Remember that this list is just a timely sampling of the many, many author resources that exist and continue to be generated. I encourage you to conduct your own exhaustive research and discover what else is out there or what new resources have been made available since this book was published.

To your success with influential authorship,
Gregory V. Diehl

All-Purpose Freelancer Platforms

Damongo – http://www.damongo.com/
Fiverr – https://www.fiverr.com/
Freelancer – https://www.freelancer.com
Guru – www.guru.com
iFreelance – https://www.ifreelance.com/
People Per Hour – https://www.peopleperhour.com/
Upwork – https://www.upwork.com/

Category and Keyword Research

Google Keyword Planner – https://adwords.google.com/home/tools/keyword-planner/
KDP Rocket – https://kdprocket.com/
KDSpy – https://www.kdspy.com/
Keyword Tool Dominator – https://www.keywordtooldominator.com/
Kparser – https://kparser.com/amazon-keyword-tool/
Merchant Words – https://www.merchantwords.com/
Ranktracer – https://ranktracer.com/best-selling-books.php
The Sonar – http://sonar-tool.com/us/
Yasiv – http://www.yasiv.com

Drafting, Editing, and Proofreading Software

After the Deadline – https://www.afterthedeadline.com/
Grammar Check Online – http://www.grammarcheckonline.net/spelling-and-grammar-check-online/
Grammarly – https://app.grammarly.com/
Hemingway App – http://www.hemingwayapp.com/
iA Writer – https://ia.net/writer
Prowriting Aid – https://prowritingaid.com/
Spellcheck Plus – https://spellcheckplus.com/

Ghostwriting Services

Association of Ghostwriters – http://associationofghostwriters.org/find-ghostwriter/
Ghostwriters Central – https://www.ghostwords.com
Ghostwriting LLC – https://ghostwritingllc.com
Hot Ghostwriter – https://hotghostwriter.com/
Reedsy – https://reedsy.com/

Editing and Proofreading Services

Dragonfly Freelance – http://writingeditingservices.com/
Kibin – https://www.kibin.com
Postscripting – https://postscripting.net
Reedsy – https://reedsy.com/
Scribendi – https://www.scribendi.com/
Wordy – https://www.wordy.com/

Dictation and Transcription Software

Dragon Naturally Speaking – https://www.nuance.com/dragon.html
Sonix – https://sonix.ai/
Speech Notes – https://speechnotes.co/
Speech Texter – https://www.speechtexter.com/

Cover Design Software

Adobe Illustrator – https://www.adobe.com/sea/products/illustrator.html
Adobe Photoshop – https://www.photoshop.com/
Canva – https://www.canva.com/create/book-covers/
KDP Cover Creator – https://kdp.amazon.com/en_US/cover-templates/
Placeit – https://placeit.net/

Cover Design Services

100 Covers – http://100covers.com/
1106 Design – http://1106design.com
99 Designs – https://99designs.com/
Design Crowd – https://www.designcrowd.com/
Reedsy – https://reedsy.com/

Print and E-Book Formatting

Adobe InDesign – https://www.adobe.com/sea/products/indesign.html
Apple Pages – https://www.apple.com/lae/pages/
Blurb – http://www.blurb.com/bookmaking-tools
Jutoh – http://www.jutoh.com/
Kindle Create – https://kdp.amazon.com/en_US/help/topic/GHU4YEWXQGNLU94T
Microsoft Word – https://products.office.com/
Pressbooks – https://pressbooks.com
Reedsy – https://reedsy.com/
Scrivener – https://www.literatureandlatte.com/scrivener/overview
Vellum – https://vellum.pub/

Audiobook Narration Software

Adobe Audition – https://www.adobe.com/products/audition.html
Amadeus Pro – https://www.hairersoft.com/pro.html
Audacity – https://audacity.en.softonic.com/
MixPad – https://www.nch.com.au/mixpad/index.html
Reaper – http://reaper.fm/
SpeakPipe – https://www.speakpipe.com/voice-recorder

Audiobook Narrators

Audio Creation Exchange – https://www.acx.com/
Voice123 – https://voice123.com/
VoiceBunny – https://voicebunny.com/
Voices – https://www.voices.com/

Nonfiction Book Review Bloggers

20 Something Reads – https://www.20somethingreads.com/
Book Geek – https://www.bookgeeks.in/
Book Reporter – http://admin.bookreporter.com/book-submission-inquiry/
Bookstoker – http://bookstoker.com/genre/non-fiction/
Consumed By Books – http://www.consumedbybooks.com
Rachel Reading – https://rachelsreading.com
SMS Nonfiction Book Reviews – http://smsnonfictionbookreviews.com/
Thirsty4Health – http://thirsty4health.com/

Promotion for Free and Discounted E-Books

Awesome Gang – http://awesomegang.com/
Book Goodies – https://bookgoodies.com/
BookBub – https://www.bookbub.com/
Books Butterfly – https://www.booksbutterfly.com/
Buck Books – http://buckbooks.net/
Choosy Bookworm – http://choosybookworm.com/
Digital Book Today – https://digitalbooktoday.com/
Free Booksy – https://www.freebooksy.com/
Kindle Nation Daily – http://kindlenationdaily.com/
The Fussy Librarian – https://www.thefussylibrarian.com/

E-Book Publishing Platforms

Barnes & Noble Press – https://press.barnesandnoble.com/
Bibliotheca – https://www.bibliotheca.com/
Draft2Digital – https://draft2digital.com/
IngramSpark – https://www.ingramspark.com/
Kindle Direct Publishing – https://kdp.amazon.com/
Kobo Writing Life – https://www.kobo.com/en/p/writinglife/
Lulu – https://www.lulu.com/
PublishDrive – https://www.publishdrive.com/
Smashwords – https://www.smashwords.com/
StreetLib – https://www.streetlib.com/

Print-on-Demand Printers and Distributors

IngramSpark – https://www.ingramspark.com/
KDP Print – https://kdp.amazon.com/
Lulu – https://www.lulu.com/
Nook Press – https://press.barnesandnoble.com/
Print Trail – https://printtrail.com/

Audiobook Publishing Platforms

Audio Creation Exchange – https://www.acx.com/
Author's Republic – https://authorsrepublic.com/
Findaway Voices – https://findawayvoices.com/
ListenUp – http://listenupaudiobooks.com/
Podium Publishing – http://podiumpublishing.com/
Scribl – https://www.scribl.com/

Book Review Assistance

Book Review Targeter – https://bookreviewtargeter.com/
Choosy Bookworm – https://www.choosybookworm.com
Enas Reviews – http://enasreviews.com
Happy Book Reviews – http://happybookreviews.com/
IndieReader – https://indiereader.com/
NetGalley – https://www.netgalley.com/
Reading Deals – https://readingdeals.com/reviews
Your New Books – https://www.yournewbooks.com/

Foreign Language Translation

Babel Cube – https://www.babelcube.com/
Click for Translation – https://clickfortranslation.com/
Harcz & Partner Ltd. Translation Company – http://www.translationcompany.org/
MINCOR – http://mincor.net/
Translators Base – https://www.translatorsbase.com/

Book Social Networking Sites

Book Talk – https://www.booktalk.org/
BookCrossing – http://www.bookcrossing.com/
BookLikes – http://booklikes.com/
Goodreads – https://www.goodreads.com/
LibraryThing – http://www.librarything.com/
Shelfari – http://www.shelfari.com/

Press Release Distributors

24-7 Press Release – https://www.24-7pressrelease.com/
eReleases – https://www.ereleases.com/
Free Press Release – http://www.free-press-release.com/
Online PR News – https://onlineprnews.com/
PR Newswire – https://www.prnewswire.com/
PR.com – https://www.pr.com/
SB Wire – http://www.sbwire.com/

Online Course Platforms

Coursera – https://www.coursera.org/
Lynda – https://www.lynda.com/
Skillshare – https://www.skillshare.com/
Teachable – https://teachable.com/
Thinkific – https://www.thinkific.com/
Udemy – https://www.udemy.com/

Acknowledgements

I am greatful to the following people who assisted in the production of *The Influential Author*:

Resa Embutin of www.ResaEmbutin.com for having the patience and talent to explore and test many different design ideas for this book's cover design, elegant section illustrations, and interior formatting style.

Keron Joseph, the aspiring author whose inherent sense of heroic meaning made him uniquely qualified to understand what I was trying to convey even when I overlooked the intended influence of my own words.

Krista Walsh of www.TheRavensQuill.com for her gentle encouragement of this book's underlying themes (punctuated by brutal honesty when certain ugly sentences or irrelevant passages needed to be entirely removed).

Susan Wenger of www.CoverToCoverLLC.com for the extreme detail she applied when providing developmental guidance on this book's overall structure, purpose, and early redundancies.

Authors Veronica Kirin, Olga Petrenko, Sean Plotkin, Becca Tzigany, and Olivier Wagner for giving me the opportunity to work with them on producing and promoting their fantastic books (and for allowing me to use snippets of their journeys in this book to teach valuable lessons about the good and bad of publishing). I encourage any reader who has been intrigued by anything they read about the real-life case study authors mentioned herein to read *Stories of Elders*, *Intimacy on the Plate*, *Get Bail Leave Jail*, *Venus and Her Lover*, or *U.S. Taxes for Worldly Americans*.

Finally, every primary ideological influence whose words have contributed to the structuring of my paradigm and values throughout the most developmental phases of my life and into the ongoing future—the names of whom would be far too numerous to list here.

About the Author

Gregory V. Diehl is the author of multiple bestselling books on identity development for businesses and individuals. He is also the founder of Identity Publications, an organization that produces and publishes books containing ideas that matter. Diehl travels to more than 50 countries, enjoys homesteading in Ecuador and Armenia, and kidnaps felines from streets around the world.

Connect with Gregory at:
GregoryDiehl.net
IdentityPublications.com

CPSIA information can be obtained
at www.ICGtesting.com
Printed in the USA
LVHW011138230120
644558LV00020BA/186